CHRISTIAN EXEGESIS OF THE QUR'ĀN

American Society of Missiology Monograph Series

Series Editor, James R. Krabill

THE ASM MONOGRAPH SERIES provides a forum for publishing quality dissertations and studies in the field of missiology. Collaborating with Pickwick Publications—a division of Wipf and Stock Publishers of Eugene, Oregon—the American Society of Missiology selects high quality dissertations and other monographic studies that offer research materials in mission studies for scholars, mission and church leaders, and the academic community at large. The ASM seeks scholarly work for publication in the Series that throws light on issues confronting Christian world mission in its cultural, social, historical, biblical, and theological dimensions.

Missiology is an academic field that brings together scholars whose professional training ranges from doctoral-level preparation in areas such as scripture, history and sociology of religions, anthropology, theology, international relations, interreligious interchange, mission history, inculturation, and church law. The American Society of Missiology, which sponsors this series, is an ecumenical body drawing members from Independent and Ecumenical Protestant, Catholic, Orthodox, and other traditions. Members of the ASM are united by their commitment to reflect on and do scholarly work relating to both mission history and the present-day mission of the church. The ASM Monograph Series aims to publish works of exceptional merit on specialized topics, with particular attention given to work by younger scholars, the dissemination and publication of which is difficult under the economic pressures of standard publishing models.

Persons seeking information about the ASM or the guidelines for having their dissertations considered for publication in the ASM Monograph Series should consult the Society's website—www.asmweb.org.

Members of the ASM Monograph Committee who approved this book are:

PREVIOUSLY PUBLISHED IN THE ASM MONOGRAPH SERIES

Runchana P. Suksod-Barger, *Religious Influences in Thai Female Education (1889–1931)*

Sarita D. Gallagher, *Abrahamic Blessing: A Missiological Narrative of Revival in Papua New Guinea*

Darren Todd Duerksen, *Ecclesial Identities in a Multi-Faith Context: Jesus Truth-Gatherings (Yeshu Satangs) among Hindus and Sikhs in Northwest India*

Christian Exegesis of the Qur'ān

A Critical Analysis of the Apologetic Use of the Qur'ān in Select Medieval and Contemporary Arabic Texts

J. Scott Bridger

American Society of Missiology Monograph
Series vol. 23

PICKWICK *Publications* • Eugene, Oregon

CHRISTIAN EXEGESIS OF THE QUR'ĀN
A Critical Analysis of the Apologetic Use of the Qur'ān in Select Medieval and Contemporary Arabic Texts

American Society of Missiology Monograph Series 23

Pickwick Publications
An Imprint of Wipf and Stock Publishers
199 W. 8th Ave., Suite 3
Eugene, OR 97401

www.wipfandstock.com

ISBN 13: 978-1-4982-0197-1

Cataloging-in-Publication data:

Bridger, J. Scott

Christian exegesis of the Qur'ān : a critical analysis of the apologetic use of the Qur'ān in select medieval and contemporary Arabic texts / J. Scott Bridger.

xii + 188 p. ; 23 cm. — Includes bibliographical references and indexes.

American Society of Missiology Monograph Series 23

ISBN 13: 978-1-4982-0197-1

1. Qur'an—Criticism, interpretation, etc.—History. 2. Qur'an—Criticism, interpretation, etc.—History—Middle Ages, 600–1500. 3. Christianity and other religions—Islam. I. Title. II. Series.

BP132 B77 2015

Manufactured in the U.S.A.

I dedicate this book to my beautiful and loving wife, Miriam, and our five children: Elijah, Isaiah, Ethan, Moriah, and Isaac. I have never been the same since meeting you in Jerusalem on Christmas Eve, 1998. You are God's gift to me—a source of blessing and encouragement through the many years of study, residency, and life overseas in oftentimes very challenging circumstances. I would not have persevered were it not for your smile.

Contents

Acknowledgments

THIS BOOK WOULD NOT have been possible without the investment of many dedicated mentors, teachers, and friends. First and foremost among them are my parents and family members. All of you have shown me undivided support over the course of many years dedicated to research, study, and residency in several different countries. I especially thank God for the prayers of my mother, which have sustained me and my family in the face of numerous challenges. Among the pastors who have invested in my life, a special word of thanks is due to Joe Drummer and Charles Farag. You taught and modeled for me a deep and sustaining devotion to Christ and an unwavering commitment to the gospel. Next, I must thank my brothers in the faith who have sharpened me over the years. Among them are Matthew Harding, Clark Sneed, Michael Liter, and Scott Newton. Several professors have left a lasting influence on my thinking while under their tutelage over the years. Although I cannot take time to mention all of them, a special word of thanks is due to the following: Keith Eitel (Southwestern Baptist Theological Seminary); John Feinberg and Harold Netland (Trinity Evangelical Divinity School); Ofer Livne, George Kanaza, Edna Kidron, Vardit Rispler, Reuven Snir, Khalid Sindawi, Ali Hussein, Arieyh Kofsky, Ibrahim Geries (University of Haifa); Gabriel Said Reynolds (University of Notre Dame); John Hammett, Ant Greenham, and especially my friend, Bruce Ashford (Southeastern Baptist Theological Seminary). Bruce urged me to tackle the question this book addresses when my inclinations were to settle for a less controversial topic. I also want to thank the many friends and members in the Body of Christ from the Middle East (or residing there) whose love, commitment, and passion for the gospel has had a lasting impact on my life. Among them are: Ibrahim Arafat, Tony Joubran, Shmuel Aweida, Freddie Drayton, the late Kamal Hussein, Bishara and Lubna Deeb, Ziad

Faraj, Khalil Fawakhri, Rani Espanyoli, Renod and Karen Bejjani, Duane Alex Miller, Brent Neely, Doug Coleman, Ray and Rosemary Register, and the many friends and colleagues whose names I cannot list here. Finally, I want to express my love and gratitude to Jesus, my Messiah, Savior, and King. You called me from the darkness into the light and have given me an incorruptible gift of faith—the faith of my father Abraham. To you alone belongs glory and honor and praise.

Abbreviations

AJCP	*Alif: Journal of Comparative Poetics*
ASTJ	*Ashland Theological Journal*
BSOAS	*Bulletin of the School of Oriental and African Studies*
CMR	*Christian-Muslim Relations: A Biographical History*. 5 vols. Edited by David Thomas et al. Boston: Brill, 2009.
DOP	*Dumbarton Oaks Papers*
EI[2]	*Encyclopedia of Islam*. 2nd ed. Edited by P. Bearman et al. Leiden: Brill, 2002.
EMQ	*Evangelical Missions Quarterly*
HTR	*Harvard Theological Review*
IJFM	*International Journal of Frontier Mission*
JAL	*Journal of Arabic Literature*
JAOS	*Journal of the American Oriental Society*
JES	*Journal of Ecumenical Studies*
JIS	*Journal of Islamic Studies*
MW	*Muslim World*
NTS	*New Testament Studies*
OC	*Oriens Christianus*
PO	*Parole de l'Orient*
REI	*Reveue des etudes islamiques*
RSR	*Religious Studies Review*
RT	*Religion & Theology*

SFM	*St. Francis Magazine*
SM	*Studia Missionalia*
TJ	*Trinity Journal*
TB	*Tyndale Bulletin*
WW	*Word & World*
XV	*Xristianskij Vostok*

1

Christian Theology and the Qur'ān

THIS BOOK AIMS TO answer the question of whether or not Christians are justified in making positive apologetic use of the Qur'ān in Arabic-speaking contexts. The originality of my approach, generally speaking, is that I seek to answer the question not solely on the basis of biblical and theological arguments, which I do address, but by examining the question from the perspective of how some Christians residing within the world of Islam treat it. Western evangelical treatments of this issue usually address it by discussing what constitutes sound missional practices for evangelicals bringing the gospel to Muslims. While my treatment does contribute to the ongoing discussion of contextually appropriate methods of evangelizing and theologizing in Islamic contexts, I believe it is vitally important to examine this issue from the perspective of Christians who have lived in the world of Islam for centuries and who continue to write and explain their theology in the language of the Qur'ān—Arabic. Many western Christians assume that Christian history in the East ends with John of Damascus (d. ca. 749). Few are aware of the cultural, intellectual, and theological achievements of Arabic-speaking Christians residing within the world of Islam. Moreover, few are aware of the benefits that those investigating contemporary theological and missiological questions, such as the apologetic use of the Qur'ān, can glean from this under-utilized source of the global church's history.

This chapter briefly surveys the history of Arabic Christianity with a focus on Christian approaches to the Qur'ān and developments within Islamic theology that set the agenda for the first few generations of Christian theologians composing their theology and apologetic responses to

Islam in Arabic. Understanding this history demonstrates the pervasive influence of the Qur'ān on all religious discourse in Arabic. It also highlights some of the challenges facing those Christians who would venture to write their theology in the language of the Qur'ān. After surveying this history, I situate the problem this work addresses within both western evangelical missiology and the emerging global theological discourse brought about by the expansion of the Christian faith in the global South and East. The basic contention of the book is that there is biblical, historical, and theological justification for Christians who make positive use of the Qur'ān when discussing the Bible and Christian doctrines in Arabic-speaking milieus. This introduction investigates some of the historical factors that elucidate and lend support to this position.

THE STORY OF ARABIC CHRISTIANITY

Arabic Christianity in Pre-Islamic Times

The story of Arabic Christianity begins in the New Testament on the day of Pentecost when the Spirit falls on those who hear Peter proclaim the gospel. The event is theologically important for its link to Babel and the "undoing" of the effects of humanity's collective rebellion against God in Genesis 11. God effects this "undoing" not through the un-confusing of human languages, but through the uniting of people from an array of ethno-linguistic groups by their common faith in Abraham's seed—Jesus. Among the people groups explicitly mentioned in Acts 2 are the Arabs: "And how is it that we hear, each of us in his own native language? Parthians and Medes and Elamites and residents of Mesopotamia, Judea and Cappadocia, Pontus and Asia . . . both Jews and proselytes, Cretans and *Arabians*—we hear them telling in our own tongues the mighty works of God" (Acts 2:8–9, 11, *italics* added). The only other mention of Arabia in the New Testament is in connection with Paul's journey there after his conversion (cf. Gal 1:15–17). Eckhard Schnabel argues that Paul's purpose in going to Arabia was to propagate the Christian faith. And there is reason to believe that Paul was successful. As Schnabel points out, "The aggressive reaction of Nabatean [i.e., Arab] officials who want to eliminate Paul suggests that people had been converted in noticeable numbers, provoking unrest in various cities that caused the intervention of the Nabatean king."[1]

1. Schnabel, *Paul the Missionary*, 64.

Historical records reveal that the first leader to convert to Christianity and proclaim his nation as a Christian nation was an Arab—King Abgar the Great of Edessa ca. 200.[2] Edessa became the spiritual capital for Syriac Christianity during the first two centuries of Christian history, and like King Abgar, some of these early "Syriac" Christians were actually Arabs. Arabic at this time was a spoken language by many in the region; nevertheless, it was not a *written* language until after the emergence of Islam. Most Arab Christians would have prayed in Greek or Syriac.[3]

According to Irfan Shahid, there were three centers for Arabic Christianity that existed prior to the rise of Islam. The first was al-Jabīya, located on the Golan Heights, capital of the famed Ghassānid tribe. The Ghassānids accepted Monophysitism in the sixth century during the reign of the Byzantine Emperor Anastasius I (d. 519). The second major center for Arabic Christianity was the city of Najrān, located in the southwestern part of the Arabian Peninsula. Christianity entered this area sometime during the fifth century.[4] The third center for Arabic Christianity was Ḥīra, located in southern Iraq. After the Roman conquest of Edessa in 243, there was a shift in the center of Arab political power to Mesopotamia. Ḥīra became the capital of the Lakhmīd dynasty, which lasted roughly three centuries. Shahid considers this era a "Golden Period" in Arab Christian history.[5] Located as it was under Sasanian control, the Christianity that flourished in Ḥīra was Nestorianism, the only branch of the faith shown periodic tolerance within the territories controlled by the predominantly Zoroastrian Persians.

Among the more notable Arab clergy in pre-Islamic times was the Monophysite bishop Jacob al-Barāda'ī (d. 577). Paradoxically, he was

2. Shahid, "Arab Christianity before the Rise of Islam," 435; cf. also Shahid, *Byzantium and the Arabs in the Fourth Century*; Shahid, *Byzantium and the Arabs in the Fifth Century*; Shahid, *Byzantium and the Arabs in the Sixth Century*. For more on the general history of Christianity in the Middle East, see Atiya, *History of Eastern Christianity*.

3. Syriac is a dialect of Aramaic but it is written in a different script.

4. Najrān is famous in Muslim sources for reportedly sending a Christian delegation to Muḥammad in 631 in order to negotiate a peace treaty, one year before his death. Additionally, according to the traditional sources, 'Umar b. al-Khaṭṭāb (d. 644), the second caliph to rule after Muḥammad's death, relocated the Christians from Najrān to Mesopotamia under pretext that Muḥammad had declared it unadvisable for two religions to be present in the Peninsula. The historicity of the Najrān delegation account is questionable. For more, see Reynolds, *Emergence*, 45–47.

5. Shahid, "Arab Christianity," 440.

ordained in the mid sixth-century with the help of the Empress Theodora (d. 548). Theodora was a proponent of Monophysitism, but she was the wife of the Emperor Justinian I (d. 565) who himself was a major proponent of Chalcedonian orthodoxy in Syria-Palestine. The Western Syriac-speaking Monophysites of what is today known as the Syrian Orthodox Church were known by the eponym "Jacobites" throughout much of the Middle Ages, preserving the memory of their Arab predecessor, Jacob al-Barādaʿī.[6]

Monastic movements were key to the spread of Christianity in this early period. Monasticism has its roots in Egypt with the famous anchorite monk Antony (d. 356), although most scholars identify Euthymius (d. 473) as the founder of monasticism in Syria-Palestine.[7] Euthymius and other monks played a key role in establishing churches among the peoples of this area, including the Arabs. This activity had the support of Bishop Juvenal of Jerusalem (f. 422–58). He instituted the "diocese of the tents" for the Arab tribes of the Judean wilderness and eventually consecrated an Arab, Sheikh Buṭrus (or "Peter"), over these tribes.[8] Buṭrus was present at the Council of Ephesus in 431 and was a member of the commission that interviewed Nestorius.[9]

It is notable that for all the missionary activity among the Arab tribes prior to the advent of Islam, there does not appear to be any evidence

6. Latourette reports that Jacob al-Barādaʿī (Jacob Baradæus) was responsible for consecrating "two patriarchs, eighty-nine bishops, and a hundred thousand priests." Latourette, *A History of the Expansion of Christianity*, 2:265.

7. Britton-Ashkelony and Kofsky, "Monasticism in the Holy Land," 272.

8. Trimingham records the account of how this took place: "One day an Arab shaikh with a party of nomads turned up at the laura and demanded to see Euthymius. Theoctistus explained to them that he only came down from his cave high up the cliff at weekends, and he suggested that they should wait a day or two. But the shaikh insisted. He brought forward his son Terebon, who was paralyzed on his right side, and told him the following story. The persecution undertaken at the end of the reign of Yazdagird I of Persia against the Christians within his dominions had caused many to seek refuge in Roman territory. The Persian authorities tried to stop this movement and sought the co-operation of the Arab tribes of their frontier zone. One powerful shaikh called Aspebet refused to hand over such refugees to Persian vengeance, but rather facilitated their flight . . . . The shaikh . . . told Theoctistus all this. He said the Persian magi had been unable to cure his son, and that the boy himself, having appealed to Christ, saw a gorge and a long-bearded, white-haired monk. On this story being relayed to Euthymius, he consented to leave his retreat and break his silence to pray for the boy, who was healed. The shaikh received the baptismal name of Peter, Buṭrus in Arabic." Trimingham, *Christianity among the Arabs*, 109–10.

9. Ibid.

of written translations of the Bible into Arabic during this period.[10] As mentioned, the ecclesiastical languages used by Arab Christians prior to Islam and even during the first Islamic century were primarily Greek, Aramaic, and Syriac.[11]

Arabic Christianity in Early Islamic Times

Sidney Griffith points out that as a result of the Islamic conquests during the first half of the seventh century, upwards of "50 percent of the world's confessing Christians from the mid-seventh to the end of the eleventh centuries found themselves living under Muslim rule."[12] Islam appeared at a time when many of these Christian communities were still defining their ecclesiastical identities in light of the Christological controversies of the fifth and sixth centuries. As noted, Chalcedonian orthodoxy had been heavily advocated by Justinian I in the decades prior to the advent of Islam and was widespread in Syria-Palestine; however, most of the Christian communities in Egypt, Mesopotamia, and the surrounding areas were either Monophysites or Nestorians. Both communities were predominantly Syriac-speaking though the Monophysites in Egypt used Coptic. The Chalcedonians were primarily Greek-speakers, but there were also Aramaic/Syriac-speakers as evidenced by their activity in the monasteries of Palestine.[13] Over time, each of the groups became identified as three distinct ecclesiastical communities: the Melkites (i.e., Chalcedonians), the Western Syriac-speaking Jacobites (i.e., Monophysites), and the Eastern Syriac-speaking Nestorians (i.e., the Church of the East). Of these, the Melkites were the first community to adopt Arabic as both their daily and ecclesiastical language under Islam.[14]

Many Christians in the region regarded the invasion by Arab armies in the first half of the seventh century as punishment by God for their sins. Abdul-Massih Saadi notes that on Christmas Eve 639 the Melkite

10. Arbache surveys the evidence for pre-Islamic translations of the Bible into Arabic and concludes that they only began to appear after the Arabic alphabet was fixed under the Umayyad Caliph 'Abd al-Malik (d. 705). See Arabche, "Bible et liturgie chez les arabes chrétiens," 37–48.

11. For more on the transition from these languages to Arabic by Middle Eastern Christian communities, see Griffith, "Aramaic to Arabic," 11–31.

12. Griffith, *Shadow*, 11.

13. See Griffith's discussion in, "Aramaic to Arabic," 13–16.

14. For a brief discussion of how Arabic became the *lingua franca* of Melkite Christians during the early Islamic period, see Blau, "Melkite Arabic," 14–16.

Patriarch of Jerusalem, Sophronius (d. ca. 640), encouraged his people to repent so that God might remove the "occupation of the Ishmaelites."[15] Others saw their presence as divine punishment for doctrinal errors. Overall, however, there was a sense among many Christians that the presence of the Arabs was temporary.

The earliest documented encounter of a Christian and Muslim[16] is the dialogue that took place ca. 644 between a Muslim Emir and the Jacobite Patriarch, John of Sedra (d. 648). The document consists of seven questions put to the Patriarch by the Muslim Emir. The Emir indicates that he accepts the Torah and he raises a number of questions about the Scriptures; however, there is no reference to the Qur'ān. Saadi states this could be an indication that it was not yet in circulation.[17] Griffith notes that John's responses to the seven questions by the Muslim Emir probably constitute the earliest Christian response to Islam. He says that they "embody the substance of the Islamic critique of Christianity and in one form or another and would be the questions Christian apologists in the world of Islam would be answering for centuries to come."[18]

Although the Qur'ān accuses Jews and Christians of distorting (*ḥarrafa*) or concealing (*katama*) the message of the Bible (*taḥrīf ma'nawī*),[19] it seems that Christians in the seventh and early eight centuries did not fully realize the implications of this accusation. Nearly all of the earliest examples of Christian-Muslim encounters are marked by appeals, on the part of the Christians, to various verses in the Bible as an apologetic strategy for defending their faith and doctrines. These scriptural *testimonia* are taken from both testaments and are frequently used to present a cumulative case for the veracity of Christian doctrines. This mode of argumentation is known as "scriptural reasoning" and is characteristic of many early Christian responses to Islam, whether in Greek,

15. Saadi, "Nascent Islam," 219.

16. Saadi notes that the terms used to refer to the Arabs (or "Muslims") during this early period varied. Among the Syriac terms are *mhaggrayê*, "immigrants" (*muhājirūn* in Arabic), and *ṭayyāyê*. Ibid., 217–18. See also Donner's discussion of the meaning of the term *muslim* in the Qur'ān and its inclusiveness of pious Christians and Jews in the early "Believers movement" in Donner, *Muhammad and the Believers*, 68–74.

17. Saadi, "Nascent Islam," 220.

18. Griffith, *Shadow*, 36. For an introduction to the text and an English translation, see Newman, *Early Christian-Muslim Dialogue*, 7–46; cf. also Bertaina's discussion and analysis of the text in Bertaina, "Theodore Abū Qurra in Debate at the Court of Caliph al-Ma'mūn," 123–39.

19. Cf., e.g., Q 2:75, 146; 4:46; 5:13, 41.

Syriac, or Arabic.[20] Use of this apologetic method demonstrates that, in early dialogues and controversies over Christian doctrines, scriptural reasoning carried weight among both Christians and Muslims. However, as the Qur'ān's accusation of scriptural tampering became more widespread and the full-blown Islamic doctrine of textual corruption (*taḥrīf lafẓī* or *taḥrīf al-naṣṣ*) was developed, the appeal to scriptural authority began to carry less weight.[21] Parallel with this was the growing sophistication of Muslim theologians in their appropriation of Greek thought and ways of constructing rational arguments. As a result, employment of scriptural reasoning by both Christians and Muslims decreased. Slowly, rational argumentation began to supplement and eventually supersede scriptural argumentation, even though in many apologetic and polemical works they are used together.

Samir Khalil Samir identifies four basic phases in the development of Arabic Christian apologetics. The first phase stretches from the mid-eighth to the mid-ninth centuries and is noted for the frequent use of biblical and qur'ānic citations. The Melkite theologian, Theodore Abū Qurra (d. ca. 830), is representative of this phase.[22] A mix of biblical citations along with philosophical reasoning characterizes the second phase, which stretches from the mid-ninth century to the beginning of the tenth. It is represented by Christian theologians such as the Nestorian, 'Ammār al-Baṣrī (d. 850).[23] The third phase is primarily philosophical and is represented by the Jacobite, Yaḥyā b. 'Adī (d. 974).[24] Samir characterizes the fourth and final phase as being spiritual and humanistic in nature. This phase is represented by the Nestorian, Elia of Nisībīs (d. 1043).[25]

20. See Bertaina's description of three forms of scriptural reasoning in Bertaina, *Dialogues*, 224.

21. Nickel has shown that the tampering motif developed gradually in Muslim polemical literature. Moreover, he shows that it developed in response to an external narrative structure (i.e., an external theological structure) that Qur'ān exegetes brought to the verses that touch on this theme. Within that narrative structure, Jews and Christians are depicted as rejecting Muḥammad's claim to prophethood and tampering with their Scriptures in order to remove any references to his predicted coming. See Nickel, *Narratives of Tampering*. For more on this topic, see Accad, "Corruption and/or Misinterpretation," 67–97; Saeed, "The Charge of Distortion," 419–36.

22. Abū Qurra's debate with the Muslim theologians in the *majlis* of al-Ma'mūn is examined in chapter three of this book.

23. See below for a discussion of al-Baṣrī's use of the "attribute apology."

24. For more, see Endress, *The Works of Yaḥyā ibn 'Adī*.

25. Samir, "Earliest Arab Apology," 109–14.

Under the Arabizing and Islamicizing campaigns of the Umayyad Caliphs, 'Abd al-Malik (d. 705) and his son al-Walīd (d. 715), policies were implemented that were designed to diminish, if not erase, Christian influence from the public sphere. As a result, Christians increasingly felt the pressure of social discrimination. Evidence of this is apparent in the writings from this period.[26] Muslim rulers, however, found justification for their policies in the Qur'ān: "Fight those who believe not in God and the Last Day and do not forbid what God and His Messenger have forbidden—such men as practice not the religion of truth, being of those who have been given the Book—until they pay the tribute [*jizya*] out of hand and have been humbled" (Q 9:29).[27] Texts like this were used to provide a legal basis for classifying Jews and Christians as *dhimmīs*, or subjugated peoples, and requiring them to pay a tribute tax for protection. This protection included allowing Christians to continue governance of their own internal affairs, according to the canon laws of each ecclesiastical community,[28] but the public sphere was now under the control of Islam. Although, historically, policies of this sort were enforced irregularly throughout the various Islamic empires, the overall effect was a diminishing of Christian influence and presence in the public domain.[29]

Over time, Christian communities were increasingly faced with a number of their fold who converted to Islam. Conversion elevated one's status from a subjugated person (*dhimmī*) to someone with normal rights and privileges. Thus, by the late part of the eighth century conversion increasingly became an appealing option for many of the social elite among Jews, Christians, and others.[30] This reality, combined with the Qur'ān's critique of the Christian teaching about God, forced Christian leaders to offer pastoral, apologetic, and polemical responses to the challenges facing their communities. Initially, these responses manifested themselves in the translation of liturgical and theological works from Syriac and

26. E.g., see Reinink's investigation of the shock many Christians felt at being conquered by a seemingly inferior people in Reinink, "Early Christian Reactions," 227–41.

27. Unless noted otherwise, translations from the Qur'ān are from Arberry with occasional modifications to update the language. Arberry, *The Koran Interpreted*.

28. The qur'ānic basis for this is found in Q 5:47.

29. For more, see Ye'or, *The Decline of Eastern Christianity*. For an exploration of the historical development of discriminatory policies towards non-Muslims in what became known as the "Covenant of 'Umar," see Tritton, *The Caliphs and Their Non-Muslim Subjects*.

30. Bulliet has investigated the rates of conversion and the time it took for Muslims to become the majority in the areas under their control in Bulliet, *Conversion to Islam*.

Greek into Arabic. But it was not long before Christians from each of the three ecclesiastical communities began authoring original compositions in Arabic. Most notable in this regard are the aforementioned theologians, Theodore Abū Qurra and ʿAmmār al-Baṣrī, as well as the Jacobite theologian, Abū Rā'iṭa al-Takritī (d. ca. 835).[31] Each of these theologians produced original works that contained within them the seeds of a contextualized Arabic Christian apologetic theology.[32]

THE CHALLENGE OF A QUR'ĀNIC AGENDA FOR ARABIC CHRISTIAN THEOLOGY

The Linguistic Challenge

The adoption of Arabic as a language for theological expression by Christians during the eighth and ninth centuries brought with it a number of challenges. By this time the terminology and concepts used for religious discourse in Arabic had already been permeated with Islamic religious significance. Terms like *hudā* (guidance), *tawḥīd* (unicity or oneness), *shakhṣ* (person), *walad* (child), *ibn* (son), *nabī* (prophet), and *rasūl* (messenger), to name just a few, came to have fixed meanings derived from the Qur'ān and developed within the distinct theological frameworks of the burgeoning class of Muslim *mutakallimūn* (theologians) and *mufassirūn* (Qur'ān exegetes and commentators).

Hudā is what God promised to guide humanity on the "straight path" (*al-ṣirāṭ al-mustaqīm*).[33] It represents the primordial *sharīʿa* (legal code) given to Adam and Eve[34] to guide them after God commanded them to be "cast down" (imper. *ihbiṭū*, dual *ihbiṭā*) to the earth when they disobeyed his command not to eat from the tree.[35] At the heart of the guidance God gave to humanity is the message of *tawḥīd*—the monadic

31. For more on al-Takritī's life and works, see Keating, *Defending the "People of Truth."*

32. Griffith, *Shadow*, 21.

33. Cf. e.g., Q 1:6, 5:16.

34. Eve is not mentioned by name in the Qur'ān but the use of the dual in texts like Q 2:35–36 implies she is known. This is an example of qur'ānic allusion to biblical persona about whom the Qur'ān assumes its audience is knowledgeable.

35. *Hudā* becomes the qur'ānic "solution" to the "fall" in Q 2:30–38; 20:115–24. But the language used to describe the "fall" in the Qur'ān is much weaker than that found in the Bible as are the consequences of Adam's (and Eve's) sin (cf. Q 7:11–25; 15:26–39; 17:61–63; 18:50; 38:71–75). For more, see Curry, "Mission to Muslims," 224–26.

unity of God.[36] From time immemorial, the role of God's prophets and messengers,[37] from Adam to Muḥammad,[38] has always been to warn and guide humanity by faithfully declaring to them the central message of *tawḥīd*. Indeed, later Muslim *mutakallimūn* and *mufassirūn* assume that the Qur'ān's emphasis on God's unity is the central message of all previous revelation (i.e., the Bible).[39] *Shakhṣ* refers to a person, or more properly, an individual, with all of the attendant corporeal qualities characteristic of individuals, and could not, at least in the *mutakallim's* mind, be used to refer to a quality attributable to one aspect of God's nature and not to the whole of it.[40] The nouns *ibn* and *walad* (along with form I of the verb,

36. The term *tawḥīd* does not appear in the Qur'ān, though later Qur'ān exegetes and Muslim theologians developed the doctrine of *tawḥīd* from verses like Q 2:163; 12:39; 112. Badawi and Haleem note that four forms of the root و/ح/د occur 68 times in the Qur'ān: *waḥd* six times, *wāḥid* 30 times, *wāḥida* 31 times, and *waḥīd* once. Badawi and Haleem, *Arabic-English Dictionary*, 1041.

37. Although it is not entirely clear in the Qur'ān itself, many classical Muslim theologians and commentators distinguished between prophets and messengers. In its classical formulation, "messengers" are understood as those who were given a "book" (*kitāb*) consisting of a "message" (*risāla*). "Prophets" are those who acted in history as "warners" to inform people of *tawḥīd* and call people to repentance or face God's impending judgment, but they were not given a book or message in the form of written revelation. Cf. e.g., Q 4:163–65. Bijlefeld has cast doubt on this distinction. See Bijlefeld, "A Prophet and More Than a Prophet?," 1–28.

38. The supposed proper name of the Muslim prophet—"Muḥammad"—("praised one") appears only four times in the Qur'ān (Q 3:144; 33:40; 47:2; 48:29). Together, the paucity of non-Islamic references to the Muslim prophet and the unreliability of Muslim historical sources have led scholars like Reynolds to question whether Qur'ān's use of the term constitutes a proper name or a messianic epithet. See Reynolds, *Biblical Subtext*, 185–99; Reynolds, "Remembering Muḥammad," 188–206.

39. The Qur'ān refers to the Bible as "scripture" (*kitāb*) and differentiates between the Tawrāt (i.e., Torah), Injīl (i.e., Gospel), and Zabūr (i.e., Psalms). The Bible's status as intact and authoritative revelation from God is assumed in the Qur'ān as evidenced by its use of terms like "revealed" (*awḥā*) and "sent down" (form II, *nazzala*; form IV, *anzala*, or the passive *unzila*) when referring to the Bible. These are the same terms the Qur'ān uses in self-referential discourse about its status as divine revelation (cf. e.g., Q 3:3; 4:163–66; 5:43–68, *et passim*). For more on the Qur'ān's notion of "scripture" and areas of continuity and discontinuity with the Bible and other works, see Madigan, *The Qur'ān's Self Image*; Jeffery, *The Qur'an as Scripture*.

40. The term *shakhṣ* does not appear in the Qur'ān in this sense. The term and the concept of God's personhood did, however, develop into a point of contention in later Christian-Muslim disputation literature. An example of this is Abū Bakr al-Bāqillānī's (d. 1013) attack on the terms Christians employ to explain the notion of hypostasity in his "Refutation of the Christians" (Thomas, *Christian Doctrines*, 169). When speaking of the hypostases some Christians opted to use an Arabic calque (sing. *uqnūm*, pl.

walada, "he/it birthed," and its passive form, *wulida*, "he/it was birthed") carry the connotation of physical lineage, thereby excluding any figurative use of these terms for indicating that God might have a "Son."[41]

These and other terms are imbedded within the Qur'ān's particular hermeneutical horizons and act, in a subversive manner, to counter the religious significance Christians might tie to these words. This fact posed a tremendous challenge for the first Christians who ventured to write their theology in Arabic during the early 'Abbāsid era (750–1258), and continues to do so today. How were (and are) they to employ the language of the Qur'ān, which Muslims considered the apogee of divine revelation, to articulate a Christian worldview? What terms were (and are) to be used to discuss certain theological realities such as the triune nature of God or the uniting of the divine with the human in Christ?

Inevitably, the choices Christian theologians made in this regard would be influenced by the parameters and concerns set for the discussion by the Qur'ān and nascent Islamic theology. Indeed, these parameters formed a hermeneutical circle within which Christians were pressed to operate. Griffith explains:

> That the Qur'ān set the parameters in the Arabic-speaking world for the discussion of important religious doctrines, even Christian ones, can be seen in the structures of the Christian *kalām*.[42] For example, the doctrine of the Incarnation is often put forward in the framework of a Qur'ānic prophetology, while the doctrine of the Trinity is inevitably discussed in terms of the *ṣifāt Allāh*, the beautiful names (*al-asmā' al-Ḥusnā*) of God as one finds them in the Qur'ān. Similarly, the collection of testimonies from the scriptures to the veracity of Christian teachings and interpretations, gathered from Torah, Prophets, Psalms and Gospel, the scriptures as they are mentioned in the Qur'ān, assumed a major importance in Arab Christian texts. It is not

aqānīm) on a Syriac loanword (sing. *qnōmā*, pl. *qnōmē*) to refer the three persons of the Godhead. For more on the background and selection of this terminology by Arab Christian theologians, see Griffith, "The Concept of al-Uqnūm," 187–91.

41. Cf. Q 112:3. This does not, however, completely rule out the figurative use of the term *ibn* since it is used quite frequently in the Qur'ān to refer to the generic "wayward one" (*ibn al-sabīl*; lit. "son of the road") without any sense of physical lineage. Cf. e.g., Q 2:215, *et passim*.

42. "*Kalām*" (lit. "speech") refers to the dialectical mode of Islamic theological discourse that developed as a response both to internecine conflicts in the nascent Muslim community and Muslim disputation with Jews and Christians. See further discussion below.

> that Arab Christians did not draw on their earlier traditions in Greek, Syriac, and Coptic to support their creed in the face of new challenges. In fact, many of their difficulties stemmed precisely from their efforts to translate the terms of the traditional doctrinal formulae into Arabic in such a way that the connotations of the Arabic words would not belie their intentions. But overall there swayed the ever-present need to present their ideas within the confines of what we might call the hermeneutical circle of the Qur'ān. In a very real way it determined the possibilities of religious discourse in Arabic in the world of Islam.[43]

The early 'Abbāsid era was a period when Muslims became increasingly eager to validate their beliefs in light of the challenges put forward by their more numerous and philosophically advanced Christian subjects. Intellectual and theological cross-pollinization were rampant during this early period, and it is within this matrix that Islamic theology, *'ilm al-kalām*, originated and matured.

The Challenge of Islamic Theology

There are two views regarding the origins of *kalām* (i.e., Islamic dialectical theology) and its relation to Christian theological discourse about the nature of God. Josef van Ess represents the first view.[44] He rejects the notion that Christian theology or theologians directly influenced the manner and style of Muslim theological reasoning. Van Ess believes that *kalām* simply evolved around the time of 'Abd al-Malik (d. 705) when Muslims were arguing over such issues as God's decrees and the qualifications for Caliph. He bases his view on an investigation of Greek texts as well as early Qadarite and Murj'ite texts—texts authored in Arabic.[45]

43. Griffith, "Arab Christian Texts," 218.

44. According to van Ess, "Kalām in Arabic is not defined by reference to its contents as, theo-logia, something about God, a logos about God, but is defined in terms of its stylistic form, the dialectical method of argumentation." Van Ess, "Islamic Theology," 105. Gardet shares a similar view to that of van Ess in Gardet, "'Ilm al-Kalām," 1141.

45. Generally speaking, the Qadarites are those who affirmed humanity's ability to make meaningful choices (i.e., free will). The Murj'ites advocated a position of delayed judgment when it came to determining who was a true believer, particularly political leaders who were accused of having committed "grave sin," thereby excluding themselves from leadership of the Muslim community. Both movements are associated with early theo-political controversies in Islamic history. However, van Ess's focus in this particular study is not on the contents or the theological positions espoused in these documents but on the form of their argumentation.

After investigating them he concludes that "Muslim civilization did not slowly develop the art of theology and especially of *kalām*, but rather grew up with it."[46] He believes that *kalām* developed as a part of a landscape that had always included discussions on theological issues: "There was something like a common stock of ideas, but there does not seem to have been any 'influence' in the sense that the Muslims were awakened to a certain problem by Christian counter arguments and that they consciously rectified their position in order to avoid being molested again."[47]

Michael Cook offers an alternative view. He situates the origins of the *kalām* within the context of Greek and Syriac examples of theological disputation comparable to the Arabic treatises investigated by van Ess. Cook criticizes van Ess for limiting himself to Greek and Arabic materials while overlooking the Syriac "questions and answers" genre.[48] In Cook's mind, these provide a convincing source of Muslim borrowing. He finds evidence for this in a set of monothelite (i.e., Maronite) treatises written against a group of dyothelites (i.e., Melkites). According to him, the dating of these sets of questions and answers makes it "implausible that we have in these texts a Maronite borrowing of Muslim *kalām*."[49] Cook demonstrates this through an investigation of linguistic constructions found in Syriac texts and then compares them with similar constructions in Arabic. He also finds similar constructs in the intra-Christian dialectical argumentation between Chalcedonians, Monophysites, and Nestorians. In the end, Cook concludes that Muslim-borrowing from Christians probably did take place, and it most likely occurred in Syria. He speculates regarding how this happened, mentioning the polemical pressure of Christianity, a thesis put forth by C. H. Becker,[50] and the influence of Christian converts to Islam. Cook finds validity in both theses and does

46. Van Ess, "Beginnings," 90.

47. Ibid., 99. Thomas seems to be in agreement with van Ess regarding the origins of *kalām*. He even argues that Christians borrowed *kalām* methods from the *mutakallimūn*. He states, "John of Damascus' dismissal in the mid second/eighth century of Muhammad as a fraud and the Qur'ān as an ignorant imitation of the Bible gave way in the third/ninth century to attempts by Arabic-speaking Christians to articulate their doctrines in terms of the distinctive kalām logic that Muslim intellectuals were currently employing." Despite their valiant efforts at contextualizing their faith utilizing *kalām* methods, Thomas believes Christians "actually failed to understand fully what they were about." Thomas, *Christian Doctrines*, 3.

48. Cf. Daiber, "Masā'il wa Adjwiba," 636.

49. Cook, "The Origins of "Kalām," 35; cf. Cook, *Early Muslim Dogma*.

50. Becker "Christian Polemic," 241–57.

not rule either of them out. He also offers a Syriac origin for the term *kalām* itself. Cook's conclusions make it apparent that *kalām* does in fact have its roots in Christian dialectical theology. He also provides insight regarding the extent to which the sectarian milieu of the late seventh and eighth centuries influenced the style and content of each community's theology as well as the apologetic approaches each adopted in order to defend their respective beliefs.

Among the early controversies that occupied Muslim *mutkallimūn* was the ontological status of God's attributes and the createdness of the Qur'ān. Undergirding these two issues is the notion that if God's attributes are posited to be eternal, then it is reasonable to argue that the Qur'ān itself, as God's speech, is eternal and thence uncreated. All Muslims affirmed that the Qur'ān was God's speech; however, there was a controversy over how the Qur'ān related to the *attribute* of speech, which must be eternal because God is eternal. Since the Qur'ān contains information about historical events and people, some Muslims reasoned that God had determined these beforehand. However, there are also verses that seem to indicate the Qur'ān has some sort of preexistence.[51] The issue was over how Muslims were to reconcile this position with their belief in the eternality of God. For those who came to assert the eternality and uncreatedness of the Qur'ān, they made a logical connection between their position in this regard and God's attribute of speech.[52]

Clearly, the discussion over God's attributes and the createdness/uncreatedness of God's Word (i.e., the Qur'ān) has a precursor in Christian discussions over the divinity and preexistence of the divine *logos*—Christ.[53] Tied to this discussion is the Qur'ān's designation of Christ as the "Word of God" and "a Spirit from him" (Q 3:45; 4:171a).[54] Forging a connection, many early Christian theologians sought to establish

51. Cf., e.g., Q 85:21–22.

52. For more on the background of this topic, see Watt, *Formative Period*, 179; 242–46. See also the discussion in chapter three.

53. Becker asserts this ["Christian Polemic," 250–51] as does Wolfson. Although Wolfson's works have been criticized for going too far in suggesting a Christian origin for nearly every development in early Islamic theology, they are insightful in terms of the theological parallels he identifies as well as the various sources he investigates in his study of *kalām*. See e.g., Wolfson, "Attributes," 1–18; Wolfson, "Philosophical Implications," 73–80; Wolfson, *Philosophy of the Kalam*.

54. O'Shaughnessy's study on the notion of the "word of God" as it relates to Christ in the Qur'ān remains helpful for understanding this designation in context. See O'Shaughnessy, *Koranic Concept*.

conceptual congruence for a defense of Christ's divinity by referencing these two verses. By affirming that God's Word is eternal and identifying Christ as God's Word (something the Qur'ān advances), Christians could affirm Christ's divinity and accuse those who objected to it of believing there was a time when God was without his Word. For many Christian theologians, this line of argumentation paved the way for them to express their Christology in a manner that comported with their Muslim surroundings.

Contextualized Christian Apologetics in the Arab-Muslim Milieu

At the heart of Islam's challenge to Christian doctrines is the denial of two core tenets of the Christian faith, the Trinity and Incarnation.[55] The Christian theologians who chose to respond to this challenge defended Christianity through a variety of approaches. Some were involved in debates,[56] while others engaged in an exchange of letters between leaders.[57] Still others wrote systematic treatises wherein they sought to provide both rational and scripturally based explanations of Christian doctrines. Others supplemented rational and scriptural reasoning with allusions to or full quotes from the Qur'ān. In rare cases, some Christians "built their apologetic arguments in behalf of Christianity on certain interpretations of particular verses from Islamic scripture."[58] A few were ostensibly willing to place the Qur'ān on the same level as the Bible, while still maintaining orthodox positions on the Trinity and Incarnation.[59]

For their part, notable Muslim polemicists, such as Abū ʿĪsā al-Warrāq (d. 861), al-Nāshi' al-Akbar (d. 906), Abū Bakr al-Bāqillānī (d. 1013), and ʿAbd al-Jabbār (d. 1025), among others, reduced their explanations of Christianity to a refutation of Trinity and Incarnation.[60] The

55. Cf., e.g., Q 4:171b; 5:17, 72–73, 116; 9:30–31; 19:35; 23:91; 25:2; 112:3–4.

56. For an examination of this apologetic strategy, see Griffith, "The Monk in the Emir's *Majlis*," 13–65.

57. The most notable in this regard is the ninth century correspondence between the Christian al-Kindī and the Muslim al-Hāshimī, which circulated widely in both the East and West. See Griffith, *Shadow*, 86–88, and the discussion below.

58. Griffith, "Arab Christian Texts," 204.

59. The anonymous tract entitled by Griffith, "*Answers for the Shaykh*," presents a highly contextualized (syncretized?) defense of the Trinity and hypostatic union. Its author frequently quotes from the Qur'ān in the context of offering reasons from "revelation" for believing these doctrines. See Griffith, "*Answers for the Shaykh*," 277–309.

60. In addition to providing editions of their polemical texts in Arabic with English

reason for this was the obvious challenge the Trinity and Incarnation posed to the monadic conceptualization of God's unity (*tawḥīd*) that is at the center of the Islam's proclamation. Commenting on al-Bāqillānī, David Thomas notes that "al-Bāqillānī uses Christianity. . . to show that as an alternative to Islam it is wrong. And like many other anti-Christian polemicists of this period he does this by attacking the Trinity and Incarnation, the two doctrines that threaten to compromise the Islamic doctrine of God."[61]

Most of the attacks the Muslim *mutakallimūn* carried out on Christianity and Christian doctrines were at the abstract level. They extracted doctrines like the Trinity and Incarnation from the Bible's narrative context within which those doctrines are developed and recast them as an assemblage of propositions that were then subject to critique by *kalām* methods.[62] Their method in this regard was undoubtedly influenced by the way the Qur'ān itself refers to Christian doctrines like the Trinity or the divinity of Christ in an elliptical manner.

In light of this, one of the main approaches Christian theologians developed for explaining the divinity of Christ and the doctrine of the Trinity was the attribute apology. The attribute apology is an apologetic strategy that appears unique to Arabic-speaking Christians living in the world of Islam. It was devised in the context of the intra-Muslim debate over God's attributes mentioned previously. Mark Swanson gives a succinct explanation of the general strategy as follows:

> 1. the assimilation of the trinitarian hypostases to the attributes of God, in particular attributes that are given in, or deducible from, the qur'ān; 2. the claim that the point of the doctrine of the Trinity is the affirmation that (1) God is (2) living and (3) speaking (knowing, wise, etc.); or, in other versions, that God is (1) an essence, or existing, (2) living, and (3) speaking (knowing, wise, etc.); 3. when necessary, the affirmation that each «adjectival» attribute (e.g., existing, living, speaking) corresponds to a nominal form (existence, life, speech) which is a reality in

translations, Thomas gives helpful biographical information and introductions to al-Nāshi,' al-Bāqillānī, and 'Abd al-Jabbār in Thomas, *Christian Doctrines*, 19–34, 119–41, 205–24.

61. Ibid., 126.

62. Thomas provides a survey of the history of the literature produced by Christians in defense of these two doctrines and Muslim critiques of them in Thomas, *Christian Doctrines*, 1–18. See also the introductions to the following two works: Warrāq, *Anti-Christian Polemic*; Warrāq, *Early Muslim Polemic*.

> God; 4. the correlation of the biblical names «Father», «Son,» and «Holy Spirit» with the attributes discussed, e.g., the Father is the Existence (al-wuǧūd), the Son is the Speech (an-nuṭq), and the Holy Spirit is the Life (al-ḥayāt); 5. an argument as to why the hypostases are only three in number.[63]

While John of Damascus may have been the first Christian theologian to suggest explaining the Trinity in terms of the divine attributes,[64] other theologians writing in Arabic seized upon the idea to build a contextualized defense of the doctrine. Among the more sophisticated versions of the attribute apology is that of the Nestorian theologian, 'Ammār al-Baṣrī. Al-Baṣrī's intention, according to Griffith, was "to utilize the discussion of the divine attributes to defend the reasonableness of the doctrine of the Trinity."[65] He offers the attribute apology as a solution to the linguistic dilemma faced by his contemporary Muslim *mutakallimūn* when they spoke of God. Al-Baṣrī believed that the locus of the problem for the *mutakallimūn* in understanding Christian discourse about the Trinity and Jesus' status within the Godhead had to do with their assumption that the physical aspects of generation, characteristic of humans, obtained when Christians spoke of God as "Father" and Jesus as his "Son." They could not tolerate attributing "fatherhood" or "sonship" to "persons" within the Godhead since these terms were qualities attributable to created beings not God. This, in turn, led to an inversion in the way they assessed Christian discourse about God. God's attributes, "knowing," "living," "speaking," etc., were thought to apply to God metaphorically when, in fact, according to al-Baṣrī, it is the other way around. They belong to God essentially and to humans metaphorically:

> . . . it is not legitimate for us, just because we see them [i.e., the attributes] as originated (*muḥdathatan*), since we are ourselves originated, to say that they belong to the Creator as originated. Rather, since they belong to the Creator in actual reality (*bil-ḥaqiqah*), and to us only on loan (*bil-isti'ārah*) from Him, we must say that they belong to Him eternally (*azaliyyatan*).[66]

63. Swanson, "Are Hypostases Attributes?," 239–40.

64. See Sahas's description of John's explanation of the Trinity in Sahas, *John of Damascus*, 78–84; cf. also Hoyland, *Seeing Islam as Others Saw It*, 486. I am assuming that John is the author of chapter 101 in his *Fount of Knowledge* though some scholars question this.

65. Griffith, "The Concept of al-Uqnūm," 183.

66. Griffith "'Ammār al-Baṣrī's Kitāb al-Burhān," 173; for the Arabic, see Hayek, *'Ammār*, 59.

For al-Baṣrī, it is inappropriate to equate the particularities of God's essence (e.g., "fatherhood" and "sonship") with the "appurtenances of human, bodily generation, which bespeak imperfection."[67] In this way, al-Baṣrī presents the doctrine of the Trinity as a solution to the linguistic dilemma faced by the Muslim *mutakallimūn*, whom he depicts as explicitly trying to avoid the Trinity.[68] In a later generation, the Jacobite theologian and philosopher, Yaḥyā b. 'Adī, would defend the Trinity along similar lines.[69]

Christian Approaches to the Qur'ān

In his investigation of Christian approaches to the exegesis of the Qur'ān from the eighth to the twelfth centuries, Paul Khoury notes that Christian apologetic responses to Islam were oftentimes characterized not by appeals to tradition, but by appeals to Scripture—to the Bible and the Qur'ān. Khoury identifies several ways in which Christian theologians employed qur'ānic passages in their apologetics. These include the use of texts to demonstrate the veracity of Christian practices, criteria for what constitutes true religion, and the use of texts to defend Christian belief in both the Trinity and the Incarnation. He points out that Christian apologetic use of the Qur'ān was frequently countered by Muslim arguments to the effect that Christian use of their book implied its divine character.[70] Christians replied to these arguments in a number of ways, chief among them was questioning the Qur'ān's origins.

In the earliest documents that record Christian encounters with the Qur'ān, there is evidence that many of the Christians were uncertain regarding its composition. Griffith notes that in ca. 720 a monk of Bēt Ḥālē is reported as distinguishing between the Qur'ān and *sūrat al-baqara*, the second *sūra* of the Qur'ān.[71] Similarly, John of Damascus, writing in Greek in the mid-eighth century, spoke of the Muslims possessing a "book" (βιβλίον), but he refers to several *sūras* independently as "scripture" (ἡ γραφή), giving the indication that he believed them to be separate works.[72] John also categorized Islam as a heresy and the Qur'ān

67. Ibid.

68. Ibid., 171.

69. Cf. 'Adī, *Jawāb 'an Radd Abī 'Isā al-Warrāq*.

70. Khoury, *Exégèse chrétienne du Coran*, 7–12.

71. Griffith, "Arab Christian Texts," 205–6.

72. Ibid., 206.

as "preposterous."[73] Moreover, he attributes Muḥammad's theology in the Qur'ān to an Arian monk.[74] Christians eventually developed the idea that Muḥammad had contact with a heretical Christian monk into a full polemical argument, naming the monk Sergius Baḥīrā and making him responsible for the Qur'ān.[75]

However, by the ninth century things began to change. As Mark Swanson notes, "arabophone Christians were learning to pray using Qur'anic turns of phrase; to relate to God's dealing with humankind in narrative filled with Qur'anic echoes."[76] This Arabization (and Islamicization) of Christianity prompted many Christian theologians to offer apologetic and polemical responses. In doing so, however, each ecclesiastical community and their theologians made use of the Qur'ān. And this should not come as a surprise given the context within which they were residing. Nevertheless, "no medieval Christian apologist would allow the Qur'ān entire freedom to speak."[77] Over time they developed a spectrum of approaches to the Qur'ān ranging from polemical attacks to more irenic approaches that included qur'ānic allusions, intertextual echoes, and quotes designed to resonate with their audience while upholding the author's belief in the veracity of Christianity.

On the polemical end of this spectrum is the well-known, though probably fictitious, correspondence between a Christian and a Muslim, *Risālat al-Kindī* (*The Apology of al-Kindī*). Composed in Arabic sometime during the ninth century and translated into Latin from Garshūnī[78] in 1141, this work contains a forceful attack on many of the central tenets of the Islamic faith, including a frontal attack on the origins, collection, redaction, and language of the Qur'ān.[79] At the other end of the spectrum is the eighth or ninth century letter from an anonymous Melkite monk

73. Sahas, *John of Damascus*, 89.

74. Ibid., 73–74.

75. Griffith, "Arab Christian Texts," 206–10; cf. Griffith, "Muḥammad and the Monk Baḥīrā," 146–74. Roggema argues that the Baḥīra legend developed in the middle of the eighth century. See Roggema, *The Legend of Sergius Baḥīrā*, 5.

76. Swanson, "Beyond Prooftexting," 319.

77. Ibid., 318.

78. Garshūnī (or Karshūnī) is Arabic written in Syriac letters.

79. For an English translation of the text itself, see Newman, *Early Christian-Muslim Dialogue*, 381–545. For a recent discussion of authorship and an extensive bibliography of the various manuscripts and scholarly studies on the text, see Bottini, "The Apology of al-Kindī," 1:585–94.

to a Muslim sheikh in Jerusalem. Griffith has entitled the letter, "*Answers for the Shaykh*."[80] What is interesting in this letter is the way the author defends his belief in the Trinity and Incarnation on the basis of references to *kutub Allāh* ("God's books"), i.e., the Bible and Qur'ān. There is no polemical attack; the author offers simple allusions and references to "revelation," giving one the impression that in discussions of Christian doctrines like the Trinity and Incarnation, "the Qur'an somehow participated virtually as an equal partner in a revelatory discourse."[81]

Despite the ambiguity regarding the revelatory status of the Qur'ān in "*Answers for the Shaykh*," overall there is very little indication that Christian writers during the first several centuries of Christian-Muslim dialogue and debate accepted the Qur'ān as revelation from God. Commenting on the use of the Qur'ān in the eighth century text, *On the Triune Nature of God* (one of the theological treatises to be analyzed in this book), Griffith states:

> So the question arises, does he [the anonymous author] consider the Qur'ān a revealed scripture on par with the Law, the Prophets, the Psalms, and the Gospel? While the answer to this question is surely "No," given the fact that throughout the treatise arguments from the Bible and Christian tradition are adduced expressly to respond to the challenge of Islamic teaching, nevertheless the fact remains that the prominence of the Qur'ān's influence in the work does testify to the Muslim scripture's active currency even among Christians in the Arabic-speaking community of eighth-century Palestine. And the author obviously thought that his quotations from the Qur'ān would have some probative value for his apologetic purposes.[82]

In his analysis of this and other texts, Griffith deomonstrates that Christian adoption of Arabic as a theological language resulted in a degree of Islamicization in the diction and phraseology of early Arabic Christian theology. Words, phrases, and even (in rare cases) the rhymed prose style (*saj'*) of the Qur'ān "suffused the religious conscious" of many Christian theologians writing in Arabic.[83] These developments reveal the

80. For a description of the letter and relevant bibliography, see Salah et al., "Masā'il wa ajwiba 'aqliyya wa-ilāhiyya," 1:661–63.

81. Griffith, "*Answers to the Shaykh*," 303. Obviously, if this is the case, a position of this sort is untenable for evangelicals.

82. Griffith, *Shadow*, 56.

83. Griffith, "Arab Christian Texts," 204.

extent to which the Qur'ān had "set the agenda" for Christians writing theology in Arabic.[84] Indeed, the whole shape and orientation of Christian theology authored within the world of Islam was impacted by the necessity of having to take Islamic frames of reference into account and defend the faith from the burgeoning class of Muslim *mutakallimūn* who, taking their cue from the Qur'ān, set out to attack the central tenets of the Christian faith.[85] Keating explains:

> The shift to Arabic forced Christian apologists to contend with the difficulties it presented as a language. Whereas John of Damascus had composed his summary of Christian doctrine and the "heresy" of Islam in the first half of the eight century in Greek . . . later writers were confronted with the problem of translating complex ideas and doctrines into an idiom that explicitly precluded their basic premises, and in the beginning, had not yet acquired the vocabulary necessary for such an enterprise. The problem was thrown into relief when Christians tried to articulate ideas in terminology already dominated by *Qur'ānic* images.[86]

It is important to mention that irenic approaches to the Qur'ān were not limited to Arabic-speaking Christians.[87] In the Latin West, Riccoldo of Monte Croce (d. 1320), author of the widely read and translated polemic against Islam, *Contra legum sarracenorum*, offered what Nicholas of Cusa (d. 1464) termed a "righteous interpretation" of the Qur'ān that enabled one to "sift" through what was false and what was true.[88] Thomas Burman notes that despite the vitriol found in Riccoldo's work, one also finds that "the Qur'ān is not entirely a catalogue of error and deceit . . . ." At times, Riccoldo strikes an irenic tone and demonstrates "that there is much in the Qur'ān that can be used by Christians to argue—as he does

84. Griffith, *Shadow*, 56.

85. For a discussion of how these phenomena shaped the theological orientation of Syriac and Arabic Christian texts from first 'Abbasid century, see Griffith, "The Prophet Muhammad," 99–146.

86. Keating, *Defending the "People of Truth,"* 23–24.

87. For a historical overview of western (i.e., European) evaluations and responses to Islam, including missionary strategies, see Tolan, *Saracens*.

88. Nicolas was known for his irenic approach both to Jews and Muslims, all the while arguing for the truth of Christianity. For more see Biechler, "Christian Humanism," 1–14.

in his tract—for the primacy of the Bible, and the veracity of the core Christian beliefs in the Trinity and Incarnation."[89]

In the modern period, many evangelicals residing in or originating from Muslim majority countries, such as Abdul-Haqq,[90] Fouad Accad,[91] and Raouf Ghattas,[92] argue that Muslims have misinterpreted the Qur'ān in numerous places and that when certain verses are interpreted correctly they affirm many of the beliefs to which Christians adhere. But this type of approach to the Qur'ān poses a number of questions. What constitutes a "correct" reading of the Qur'ān? Can Christians interpret the meanings of select qur'ānic verses apart from the history of their interpretation developed within the classical corpus of Muslim *tafsīr* literature?[93] Can they use the Qur'ān in any way to support their doctrines? If they do, are they implicitly elevating the status of the Qur'ān to that of the Bible? What is the apologetic strategy envisioned by Christians who make positive use of the Qur'ān?

89. Burman, "Polemic, Philology, and Ambivalence," 182.

90. Abdul-Haqq, *Sharing Your Faith*, 39, *et passim*.

91. Accad, *Building Bridges*, 59–62, *et passim*.

92. Ghattas and Ghattas, *Guide to the Qur'an*, 32, *et passim*.

93. "*Tafsīr*" refers to the genre of classical exegetical and interpretive literature on the Qur'ān. The word itself is the verbal noun of form II of the verb *fassara* ("to interpret") and corresponds to the Hebrew cognate in the pi'el פרש. Norman Calder provides a good description of *tafsīr*: "*Tafsīr* is a literary genre with definable formal characteristics. The most fundamental of these is the presence of the complete canonical text of the Qur'ān (or at least a significant chunk of it), segmented for purposes of comment, and dealt with in canonical order. In a work of *tafsīr*, passages of comment invariably follow canonical segments. Canon and segmentation, lemma and comment: where these are not systematically present, then a work is not an example of the central tradition of *tafsīr*, though it may belong to the margins of that tradition. This formal structure is so fundamental as to require no exemplification." See Calder, "*Tafsīr*," 101. Over the centuries, the body of *tafsīr* literature developed into an enormous corpus. Today it is generally believed that this corpus contains the final and authoritative interpretation of the Qur'ān's meaning. The problem, however, is that the methods for interpreting the Qur'ān employed by various *mufassirūn* have varied throughout the centuries and, in many cases, they fail to understand the meaning of many passages. See the discussion in chapter five.

MAJORITY WORLD CHRISTIANITY[94] AND CHRISTIAN EXEGESIS OF THE QUR'ĀN: THE CONTROVERSY IN WESTERN EVANGELICAL MISSIOLOGY

The Emergence of a Global Theological Discourse

The question in western evangelical missiology over the apologetic use of the Qur'ān is partly attributable to the ongoing shift in the centers of global Christianity from the West to the global South and East. This has resulted in what Timothy Tennent has described as the "emergence of a global theological discourse."[95] Although western evangelicals are now a numerical minority in the world, they nevertheless retain a tremendous influence on global evangelicalism. That influence extends to evangelicalism's discourse and its theological agenda due largely to the continued ascendancy of western theological institutions. Yet, as western theologians are increasingly faced with questions posed by majority world Christians residing in predominantly non-Christian milieus, many of these theologians are struggling to respond to their questions in ways that are faithful to the gospel while appreciating the particularities of each individual situation. In many cases, western theologians find themselves ill-equipped to provide answers to the theological questions majority world Christians are now posing, particularly questions that are generated by issues related to their birth religions or pre-Christian backgrounds.

One question that looms large for majority world Christians is related to the status of the sacred or authoritative texts of their birth religions.[96] Many Christian theologians writing in these contexts display nuanced understandings of these texts, and they use their knowledge of them to provide points of contact for communicating the gospel. Points of contact are defined in this book as locutions (i.e., ideas, words, phrases, or texts), in particular those derived from the Qur'ān, that exhibit linguistic

94. Terminology like "majority world Christianity" or the "majority world church" refers to Christians in the non-western world, primarily Asia, Africa, and Latin America, who now make up the majority of the world's Christian population. For a discussion on the background of this terminology, see Tennent, *World Christianity*, xviii–xx. For more on the shift in the numbers of professing Christians currently taking place from the West to the global South, see Jenkins, *The Next Christendom*. For evangelical perspectives on issues related to the globalization of the Christian faith and its impact on theology, see Ott and Netland, *Globalizing Theology*.

95. Tennent, *World Christianity*, 1.

96. Tennent discusses this issue in ibid., 53–73. I make use of Tennent's criteria for evaluating Christian uses of non-canonical texts in chapter two.

and/or conceptual congruence with biblically conceived ideas. Christian theologians use this congruence to construct biblically enriched locutions that are then directed back into the Bible's hermeneutical and theological horizons. Their goal in such endeavors is to communicate the gospel in a comprehensible way. No presentation of the gospel exists in a vacuum, nor does any explication of Christian doctrine. For this reason, many majority world Christian theologians make use of their linguistic, cultural, and theological familiarity with other sacred texts in order to explain and communicate biblical teaching. In doing so, many of them adopt a "positive" or "irenic" approach to these other texts.[97] This does not mean that they affirm the system of belief signified by these texts. It does mean, however, that enough linguistic and conceptual congruence exists in the language, ideas, or meanings of the verses or texts they are citing to make positive use of them in their apologetic theology.

This type of approach has numerous precedents in church history. In addition to the attribute apology developed by Christian theologians residing in the world of Islam discussed previously, a well-known example is Justin Martyr's use of the *logos spermatikos* derived from Greek philosophy to discuss Christology in the second century.[98] Another example in a Hindu context is Brahmabandhav Upadhay's restatement of the doctrine of the Trinity in Upanishadic categories.[99] Practices of this sort raise a number of questions for Christians, particularly western evangelicals, examining them. Is it possible to advocate "Christian" readings of others' religious texts? What about using their language or theological categories to couch an explanation of Christian doctrines? Can their texts be appealed to in order to "prove" the veracity of core Christian beliefs like the divinity of Christ?

97. Within the context of religious studies, I do not mean by "irenic" what Rippin reports that Adams has stated as being a "greater appreciation of Islamic religiousness and the fostering of a new attitude toward it" [Rippin, "Literary Analysis," 159]. Rippin has rightly pointed out that such an approach avoids asking hard questions of the sources in question, in this case the Qur'ān. For Christians working in Islamic contexts, this particular understanding of "irenic" has the potential of subverting the uniqueness of God's revelation to humanity in Christ and the story of redemption.

98. For more, see Osborn, "Justin Martyr," 143–59.

99. See Tennent's discussion of both Justin Martyr's use of *logos spermatikos* and the use of the Upanishads in Tennent, *Christianity at the Religious Roundtable*, 199–229.

The Ongoing Debate

In a 2010 New York Times article,[100] Jerry Rankin, former president of IMB of the Southern Baptist Convention, was castigated by a former Muslim turned evangelical, Ergun Caner, for advocating evangelistic approaches among Muslims that employ qur'ānic passages as points of contact. The approach Caner criticized, known as the "CAMEL" method, uses qur'ānic passages as points of departure for sharing the gospel.[101] Advocates claim it is a contextualized approach for locating "persons of peace" who show evidence of the Spirit's work in their lives. Detractors, on the other hand, like Caner, claim that using qur'ānic passages in the context of testifying to the uniqueness of Christ compromises the gospel message. He also contends that the differences between the God of the Bible and the God of the Qur'ān are so stark that even using the Arabic word *Allāh* to refer to the biblical God distorts the Bible's teaching about his true identity.[102]

100. Oppenheimer, "Dispute on Using the Koran."

101. "CAMEL" is an acronym which stands for "Chosen," "Announced by Angels," "Miracles," and "Eternal Life." It is based on Q 3:42–55. Advocates of the method interpret these verses in a manner that identifies Jesus as the chosen one proclaimed by angels who knows the way to eternal life. See Greeson, *Camel*, 104–10. The current study is not an endorsement of the Camel method nor the Camel book *per se*, but it does engage in a biblical, historical, and theological analysis of the premise upon which the Camel method is based—using qur'ānic texts as points of contact in Christian theological writing or evangelistic presentations. How it is employed in the Camel method is a point of controversy not directly addressed in this book. Feeding that controversy, however, is the fact that many advocates of the Camel-like methods provide inadequate biblical, historical, and theological justification for their practices.

102. While many evangelicals are right to question the theological pluralism advocated by scholars like Miroslav Volf in his book *Allah: A Christian Response*, the approach of evangelicals like Caner leaves much to be desired. Ergun Caner and his brother, Emir Caner, have co-authored a polemical work against Islam wherein they criticize Christians who use "*Allāh*" to refer to the God of the Bible in Arabic. They purport that, "Many Arabic-speaking Christians use the Persian term *khudu* for God, rather than cause confusion by calling Allah the name *God* [sic]." Caner and Caner, *Unveiling Islam*, 106, *italics* original. The Caners' position in this regard is rather odd given that Arabic Christianity appears to originate in the New Testament itself (cf. Acts 2:11) and in light of the continued use of *Allāh* to refer to the God of the Bible by *all* Arabic-speaking Christians (and Jews) residing in the Middle East regardless of ecclesiastical affiliation. Granted, there are different conceptions of God's character in Christian and Muslim minds. But in Arabic these conceptions are not inherently tied to the term *Allāh* anymore than the numerous conceptions of "God" current in English-speaking contexts are tied to the word "God." In America, for instance, evangelicals, Catholics, Jews, Mormons, Jehovah's Witnesses and atheists alike all use the

Other evangelicals have been more nuanced in their approach to Muslim evangelism. In 1980, the Lausanne Committee for World Evangelization met in Pattaya, Thailand. Among the issues evangelicals discussed was Christian witness to Muslims. One of the mini-consultation meetings held during the conference issued a paper describing five different approaches to the Qur'ān advocated by evangelicals:

(a) The Qur'an should never be used in discussion with the Muslim, because using it implies that we accept it as inspired, and are putting it on the same level as the Bible.

(b) The Qur'an should be studied, but only to help us to know and appreciate what Muslims believe, and to enable us to learn Muslim terminology.

(c) The Qur'an should be used against itself, to demonstrate that it is self-contradictory. Such a polemic use of the Qur'an will show its weakness and create a hunger for something better.

(d) The Qur'an should be used as a starting point; e.g., the many verses that speak about Jesus and other biblical characters can be used to point to the biblical version of these same stories.

(e) The Qur'an can be used as a source of truth. Our recognition of all the truths which the Qur'an does contain makes the Muslim much less defensive and more open to read the New Testament. Since the Muslim has been told that the Bible has been corrupted, it is an enormous step forward for him even to read the Bible alongside the Qur'an.[103]

These five approaches demonstrate that contemporary evangelicals, like their predecessors in Christian history, display a spectrum of attitudes towards the Qur'ān. They also show that striving for a one-size-fits-all approach to the Qur'ān is complicated by numerous factors. Among those factors are the language and cultural setting of the church (or churches) posing the question and the relative size and proximity of the Muslim populations to where Christians live. In situations where

---

same word for God in English, which is not a controversy. The difference is in their conceptions of God's nature and character. Despite the Caners' contention, the referent "God" in English and "*Allāh*" in Arabic is one and the same, though the character of the referent may differ depending on usage. For more, see Tennent's discussion in, Tennent, *World Christianity*, 25–49; cf. also Brown, "Who Was 'Allah' before Islam?," 147–78.

103. *LOP*, "Christian Witness to Muslims," 12–13.

Christians are the majority and the predominant language and culture of the land has been shaped for centuries by a religious tradition other than Islam, adopting a position like (a) is understandable and, indeed, may be advisable.[104] But in situations where Christians are the minority and the predominant language and culture of the land has been shaped for centuries by terms, phrases, concepts, and diction influenced by the Qur'ān, the situation is more complex. This is especially the case for Christians from Arab-Muslim backgrounds. Are there any grounds—biblical, historical, and/or theological—for adopting a position like (b) or (d) or (e)? Or is (c) the only prudent option for evangelicals to adopt? If so, how should Arabic-speaking Christians approach the Qur'ān, especially those residing in the world of Islam who are seeking to engage Muslims in meaningful discourse on the Bible and Christian doctrines? Moreover, how should western evangelicals evaluate and respond to these practices?

Theological Method and Hermeneutics in Arab-Muslim Milieus

In his book, *Missiological Models in Ministry to Muslims*, Sam Schlorff argues that Christians seeking to contextualize the message of the gospel for Muslim peoples should not use anything in the Qur'ān or Islamic culture to do so. At the heart of the Betrothal Model of contextualization advocated by Schlorff are two central issues, the notion of "theological starting points" and hermeneutics.

First, building on J. H. Bavinck's conception of points of contact, Schlorff argues that the Christian Scriptures should be the sole contextual or theological starting point for evangelicals.[105] By contextual starting point, Schlorff means "the sources, whether theological or cultural, that will be used in the contextualization of the gospel and the church. The

104. I would disagree, however, with the idea that referencing the Qur'ān automatically implies someone accepts it as inspired (see chapter two). That being stated, it is important that this book not be construed as promoting the idea that Christians should reference the Qur'ān in *all* conversations with Muslims. In many circumstances there is no need to reference the Qur'ān when talking about the Bible, Christian doctrines, or sharing the gospel with Muslims. This can even be the case, under certain circumstances, with Arabic-speaking Muslims. Thus, I am not *prescribing* qur'ānic referencing as a necessary part of sharing the gospel or explaining the tenets of Christianity in Islamic contexts in all places and at all times. I am arguing that it is justifiable under certain circumstances, particularly for indigenous Christians residing in the world of Islam.

105. Bavinck, *Science of Missions*, 132–40. Schlorff follows Bavinck's approach throughout.

choice of starting point [in Schlorff's estimation] controls the hermeneutical method that will be used for interpreting the biblical message within the receptor culture."[106] He goes on to conclude that there is no biblical precedent for using "the receptor culture as [a] starting point for the contextualization either of theology or of the church."[107] Therefore, "One cannot use the Qur'an as a source of truth for proclaiming the gospel or try to fill Muslim forms with Christian meanings."[108]

Second, Schlorff argues that the two hermeneutical methods traditionally employed by Protestant missionaries for referencing the Qur'ān in Muslim contexts, the prooftexting method and what he calls the "new hermeneutic," are essentially syncretistic.[109] The first method aims to read Christian meanings into select qur'ānic passages while the second method "envisages a two-way synthesis where both the Qur'an and the Bible are opened up to meanings from the other."[110] Schlorff objects to the use of both methods on three grounds. First, these methods remove the passages from their qur'ānic contexts. Second, they cut the texts off from their "original meaning," offering "sectarian" interpretations of key verses. And third, such methods introduce an authority conflict into the young church. Schlorff believes that beginning any theological conversation by referencing the Qur'ān, such as during an evangelistic encounter or in Christian theological writing, implies one sees the book as a source of religious authority.

The solution, according to Schlorff, is to engage in an analytic method of Qur'ān interpretation that is consistent with how one interprets the Bible. This method is guided by three principles. First, the meaning of a text is determined by analyzing the original language. This entails investigating how various terms are used within the context of the Qur'ān's original language system and cultural context. The result, Schlorff states, is that "Qur'anic language may not be interpreted in terms of what one

106. Schlorff, *Models*, 115.

107. Ibid., 122.

108. Ibid., 149. As an evangelical, my assumption throughout this book is that the Qur'ān is a product of its environment. Though it is clearly in conversation with biblical and extra-biblical literature and legends, it is not an inspired document from God. This does not mean, however, that there are not true statements in the Qur'ān. For more, see the discussion in chapter two. For a discussion on the revelatory status of the Qur'ān from an evangelical perspective, see Coleman, "The Insider Movement Paradigm," 92–138.

109. Cf. also Schlorff, "The Hermeneutical Crisis," 143–51.

110. Schlorff, *Models*, 126.

might think similar biblical language might have meant. It cannot be filled with Christian content."[111]

Second, Schlorff says that all interpretations of the Qur'ān must begin with the presuppositions of the believing community—the Muslim community. For Schlorff,

> This does not mean that we ultimately accept the presuppositions of the community as being true in themselves. Nor does it mean that we reject out of hand historical-critical methods for the study of the Qur'an . . . . What it *does* mean is that we take the presuppositions of the Muslim community as the starting point to understanding the Qur'an's meaning, and, therefore, basic to our use of the Qur'an in presenting the gospel.[112]

Indeed, for Schlorff, "This should be considered the *sine qua non* of our use of the Qur'an in communicating the gospel to Muslims."[113]

The third principle is that the believing community of the book is central to its interpretation. In other words, Christians must interpret the Qur'ān in a manner that accords with the corpus of classical Muslim *tafsīr* literature. Schlorff argues that Christians must "respect the primacy of the Islamic tradition of Qur'anic interpretation" if we expect Muslims to "respect the primacy of Christian tradition of biblical interpretation."[114] Schlorff believes that the method of analysis he advocates will enable Christians to avoid the syncretizing tendencies endemic to the prooftexting method and the new hermeneutic.

Doug Coleman has also urged caution for evangelicals using the Qur'ān in the context of evangelistic encounters and discussions about Christian doctrines. He argues that those who advocate referencing the Qur'ān as proof for the veracity of Christian doctrines, like the Trinity and Incarnation, create "epistemological confusion" in the nascent church.[115] Though Coleman, unlike Schlorff, makes room for evangelicals who qualify their use of the Qur'ān in Islamic contexts,[116] both believe that those who do so have yet to provide adequate hermeneutical

111. Ibid., 133.

112. Ibid., 135; emphasis original.

113. Ibid.

114. Ibid., 136.

115. Coleman, "Insider Movement Paradigm," 107–13.

116. Ibid., 109.

and theological justification for their practice.[117] Moreover, both are particularly sensitive to those who appeal to the Qur'ān as evidence for the truth of the Bible and the specially revealed doctrines found therein, particularly the Trinity and Incarnation.

There are a number of problems both with Schlorff's approach to theological method and hermeneutics that I hope to address throughout the course of this book, particularly in chapter five. Before proceeding, however, it is important to note that, historically, evangelicals seeking answers to questions like whether there is justification for making positive use of the Qur'ān have oftentimes turned to the history of Protestant interaction with Islam for answers. For years the works of pioneers like William St. Clair Tisdall (d. 1928), Samuel Zwemer (d. 1952), Kenneth Cragg (d. 2012),[118] and others have shaped the approach evangelicals have taken towards Islam, the Qur'ān, and contextualization. Undoubtedly, their works contain many valuable insights into the Muslim worldview and how to communicate the gospel in such contexts. Rarely, however, have western Christians, especially evangelicals, turned to Eastern Christianity,[119] particularly Arabic Christian texts, in order to provide answers to contemporary missiological questions. What continues to plague evangelical theological reflection on Islam and discussions of

117. Schlorff and Coleman's critiques are aimed primarily at western missionaries laboring in Muslim contexts and advocating ecclesiological models that diminish the need for believers to meet in distinct groups (i.e., churches), united by their common faith in Christ. Such approaches have been termed "Insider Movements" given the fact that many of these professed followers of Jesus remain "inside" their birth religions. Discussion of Insider ecclesiology, soteriology, etc., is beyond the scope of the present book and has been thoroughly treated by Coleman and others. However, it is important to point out that the positive use of the Qur'ān investigated here is advocated by many who consider themselves proponents of the Insider Movement Paradigm, such as Maẓhar al-Mallūḥī (see below). But the approach is not limited solely to Insider Movement advocates as the historical section of this book clearly demonstrates.

118. Griffith has pointed out that Cragg, in his book, *The Arab Christian*, displays a lack of appreciation and knowledge of the accomplishments of Christians writing in Arabic from the eighth century onward. Cragg's basic conclusion is that Arabic Christianity "failed to marry itself to the Arab psyche." Griffith has criticized Cragg for failing to read the works of Arab Christians on their own terms and showing "no reluctance to sit in judgment on centuries of Christian life in the Arab world for not having perceived the desirability of relating to Islam in ways similar to those Cragg himself had developed so notably in his career." See Griffith, "Kenneth Cragg," 31; cf. also Cragg, *The Arab Christian*.

119. An important exception to this among evangelicals is Greear, "*Theosis* and Muslim Evangelism."

contextualization in the Muslim world is the dearth of studies examining how indigenous Christians residing in these areas have addressed many of the very questions and issues now facing those in the West. Their emic perspectives are crucial for arriving at a position on an issue like Christian exegesis and apologetic use of the Qur'ān that is faithful to Scripture, historically well informed, and contextually relevant to the Arab-Muslim milieu. Griffith's urgent appeal is pertinent in this regard: "Now is the time for westerners to consider the lessons to be learned from the experience of Christians who have lived in the world of Islam for centuries."[120] This book aims to explore what western evangelicals can learn about the apologetic use of the Qur'ān in medieval and contemporary Arabic Christian theological writings.[121]

STATEMENT OF THESIS

This book argues that in Arabic-speaking Muslim milieus Christians are justified in making positive apologetic use of qur'ānic points of contact in religious discourse about the Bible and Christian doctrines, including Christology.

METHODOLOGY, LIMITATIONS, AND THE TEXTS

Methodology

The primary method for defending my thesis is an examination, interpretation, and theological analysis of written sources. The chapters are arranged so as to offer three grounds of defense for my thesis: (1) an exegetical argument based on Acts 17 (chapter two), (2) historical and textual arguments based on representative examples of positive uses of qur'ānic points of contact selected from two medieval and two

120. Griffith, *Shadow*, 179.

121. Oftentimes one gets the impression from some majority world Christians, or their western advocates, that western evangelicals are obliged to accept their positions on issues of contextualization without critique simply because they are "insiders" and westerners are "outsiders." While western Christians would do well to remember that ultimate responsibility for contextualizing the gospel lies with majority world Christians (see chapter five), majority world Christians and their western advocates must remember that their faith in Christ unites them to the global body of Christ. This union obligates them to listen carefully to the reservations many evangelicals (western or otherwise) exhibit towards certain practices, even if they disagree with them. Doing so demonstrates their commitment both to Christ and his body. One cannot be separated from the other.

contemporary Arabic Christian texts (chapters three and four), and (3) a theological argument based on the dialogical method of contextualization, which includes a critique of Schlorff's theological and hermeneutical method (chapter five). It is upon these three bases that I determine that there is justification for Christians who make positive use of qur'ānic texts as points of contact in Arabic-speaking milieus.

The first part of this chapter demonstrates that historically those who sought to engage in meaningful discourse in Arabic about Christian doctrines could not avoid what the Qur'ān says. Today, many Christians residing within the world of Islam argue that more has to be done if Christians are to articulate an understanding of their faith that speaks in language and categories that Arab Muslims understand. Many of them are writing their apologetic theology for the nascent Muslim-background church and the broader Arab Muslim populace. For some of them, the question is not how one can avoid the Qur'ān. The issue is how one is to go about referencing the Qur'ān in such a way that the Bible's world of discourse is allowed to subsume (i.e., to confirm, correct, challenge, and ultimately critique) the Qur'ān's world of discourse and the attendant misconstrual of salvation history developed by Muslim scholars.

Chapter two looks at Paul's Areopagus speech in Acts 17, a passage that both proponents and detractors of qur'ānic points of contact often cite in their treatment of this issue. Close analysis of this passage demonstrates that Paul repositions quotes from Greek literature, originally intended and written in praise of Zeus, within a hermeneutical context with biblical horizons. Paul's practice in this regard, so it is argued, offers us a precedent for how to approach others' religious texts. Timothy Tennent has analyzed this subject and offers hermeneutical guidelines for the apologetic use of sacred and authoritative literature from other religious traditions. I discuss his guidelines in chapter two and expand on them for use with the Qur'ān.

Chapters three and four serve to illustrate examples of positive uses of qur'ānic locutions in Arabic Christian texts selected from two of the most fruitful and creative periods of Arabic theology in history, the 'Abbāsid era (750–1258) and the modern era. In my analysis of the texts, both the medieval ones and the contemporary ones, I do not investigate each and every instance of qur'ānic borrowing, prooftexting, or allusion. Nor do I investigate problematic instances of qur'ānic referencing. My focus is limited to exploring representative examples of positive uses of qur'ānic points of contact in the context of discussing three broad

Christological themes: the divinity of Christ, the Incarnation, and Jesus' crucifixion and resurrection.

The final chapter draws from the insights of evangelical theologians like David Clark and Kevin Vanhoozer in order to critique Schlorff's view of theological method and contextualization. I also build on the insights of critical scholarship on the Qur'ān and the origins of Islam, in particular that of John Wansbrough and Gabriel Said Reynolds, to justify distancing the Qur'ān from how it is interpreted in the classical *tafsīr* literature. That literature contains within it the Muslim construal of salvation history. One of the conclusions of chapter five and broad implications of this book is that there is apologetic value for Christians who interpret the Qur'ān in ways that separate it from the corpus of classical literature normally utilized by Muslims to interpret it.

Ultimately, the goal of any truly Christian apologetic theology authored in an Arabic-speaking context must be to subvert the Qur'ān-based, theological infrastructure that supports the Muslim construal of salvation history. That depiction of salvation history denies Christ's work on the cross and subverts the grand biblical narrative at several key points. Obviously, this means that there are limits to the positive use of qur'ānic texts as points of contact. Those points of contact must give way to points of contrast and even contradiction. Nevertheless, in order to communicate the gospel effectively in Arabic-speaking milieus, must one adopt a strictly polemical approach to the Qur'ān? Is this the only approach that can rightly be considered "Christian" or "evangelical?" Or is there room for positive uses of qur'ānic texts even if we assume, as all Christians should, that the Qur'ān is not inspired nor can it lead one to saving faith in Christ?

Limitations

My primary focus in this book is to demonstrate and defend the positive use of select verses from the Qur'ān as a point of contact; however, I recognize this approach has limits. I indicate some of the boundaries to the positive use of the Qur'ān in the guidelines I adopt in chapter two. It is important to understand, however, that I am not attempting to offer a comprehensive approach to the Qur'ān, nor am I trying to delineate each and every way Christians can make positive use of the Qur'ān or critique each and every negative use of the Muslim scripture. With those points in mind, there are two broad limitations that are important to mention at the outset. First, I am limiting my discussion of this topic to Arabic-speaking contexts since this is the only Muslim context within which Christians have to articulate their theology in the sacred language of the Qur'ān—Arabic. Extrapolations from this work to other contexts may be justifiable; however, I do not discuss the implications of my findings for other contexts. Second, I am limiting myself to positive uses of the Qur'ān since these are illustrative of what my thesis aims to demonstrate. This should not be construed as an endorsement of how the authors examined here reference the Qur'ān in each and every case. In my estimation, there are problematic uses of the Qur'ān in each text. However, the existence of negative examples does not automatically invalidate approaches that make positive use of the Qur'ān. These caveats are particularly important to remember when it comes to the two contemporary Bible commentaries examined here.

Both of the commentaries were published by the al-Kalima School, based in Beirut, Lebanon.[122] Maẓhar al-Mallūḥī is the pioneer of al-Kalima's efforts to produce Bible commentaries that take seriously Arab-Muslim frames of reference. And he is to be commended for his efforts. However, many evangelicals have rightly criticized Paul-Gordon Chandler's biography of Mallūḥī, *Pilgrims of Christ on the Muslim Road*.[123] Chandler's treatment of several issues in this biography raises a number of theological questions for Christians committed to the finality of God's revelation to humanity in Christ as revealed in the Bible. This is particularly the case when one looks at Chandler (or Mallūḥī's?) apparent championing of a separation between ecclesiology and soteriology in an attempt to justify what many have labeled "Insider ecclesiology," a reference to the Insider Movement Paradigm.[124] Examining and critiquing

122. The "al-Kalima School" represents a group of Christian and Muslim scholars based in Beirut, Lebanon. They are led by Maẓhar al-Mallūḥī, a self-described Syrian Muslim follower of Christ, and are working on a set of commentaries and a new translation of the Bible that aim to "bridge the the chasm of misunderstanding between Muslims and Christians . . ." (Al-Kalima, "Translation Project").

123. Chandler, *Pilgrims of Christ*. Chandler's treatment of the issues he raises in his book is haphazard. Exacerbating the issue is the difficulty one has in determining what constitutes the position of Mallūḥī and what constitutes the opinions of Chandler himself. Much of the problem stems from the antagonistic attitude the book (and Mallūḥī?) displays towards conservative evangelicals (cf., e.g., 39, 79, 185). Again, it is difficult to discern if this is in fact the position of Mallūḥī or Chandler. For a reviews of the book see, Simnowitz, Review of *Pilgrims of Christ*, by Paul-Gordon Chandler; Engdahl, Review of *Pilgrims of Christ*, by Paul-Gordon Chandler.

124. Chandler, *Pilgrims*, 40, 115, *et passim*. Cf. also Mallouhi, "Comments on the

these issues is beyond the scope of the present work. Nevertheless, support for how certain authors from the al-Kalima School, including Mallūḥī himself, use the Qur'ān should not be interpreted as endorsement of all their theological positions.

My focus here, in fact, is much narrower. I am interested in demonstrating that, within certain boundaries, Christians in Arabic-speaking contexts are justified in making positive use of qur'ānic texts when discussing the Bible, Christian faith, and the specially revealed doctrines unique to Christianity. As the historical overview of Arabic Christianity demonstrated, Christians residing within the world of Islam faced a unique set of circumstances when it came to adopting Arabic as a language of Christian theological discourse.[125] Their theology instinctively reflects and responds to qur'ānic critiques and Islamic themes and, in many cases, employs qur'ānic language and verses in defense of Christian beliefs and practices. Those elements are also evident in the writings of some contemporary Christian theologians residing in the Arab world who are aiming to write a theology that speaks the language of the broader Muslim populace, while addressing the barriers that prevent them from understanding the gospel. The goal of this book, therefore, is to defend the principle that, within certain boundaries, positive apologetic use of the Qur'ān as a point of contact is justifiable. The textual case studies in chapters three and four illustrate some of the ways this has been done and is being done in the theology of Arabic-speaking Christians.

The Texts

Two criteria have been used to choose the selected texts. First, they all exhibit a generally positive or irenic approach to the Qur'ān versus a direct polemical attack. Second, the medieval texts were chosen because they affirm dyophysite Christology (i.e., they are all from the Chalcedonian or Melkite community). Granted, during the early 'Abbāsid period, a number of apologetic works featuring positive uses of the Qur'ān were authored by representatives from the other two ecclesiastical communities in the Middle East—the Jacobites and the Nestorians. But given that the

Insider Movement," 3–14. Tennent has analyzed and critiqued the problems of the Insider Movement and noted the crucial link between ecclesiology and soteriology in Tennent, "Followers of Jesus," 101–15; Tennent, *World Christianity*, 193–220.

125. For more on the subject of Arabic as a "Christian" language, see Swanson, "Arabic as a Christian Language"; Swanson, "Early Christian-Muslim Theological Conversation."

dyophysite Christology of the medieval Melkites is consistent with that of the modern al-Kalima School and the two Bible commentaries they have published, it is important to see how the modern community has appropriated that Christology given the similarity of apologetic strategy vis-à-vis the Qur'ān.

Regarding the medieval texts, the two works selected date from the first 'Abbāsid century and represent two genres of Christian apologetic literature. One is from the "systematic treatise" genre, and the other is representative of the "monk in the Emir's *majlis*" genre.[126] The early 'Abbāsid era was a period when Muslim scholars had yet to reach methodological consensus regarding how to interpret and apply the Qur'ān.[127] It appears there was openness among some to entertaining a variety of interpretations. This openness would decline as Muslim scholars reached agreement regarding the role that *ḥadīth* would play in determining the meaning of the Qur'ān. Part of the motivation for reaching a methodological consensus was to curtail what many Muslims viewed as sectarian interpretations of the Qur'ān. Today, there is a new openness among some in the Middle East to entertaining alternative interpretations of the Qur'ān and distancing its interpretation from the *ḥadīth*. Partial evidence of this can be seen in the growing "Qur'ānist" movement.[128] But the apologetic value of advocating such alternative interpretations has yet to be fully analyzed by Christians.

The first text, *On the Triune Nature of God*, was mentioned previously. It is an anonymous systematic theological treatise and represents one of the oldest apologies for the Christian faith in Arabic. It dates to 755 or 788.[129] Given its antiquity, it deserves the attention of evangelicals. The second text is Theodore Abū Qurra's debate with Muslim *mutakallimūn* in the *majlis* of the 'Abbāsid Caliph, al-Ma'mūn (d. 833).[130] It reportedly

126. Griffith identifies and labels four genres of Christian theological and apologetic literature. They are: (1) the systematic treatise, (2) questions and answers, (3) the monk in the Emir's *majlis*, and (4) the epistolary exchange. Griffith, *Shadow*, 75–92.

127. Schacht demonstrates this in his classic study on the role *ḥadīth* played in the early systematization of Islamic legal thought. See Schacht, *Muhammadan Jurisprudence*.

128. For more, see www.quranists.net; Reynolds, *Emergence*, 43, 91–92, 207–8.

129. Griffith argues it dates from 755 and Swanson calculates the date to be around 788. See Griffith, *Shadow*, 53–57, 89–90n47; Swanson, "Dating," 115–41. For a partial publication of the treatise and an English translation, see Gibson, ed.,'*On the Triune Nature of God*.' Cf. also Swanson, "Apology."

130. The Arabic edition of this text used in this book was edited and published by

took place in Ḥarrān ca. 829. Abū Qurra is the first named theologian to author original theological treatises in Arabic.

The contemporary texts come from two commentaries on the Gospel of John and the Gospels and Acts published by the al-Kalima School—*A Sufi Reading of the Gospel of John*[131] and *The True Meaning of the Gospel and Acts in Arabic*.[132] All the commentaries and books published by al-Kalima have the explicit aim of helping Arabic-speaking Muslims, especially those who have chosen to follow Christ, understand the Bible. They aim to "re-present the Scriptures as the ancient Middle Eastern sacred writings that they are—returning them to their authentic cultural origin."[133] Several articles treating questions and topics pertinent to Arabic-speaking Muslims preface each of the two Bible commentaries. Given that al-Kalima's authors wrote the two commentaries with the explicit aim of offering a contextually sensitive reading of the Bible for the Arab world, these articles offer an excellent place to examine contemporary Arabic Christian approaches to biblical and theological interpretation.[134]

CONTRIBUTION TO THE FIELD

Over the past several decades, evangelicals and others have produced a number of books, articles, and dissertations addressing various aspects related to communicating the gospel in Muslim contexts and Muslim conversion to Christianity. Some have dealt explicitly with communication strategies,[135] while others have treated issues like baptism,[136] conversion and

Dick, *Mujādalat Abī Qurra*. See discussion below.

131. al-Mallūḥī et al., eds., *Qirāʾa Ṣūfīya*.

132. al-Jaṭlāwī et al., eds., *al-Maʿnā al-Ṣaḥīḥ*.

133. Chandler, *Pilgrims*, 68. The translation philosophy of the al-Kalima School is not treated at any depth in the present work. It is apparent, however, that some, including Jay Smith, have mischaracterized their works as "Muslim compliant translations." See al-Kalima Editorial Committee, "Response to Jay Smith," 15–20.

134. It is important to state that some of the al-Kalima authors would not self-identify as "Christians." With that in mind, I use the term "Christian" in a general manner to describe all those who affirm the historic tenets of the faith and view Christ as God's definitive revelation to humanity. Taken as a whole, this is the stance all of al-Kalima's publications and the articles found therein.

135. E.g., Register, *Dialogue and Interfaith Witness*; cf. also Accad, "Christian Attitudes toward Islam and Muslims," 29–48.

136. E.g., Wilson, "The Stigma of Baptism."

identity issues,[137] and evangelism.[138] There have also been studies on ecclesiology and church planting.[139] Still other studies have focused on the most effective means of contextualization in Muslim contexts[140] and evaluating various theological and missiological models.[141] Some of these have been historical studies, examining the strategies of Protestant missionaries.[142] But to date very few have examined the theology and apologetic strategies of indigenous Christians residing in the world of Islam and writing their theology in the language of the Qur'ān—Arabic. Moreover, the various historical and philological studies done on early Arabic Christian texts have oftentimes overlooked the theological and missiological implications these texts hold for evangelicals writing theology in the Middle East, particularly the nascent Muslim-background church.[143]

Some evangelical scholars, like Martin Parsons, seem to think that very little was done by indigenous Christians living within the world of Islam to contextualize the gospel. In his treatment of Christology, Parsons writes that "it has been already been well documented that where the ancient churches do exist in the Islamic world, they have clung tenaciously to the liturgical forms and creedal expressions such as the Nicene Creed that were in use prior to the advent of Islam with little attempt at any form of contextualisation."[144] Parsons apparently believes that all

137. E.g., Gaudeul, *Called from Islam to Christ*; Greenham, "Muslim Conversions to Christ"; Kraft, "Community and Identity"; Dunning, "Palestinian Muslims"; Qureshi, *Seeking Allah*.

138. E.g., Parshall, *New Paths*; Miller, "Living among the Breakage."

139. E.g., Stephens, "Muslim Background Believer Groups in Arabland."

140. E.g., Parshall, *Muslim Evangelization*; Parsons, *Unveiling God*; Stern, "Contextualization in Muslim Ministry."

141. E.g., Harlan, "Theologizing in Arab Muslim Contexts"; Schlorff, *Missiological Models*. Harlan's treatment of the Qur'ān as a point of contact leaves much to be desired. It spans merely one page (pp. 231–32) and concludes by asserting that the Qur'ān is a legitimate source of "spiritual edification for Christian and Muslim background followers of the Messiah." He goes on to state that he is uncomfortable in viewing Islam strictly as a man-made religion "because its origins seem to have been supernaturally initiated" (244). Harlan's positions are not endorsed in this book.

142. E.g., Pikkert, *Protestant Missionaries*.

143. An encouraging exception to this is the Protestant Egyptian Scholar, Wageeh Mikhail, who has argued that much can be gleaned from early Arabic Christian theology. See Mikhail, "The Missiological Significance of Early Christian Arab Theology."

144. Parsons, *Unveiling God*, 34n2.

constructive theological activity ceased after Muslim armies captured the ancient heartlands of Christendom.[145]

Mark Beaumont's book, *Christology in Dialogue with Muslims*,[146] is an important exception to this general pattern. In addition to looking at contemporary Protestant and Catholic approaches to Christology in Muslim contexts, he examines how three medieval Arabic-speaking Christians explain the Incarnation. Among the texts he examines are several by Theodore Abū Qurra.[147] However, he does not examine Abū Qurra's debate in the *majlis* of al-Ma'mūn nor is he concerned with how the texts he evaluates use the Qur'ān.

Wafik Nasry has studied Abū Qurra's debate and prepared a critical edition of the Arabic text based on several extant manuscripts.[148] While his work provides a helpful index of qur'ānic verses used in the debate, his study is primarily concerned with collating the extant manuscripts to produce an eclectic edition of the Arabic text along with an English translation.[149] In doing so, he incorporates the Arabic edition of the text prepared by Ignace Dick,[150] which is the version used here since Nasry's edition was not yet available when I commenced this study. Nasry's work also provides a helpful historical study on Abū Qurra and the circumstances surrounding the text.

David Bertaina's dissertation builds on Griffith's examination of Abū Qurra's debate.[151] But his primary concern is with editing and translating a Garshūnī recension of the text. Bertaina's book on Christian-Muslim dialogues analyzes and comments on Abu Qurra's use of the Qur'ān in the debate text under examination in this book; however, he does not

145. Parsons begins his study with a historical overview of the Church Fathers and their Christology. He then jumps to nineteenth century Protestant missionary approaches to Christology in Muslim contexts, apparently concluding that no creative attempts were made to explain Christ to Muslims during the intervening centuries. Parsons's oversight in this regard is representative of the broad unfamiliarity many evangelicals display towards Arab Christian history and theology.

146. Beaumont, *Christology in Dialogue with Muslims.*

147. The Arabic texts he examines are from Bacha, *Les oeuvres arabes de Théodore Aboucara.*

148. Nasry, *Abū Qurrah wa al-Ma'mūn.*

149. Nasry, *The Caliph and the Bishop.*

150. See the discussion in ch. 3.

151. Bertaina, "Arabic Account"; and Griffith, "Arab Christian Texts."

reflect on how Abū Qurra's use of the Qur'ān might pose problems for those with evangelical convictions.[152]

Clare Wilde's dissertation is similar. She evaluates the apologetic strategies used to interpret the Qur'ān in three medieval texts.[153] Her investigation focuses on analyzing how the Qur'ān was used to "prove" Christian truths by the respective authors.[154] But like Bertaina, her study does not evaluate how the use of the Qur'ān as a point of contact in the discussion of the Bible and Christian doctrines poses potential problems from an evangelical perspective.

Mark Swanson[155] and Samir Khalil Samir[156] have both examined the numerous allusions to and quotes from the Qur'ān in the treatise, *On the Triune Nature of God*. My treatment of the text highlights the pertinent aspects of their studies and examines parts of the treatise they do not address. Additionally, I use the guidelines established in chapter two to illustrate how the author uses the points of linguistic and conceptual congruence he finds in the Qur'ān in order to construct a defense of core Christian doctrines and the Bible's construal of salvation history.

Analyzing how the Qur'ān impacts religious discourse in Arabic is important for those who are aiming to write contextually relevant theology for the Arab world. In order to advance that goal, it is imperative that evangelicals become aware of the rich history of theology written by Christians residing within the world of Islam. This is important for many reasons but it is especially important for those discipling converts to the faith from Muslim backgrounds. Converts are in need of connecting with Arab Christian history and learning positive examples of how Christians have witnessed to their Muslim neighbors. These are also issues Christians in the West increasingly have to address and who better to learn from than Middle Eastern Christians who have dealt with these issues for over a millennium.

152. Bertaina, *Dialogues*, 212–28.

153. The three texts she investigates are Theodore Abū Qurra's debate in the court of the Caliph al-Ma'mūn (examined here), the unpublished Arabic manuscript from the 9th c., Sinai MS 434, entitled, "*Answers for the Shaykh*," and Paul of Antioch's letter, *Letter to a Muslim Friend*.

154. Wilde's dissertation is also interested in what evidence scholars can garner from the texts she examines for the existence of what she describes as "non-'Uthmānic Qur'ān codices." Cf. also, Wilde, "Evidence for Non-'Uthmānic Qur'ān Codices," 358–71.

155. Swanson, "Beyond Prooftexting."

156. Samir, "Earliest Arab Apology."

2

The New Testament and the Apologetic Use of Noncanonical Sacred Literature

As the previous chapter noted, many Arabic-speaking Christians residing in the world of Islam relate to the Qur'ān in nuanced ways. Undoubtedly, this stems from their intimate familiarity with the language, concepts, and the worldview represented in the Muslim scripture. It is not surprising, therefore, that many of these Christians display scant aversion to referencing qur'ānic texts as points of contact in their discussions of Christ with their family, friends, and neighbors. Nor should it surprise us that theologians writing for Muslim audiences in these contexts make positive use of the Qur'ān in their discussions of the Bible and Christian doctrines.

Analyzing and illustrating examples of how Arabic-speaking Christians have done this will be the subject of chapters three and four in this book; however, before looking at those historical and contemporary examples, it is important from an evangelical perspective to pose and answer two questions: First, are there any biblical models or precedents for referencing noncanonical sacred texts in evangelistic encounters and theological writings? Second, can we deduce any guidelines from Scripture that provide direction for evangelicals referencing texts like the Qur'ān? Below I argue that Acts 17 provides both a biblical precedent and guidelines for evangelicals analyzing apologetic uses of the Qur'ān. But before looking at Acts 17, it is first important to comment generally on the New Testament's interaction with other texts.

OTHER TEXTS AND THE NEW TESTAMENT

In his book, *Theology in the Context of World Christianity*, Timothy Tennent addresses the issue of the Bible's use of noncanonical sacred literature.[1] His discussion identifies four ways in which the New Testament interacts with other texts. In what follows I will summarize the four ways Tennent mentions and then focus on the third since it provides a precedent for referencing noncanonical sacred literature in the context of discussing God's revelation to humanity in Christ.

The first way consists of canonical borrowing. Two examples can be offered in this regard. The first one is not surprising; it is the extensive quotation from and allusion to the Hebrew Bible found in the New Testament.[2] All Christians and Bible scholars would agree that the Hebrew Bible is the foundational document from which the New Testament authors draw in order to demonstrate that Jesus is the long-awaited Messiah and King of the world. In light of Hebrew Bible's inclusion within the canon of Christian Scripture and its foundational role in narrating the origins of the universe, the fall of humanity into sin, and God's plan of redemption and restoration, it is understandable that the writers of the New Testament would quote from and allude to it liberally. The second example of canonical borrowing is the incorporation of a large portion of Mark's gospel into both Matthew and Luke. Carson and Moo estimate that Matthew makes use of about 90 percent of Mark while Luke uses roughly 55 percent.[3] In both cases, one canonical book in the Bible, Mark, serves as the primary source for two other books, Matthew and Luke.

The second way identified by Tennent whereby the New Testament interacts with other texts also concerns Matthew and Luke. Scholars have long postulated a common source to explain the verbal parallelisms for the non-Markan material in the two gospels. The source of this "Jesus Material" is oftentimes referred to as "Q" or *Quelle* ("source" in German). Though the existence of Q is pure conjecture, it continues to be used to explain certain structural and linguistic similarities between Matthew and Luke, even by evangelical scholars.[4] Related to this is Luke's admitted reliance upon sources in order to "compile a narrative of the things

1. Tennent, *World Christianity*, 55–60.

2. In some cases the biblical authors quote from or paraphrase the Septuagint. In other cases they quote from or paraphrase the Hebrew Bible. For an introduction to this topic, see Berding and Lunde, *New Testament Use of the Old Testament*.

3. Carson and Moo, *Introduction to the New Testament*, 212.

4. Ibid., 98–101.

that have been accomplished among us." (Luke 1:1). It is conceivable that Luke's research would have included an examination of eyewitness reports, verbal testimonies, and written records.[5] Each case, however, constitutes an instance of borrowing from sources that are intimately related to the life and history of God's people. Even Jude's use of the non-canonical book 1 Enoch is explicable by the fact that he is referencing a text that is tangentially related to the life and experience of God's people.[6] But there are a few cases where the New Testament authors reference texts that have no connection whatsoever to Israel's past.

Describing this third category of texts, Tennent points out that they have "no natural connection to the Christian movement . . . ."[7] Notable in this regard are Paul's quote from the Greek comedy *Thais* in 1 Cor 15:33 and his quotation of Epimenides in Titus 1:12.[8] Two other references found in Acts 17, however, are more illustrative of how Paul uses the sacred texts of pagan religious traditions in the context of sharing the gospel. For this reason, we will investigate more closely how Paul references those texts in order to determine if, in fact, they provide a precedent and hermeneutical guidance for Christians referencing the Qur'ān. But before proceeding, there is one final category of texts that warrants discussion.

Tennent's fourth category involves a discussion of biblical texts that appear in the sacred texts of other religions. His primary example in this regard is the Qur'ān. Tennent notes that the Qur'ān contains numerous allusions and references to events and personalities from the Bible. However, there are no direct quotations from Scripture that one can point to in the Qur'ān. The references to biblical topoi are likely the result of oral contact with Jews and Christians. But even if the Qur'ān did contain direct quotations from the Bible (as the Book of Mormon does), would this constitute grounds for considering the book inspired or revealed in the Christian sense?

If biblical quotations or even ideas find their way into the text of another religion and those quotations are used to undermine any of the

5. Ibid., 212–13.

6. For more on Jude's use of 1 Enoch see Charles, "Jude's Use of Pseudepigraphical Source Material," 130–45. Tennent includes Jude's use of 1 Enoch in his third category of texts; however, given the text's relationship to the life and experience of God's people, I think it is more helpful to include it in the second category.

7. Tennent, *World Christianity*, 58.

8. Ibid.

"great turning points in redemptive history," as D. A. Carson terms them, they cannot be spoken of as inspired or revealed.[9] As Tennent states, "From a Christian point of view, since these texts have been taken out of their Christological and ecclesiological context when brought into the Qur'ān, they may no longer be spoken of as either inspired or revealed, even though those particular statements that the Qur'ān has incorporated into its text without distortion remain trustworthy and true."[10] In other words, Christians can affirm the truth of select verses, statements, or ideas in the Qur'ān, including those that reference biblical or Christian topoi, without believing they are inspired or revealed. For the Christian, the only inspired and revealed book is the Bible and, as such, it is true in its entirety. However, not all true statements (or ideas) are inspired or revealed by God, but this does not in any way undermine their truthfulness. With this in mind we now turn to investigate Paul's positive use of a pagan object of worship and pagan literature in his defense of the gospel.

PAUL'S APOLOGETIC STRATEGY ON MARS HILL

The use of noncanonical literature in the Bible is a reminder of the missional context within which God revealed his Word to his followers. The Christian faith is unique in the way it interacts with and adheres to each cultural and linguistic context where it is accepted. The uniqueness of the faith is found in its ability to cross every conceivable cultural and linguistic boundary to penetrate and find a home in environments hostile to the faith. A case in point is Paul's interaction with the Athenian philosophers in Acts 17.

Paul's Areopagus speech is considered by many to provide *the* model for Christians examining biblical examples of intercultural evangelism, apologetics, and contextualization.[11] Most scholars view the speech as paradigmatic for Christians communicating and contextualizing the gospel in highly complex cultural and philosophical settings. The reason for this is found in Paul's ability "to clothe biblical revelation in a cultured

9. These include but are not limited to: the Trinity, creation, the fall, the call of Abraham, the Incarnation, the substitutionary atonement of Christ, the bodily resurrection, and the coming Kingdom (Carson, *Christ and Culture*, 43 *et passim*). See the discussion in chapter five.

10. Ibid., 67.

11. For in-depth studies on the speech, see Conzelmann, "The Address of Paul on the Areopagus," 217–30; Dibelius, *The Book of Acts*, 95–128; Gärtner, *The Areopagus Speech*; Stonehouse, *Paul before the Areopagus*.

and relevant argument to his pagan contemporaries."[12] Paul understood their language and worldview and used his knowledge to communicate the gospel clearly and effectively.

Foundational to understanding what Paul does in Acts 17, however, is dispelling the notion that he was a "cross-cultural missionary." In some cases, theologians may depict him in this way in order to lend support to the idea that Paul found no points of contact with the Athenians since he was a representative of "Jerusalem" not "Athens." Greg Bahnsen's perspective is representative in this regard:

> One can hardly avoid the conclusion that Paul was *not* seeking areas of agreement or common notions with his hearers. At every point he set his Biblical position in *antithetical contrast* to their philosophical beliefs, undermining their assumptions and exposing their ignorance. He did not seek to add further truths to a pagan foundation of elementary truth. Paul rather challenged the foundations of pagan philosophy and called the philosophers to *full repentance* (v. 30).[13]

While it is true that Paul counters many of the Athenians' beliefs and calls them to repentance, Bahnsen's portrayal of Paul's approach suggests that he found nothing in common with the Athenians—no points of contact, only points of contradiction. Bahnsen's perspective appears to be fueled by the underlying dichotomy he posits between "Jerusalem" and "Athens." But depicting Paul in this light fails to understand the complexities of Paul himself as well as the context within which the New Testament was authored. Furthermore, he assumes there was a major cultural divide (in addition to the theological divide) between the Jewish culture of Palestine and the Hellenism of Athens in the first century. I will have more to say on this below, but for now it is worth noting that Paul himself was nurtured in the same culture as the Athenians. As Schnabel points out,

> Paul spoke their language, he had some experience of the same educational system, he shared the political tradition of the last one hundred years . . . he knew their philosophy and their poets. . . The "culture" of the Jews in Tarsus, and the "culture" of the Greek-speaking Jews living in Jerusalem was in many ways

12. Charles, "Paul's Encounter," 47–62.

13. Bahnsen, "The Encounter of Jerusalem with Athens," 34; italics original. The pitting of "Jerusalem" against "Athens" dates back to Tertullian (d. 225) and his famous question, "What does Jerusalem have to do with Athens?"

> largely indistinguishable from the "culture" of the citizens of Antioch, Ephesus or Corinth. When Tarsian Jews conversed with their Greek neighbors about their faith in one true and living God, this was as little "crosscultural" as was Paul's conversation with fellow Jews about faith in Jesus as the promised Messiah.[14]

Paul's knowledge of the Greek worldview stems from the fact that he was a product of the very culture and the people God had called him to reach. Paul was intimately familiar with their history, philosophy, and literature. He grew up in Tarsus, which was well known in the ancient world as the birthplace of the Stoic philosophers Zeno (d. ca. 200 BC) and Antipater (d. ca. 130 BC). And although he knew Aramaic and Hebrew, he was, for all intents and purposes, a native Greek-speaker. Paul's background, upbringing, and his discipleship in the church of Antioch (cf. Acts 11:25; 13:1–3) provided the training he needed to communicate effectively with his Athenian audience.

Schnabel notes that Paul's knowledge of the Athenians' philosophy and literature enabled him to establish points of contact (*Anknüpfung*) *and* points of contradiction (*Widerspruch*) in his presentation of the gospel.[15] Paul utilizes both so that the gospel would connect with and counter those aspects of the Athenians' worldview that were at variance with biblical faith. Hemer notes that Paul "is meeting his audience on their own ground to respond to them there, endorsing what he can in their terms, but effectually also submitting their ideas to a profound critique."[16] Charles states that the message Paul presents "achieves continuity (kinship with God) as well as radical discontinuity (transcendence) with the Hellenistic worldview."[17] Schnabel isolates both the areas of contact and the areas of contradiction:

> The "elements of contact" as we may call them include (1) the description of God (vv. 22–23, 24–28), (2) the critique of man-made temples (v. 24), (3) the critique of sacrifices (v. 25), (4) humanity's search for God (vv. 27–28), (5) the critique of idol images (v. 29).
>
> The "elements of contradiction" include (1) significant elements of Paul's critique of Greco-Roman religiosity, in particular his

14. Schnabel, *Paul the Missionary*, 331.
15. Schnabel, "Contextualising Paul in Athens," 178.
16. Hemer, "The Speeches of Acts II," 254.
17. Charles, "Paul's Encounter," 57.

> foundational argument that there is a Creator God who made the universe and who is the Lord of heaven and earth (vv. 24–26), (2) the call to turn away from the idols to the one Creator God (v. 30), (3) the reference to God's universal judgment through a man (v. 31), (4) the reference to the one who was raised from the dead (v. 31).[18]

In summary, Paul used points of contact to communicate with the Athenians due to the linguistic and conceptual congruence he found between aspects of biblical faith and aspects of their beliefs, religious practices, and literary traditions. But these points of contact were used in a way to challenge the Athenians' beliefs and call them to repentance and faith in Christ. Additionally, Paul's general demeanor—his respectful engagement of their ideas—combined with the points of contact to pave the way for drawing distinctions between what they believed and biblical faith. In other words, Paul's positive references to the Athenians' religious practices (i.e., the "altar to an unknown god") and literary traditions (i.e., the two references to Greek literature) enabled him ultimately to subvert the message these traditions signified.

Analysis of Acts 17:16–34

Luke's positioning of Paul's speech in Acts 17 illustrates that he views it as "a model of missionary preaching to educated pagans."[19] Acts 17 furthermore demonstrates God's intention for the gospel to cross every conceivable boundary in order to reach the uttermost parts of the earth. Yeo situates the speech within the broader context of Luke-Acts:

> Acts 17:22b–31 is an integrated unit of speech which is persuasive in its argumentation. The unit is set within the context of a larger unity, that is, Acts 17:15–32, which tells of Paul traveling between Beroea and Corinth, waiting in Athens for Silas and Timothy. This context-unit is set within the larger unit of Acts 13:1–21:14, which narrates Paul's missionary journey to the Gentile world and which portrays Athens as one of its most important cities. The ministry of Paul at Athens represents the pivotal point of his ministry in the whole Gentile world, as Luke tells it. The larger unit is Luke's conscious portrayal of the movement of the gospel from Jerusalem to Rome as the gospel

18. Schnabel, *Paul the Missionary*, 171.

19. Flemming, *Contextualization*, 81–82.

of Christ is preached so that "all flesh shall see the salvation of God" (Lk 3:6).[20]

Acts 17 opens with the scene of Paul proclaiming the death, burial, and resurrection of Jesus as the long-awaited Messiah in a Thessalonian synagogue (17:2). Luke reports that a number of Greeks and women were converted, which in turn led to a violent reaction by the Jewish leaders of the city (17:4–5). This set them on a collision course with Jason, a believer and resident of Thessalonica, whose house was attacked. Upon hearing of the conversions, the Jewish leaders instituted a round up and dragged a number of the believers before the city authorities (17:6). This led to the accusation that Paul and these men who have "subverted the world," or "turned the world upside down" (οἱ τὴν οἰκουμένην ἀναστατώσαντες), have come to Thessalonica too. Eventually, the brothers send Paul and Silas to Berea where they saw a similar receptivity to the gospel message by Greek women and a similar response by Jews who came from Thessalonica to stir up the crowds. Fearing for Paul's life, the believers respond by sending him to Athens to await Silas and Timothy who are planning to join him there (17:14).

While he is waiting in Athens, Luke describes Paul's spirit as being "provoked" (παρωξύνετο τὸ πνεῦμα) at the sight of all the idols (17:16). Paul is obviously disturbed by the idolatry he encounters in Athens and this provides the impetus for him to "reason with" or "dialog with" (διελέγετο) Jews and others in the marketplace every day (17:17). In the course of his conversations, it comes to the attention of some Epicurean and Stoic philosophers[21] that Paul "seems" (δοκεῖ) to be proclaiming "foreign" or "strange deities" (ξένων δαιμονίων). Their curiosity was undoubtedly raised by the content of Paul's proclamation, which centered on "Jesus and the resurrection" (τὸν Ἰησοῦν καὶ τὴν ἀνάστασιν εὐηγγελίζετο) (17:18). According to Kavin Rowe, it appears that many of his interlocutors "heard Paul's preaching with polytheistic ears" and interpreted "Jesus" (masc.) and "Resurrection" (fem.) as two different and hence "new" or "strange" deities (17:18–20).[22] As a result, Paul is seized by the Athenians and brought before the Areopagus council where he is

20. Khiok-Khng, *What Has Jerusalem to Do with Beijing*, 166–67.

21. See Schnabel's discussion of Epicurean and Stoic thought in Schnabel, "Contextualising Paul," 178–83.

22. Rowe, *Upside Down*, 28. Cf. also Schnabel, "Contextualising Paul," 175.

asked to give an account of his teaching (17:20–21).[23] This sets the stage for Paul's speech, which should be evaluated against the backdrop of his attempt to dispel the notion that he is proclaiming something new or strange.

Paul begins his speech with an introduction that has the practical effect of establishing "rapport and credibility with his listeners."[24] He states that he has observed their religious practices and concluded that they are "very religious" (δεισιδαιμονεστέρους) (17:22). Scholars have noted that the use of this term is somewhat ambiguous, but its ambiguity served Paul's purpose by enabling him to gain a hearing whereby he could more fully explain how the gospel challenges the very religious practices and beliefs Paul appears to be complimenting.

Structurally, Paul's speech and the terms he uses conform to the general contours of Hellenistic discourse. Paul was a product of his culture and it should come as no surprise that he used culture, even a culture's rhetorical conventions, as a vehicle to convey the message of the gospel. For this reason, many have noted the similarities between Paul's Areopagus speech and other examples of Greco-Roman rhetoric.[25] Clearly, Paul's speech has a very Greco-Roman structure. Flemming observes the following elements:

> (1) an opening *exordium*, designed to gain a hearing from his listeners (Acts 17:22–23a); (2) a thesis (Acts 17:23b), stating the desired goal of the speech—to make the unknown God known to the Athenians; (3) the main proof (*probatio*, Acts 17:24–29), in which he argues his case; and (4) a concluding exhortation (*peroratio*, Acts 17:30–31), which attempts to persuade the audience to take the right course of action, namely, to repent (Acts 17:30).[26]

Bock labels the elements somewhat differently. He divides the speech along the following lines: *captatio benevolentiae* (17:22–23), *narratio* (17:24–26), *argumentatio* (17:27–28a), and a *reprehensio* (17:29b).[27] But regardless of how one labels the various elements of the speech, the

23. Rowe, *Upside Down*, 30–32. Cf. also the discussion in Bock, *Acts*, 562–63.

24. Flemming, *Contextualization*, 75.

25. Losie discusses the features that distinguish Paul's speech and the way they conform to the expectations of Paul's audience. See Losie, "Paul's Speech on the Areopagus," 226–30.

26. Flemming, *Contextualization*, 74.

27. Bock, *Acts*, 558.

point is Paul was a skilled rhetorician and he consciously conformed his language, style, and manner of speech to Greek expectations in order to be heard by his audience. His goal was to establish rapport with his audience in order offer a clear presentation of the gospel that challenged the obstacles within their worldview that impeded them from properly assessing the truth of the message. Paul "accomplishes this not by overtly attacking pagan doctrines, but rather by positively confessing the God of the Scriptures."[28]

At the heart of Paul's strategy for achieving his apologetic purpose is his reference to an object of pagan worship, the "altar to the unknown god" (17:23), and an allusion to and a quote from pagan literature written in praise of Zeus (17:28). Regarding the altar, Paul says that that which the Athenians worship as unknown, "this I proclaim to you" (ἐγὼ καταγγέλλω ὑμῖν) (17:23). Paul then grounds his proclamation of the gospel in verses 24–27 in creation and identifies the true object of the Athenians' longing as the God of creation—the God of Israel. As Rowe notes,

> Paul specifies this unknown god as "the God who made the world and everything in it," thus locating the ultimate basis of his proclamation in the origin of the cosmos. To link the identity of the unknown god with creation is to undermine in the most radical way possible the charge of preaching a new divinity. Bluntly put, it can scarcely get older than this: the God about whom Paul speaks created the world in which Athens exists.[29]

Framing his proclamation in this way enables Paul to avert the charge that his teaching was new or novel. But the means Paul uses to achieve his end are telling. To begin with, Paul references an object that "was a monument to polytheism" and turns it "in a monotheistic direction."[30] Paul seemingly affirms the Athenians' sense of the *mysterium tremendum* demonstrated in their desire to know the divine.[31] However, Paul uses it

28. Flemming, *Contextualization*, 78.

29. Rowe, *Upside Down*, 34.

30. Bock, *Acts*, 565.

31. Corduan employs the notion of the *mysterium tremendum* ("overwhelming mystery") in his analysis of religious experience to explain why people across religious traditions have similar experiences. He notes that although there are similarities in experiences, the object of some people's worship is not real (e.g., the Athenians' belief in the pantheon) while the object of others' worship is real (e.g., Christians' worship of the God of the Bible). Corduan, *Tapestry of Faiths*, 203–5.

to critique their construal of divine reality. This is an instance where Paul's apologetic use of a point of contact paves the way for his critique of the meaning the Athenians attach to the object he is referencing. In referencing altars and shrines "made by man" or "hand-made" (χειροποιήτοις) (17:24), Paul makes positive use of an object within their religious system that has meaning and authority. But he does so ultimately to undermine the meaning and authority the Athenians attribute to very object he is referencing, even if he does so in a subtle and non-overt fashion.[32]

Paul's first reference to pagan literature is found in Acts 17:28a where he makes an interesting statement about the creator-God whom he is proclaiming in verses 24–27. He says, "in him we live and move and have our being" (ἐν αὐτῷ γὰρ ζῶμεν καὶ κινούμεθα καὶ ἐσμέν). Many scholars have attributed this saying to Epimenides; however, the exact wording is somewhat ambiguous. Rowe explains:

> Scholars have attempted to derive this phrase ultimately from Plato or from the remaining fragments of Epimenides or Posidonius, but—given the flexibility of the precise meaning of the formula—the wiser course is to attribute the lack of an exact verbal parallel to Luke's careful realization of the power of general allusion. By accessing a range of plausible philosophical or theological positions, Luke avoids identifying directly the God of Israel with any particular pagan construal of θεῖος (e.g., the Stoic one) and thus preserves the space in which to maintain his critique of idolatry.[33]

Despite the ambiguity in the wording, the Athenians would have immediately recognized the allusion to a text written in praise of Zeus. Paul is resignifying the particular locutions he finds in their texts to affirm his belief about the world and, ultimately, Christ. In essence, Paul is affirming "that what pagans believed about Zeus is really true only of the God of the Old Testament, who has revealed himself through Christ."[34] But lest one conclude from this that Paul agrees with the pagans regarding their beliefs about human kinship with God, it is important to recognize with Schnabel that Paul is making a "a creation-theological

32. Rowe notes that the Athenians viewed the images housed in the shrines and temples as actual gods whose "actions were supernatural, its utterances oracular." Rowe, *Upside Down*, 36.

33. Ibid., 37.

34. Beale, "Other Religions," 88.

statement" that "is expressed in Hellenistic philosophical terminology."[35] Paul is not stating something that cannot be found in the Hebrew Bible in texts like Isaiah 55:6: "Seek the Lord while he may be found; call upon him while he is near." For this reason, Greg Beale notes that it is an oversimplification to assume Paul is identifying only with aspects of Hellenistic thought derived from general revelation or natural theology. Indeed, Paul is "thinking of the 'special revelation' of God's salvation to the nations and not merely saying that the truths of 'natural' or 'general revelation'—which pagans attributed to Zeus—are applicable only to the God of Jesus Christ."[36] In other words, Paul is making positive use of the linguistic and conceptual congruence he finds in certain aspects of the Athenians' thought, but he does so in order to serve his apologetic interests and to proclaim the uniqueness of Christ. The fact that he accomplishes this by referencing pagan ideas in close proximity to biblical ideas is telling. Again, Beale explains:

> It is remarkable to find the Acts 17 passage combining allusions to the Genesis commission for Adam to Deuteronomy about Babel, to Isaiah, and to pagan religious claims about Zeus. Also significant is the inclusion of Old Testament allusions in the midst of allusions to pagan religion. Acts 17 appears, in fact, to contain a pastiche of Old Testament allusions. . . . What Paul meets in his pagan religious environment seems to be the influence leading him back to particular relevant parts of the Old Testament. Consequently, Paul's polemic against pagan religions appears to include not merely applying pagan claims about Zeus to God, but backing up the polemic with similar Old Testament claims about Yahweh. Moreover, in the case of Acts 17, the Old Testament allusions also convey truths about God's "special" redemptive revelation.[37]

Regarding the second reference to pagan literature, it comes on the heels of the first one and is found in the same verse, Acts 17:28b. Although Paul's first reference in 17:28a presents an allusion to pagan literature, here he intentionally references what the Athenian poets have written—"as even some of your own poets have said . . ." (ὡς καί τινες τῶν καθ' ὑμᾶς ποιητῶν εἰρήκασιν). Paul uses the quote, "For we are indeed his offspring" (Τοῦ γὰρ καὶ γένος ἐσμέν) (17:28b), to convey the idea that

35. Schnabel, "Contextualizing Paul," 181.

36. Beale, "Other Religions," 88.

37. Ibid., 90.

human origins can be traced back to a transcendent creator who cannot be "formed by the art and imagination of man" (17:29).

There is more scholarly agreement that the statement Paul cites in 17:28b is a quotation from Aratus's *Phaenomena*, though Cleanthes's *Hymn to Zeus* probably influenced Aratus and the wording of this statement.[38] Rowe notes that the Jewish philosopher Aristobulus used this quote to "posit an ultimate metaphysical identity between the high god of the pagans (Zeus) and the high god of the Jews (God of Israel)."[39] However, Paul uses this statement "to criticize the basic theological error in pagan idolatry, namely, that because human beings are the 'offspring' of divinity, they can image God in their form."[40] The basic error of the pagans was one of direction. They assumed that the "correspondence implied in the divine-human relation (offspring) allows humans to read 'god' (τὸ θεῖον) off the face of their humanity."[41] However, as Rowe states, "The human arts and faculties are prone to ignorance (ἄγνοια) and superstition (δεισιδαιμονία) with the result that God comes to be conceived as like gold, silver, or stone—in short, a representation by human technical skill and imaginative power (17:29)."[42]

Paul's reference to the pagan altar and his quotation of pagan literature has led many scholars to describe Paul's apologetic strategy and use of points of contact as one of identification and translation. As Schnabel states, "The point of contact, or agreement, consists in the fact that Paul uses a vocabulary with whom his listeners are familiar, but which gives a new meaning to old words . . . ."[43] Paul is viewed as translating biblical ideas into a Greek conceptual matrix that at its heart is repugnant to the very ideas Paul is incorporating.

But Paul is not simply translating biblical faith into Greek philosophical terms. He is using the language and concepts he finds there ultimately to subvert the intended meaning of that which he references. The way Paul accomplishes this is by removing the allusions and quotes "from their original interpretive frameworks" and situating them within a framework "that stretches from Gen I through the resurrection of Jesus

38. Rowe, *Upside Down*, 37–38.

39. Ibid.

40. Ibid.

41. Ibid.

42. Ibid.

43. Schnabel, "Contextualizing Paul," 183.

to the last day (ἡμέρα, v. 31)."[44] Paul's justification for doing this is based on the fact that individual words and phrases are not inherently tied to a system of religious belief. If used to articulate the broader significances of a particular system, then they take on the meaning that system gives them. But removed from that system they are simply words and phrases. Rowe explains:

> To note this change of interpretive context is implicitly to realize the point that particular words or phrases are not in and of themselves Stoic, Epicurean, Platonist or anything else. Rather, they are "Stoic" because of the interpretive framework in which they occur, viz. "Stoicism." In a significant sense, therefore, with the change of a comprehensive hermeneutical framework the pagan philosophical phrases have *sensu stricto* ceased propounding pagan philosophy. No longer do they speak the thoughts of a system whose intellectual basis exists outside of Luke's story. . . . To the contrary, by changing the hermeneutical context of the allusive phrases, Luke alters, even subverts, the intent of the phrases in their original interpretive structure(s). He thereby changes profoundly (and with rhetorical subtlety) their meaning: drafting pagan testimony into the service of the gospel allows pagan philosophy to speak truth not on its terms but on Luke's. . . . To agree with the logic of the Areopagus speech in the end, therefore, is not to see the truth of the gospel in pagan philosophical terms (translation) but to abandon the old interpretive framework for the new. It is, plainly said, to become a Christian.[45]

Paul's strategy in Acts 17 thus provides those who would venture to engage others' religious texts with a biblical precedent and hermeneutical guidance for how to do so. Granted, the wisdom of adopting such an approach must be carefully considered, particularly if one is unaware of the connotations carried by the words, phrases, and verses one is referencing within those religious texts. Nevertheless, in principle, evangelical dismissal of the practice on biblical grounds is indefensible.

44. Rowe, *Upside Down*, 40.

45. Ibid., 40–41.

ARGUMENTS AGAINST ACTS 17 AS PROVIDING A BIBLICAL PRECEDENT FOR USING THE QUR'ĀN AS A POINT OF CONTACT

As observed above, many scholars view Paul's apologetic strategy in Acts 17 as a model for how Christians can effectively engage those around them. Within Muslim contexts, however, a number of scholars have denied that Acts 17 provides hermeneutical justification for referencing the Qur'ān in discussions of the gospel. It is important to address their concerns in light of the previous discussion and with specific reference to the Qur'ān.

Schlorff preferences his analysis of Acts 17 with a comment that he sides with scholars who view the New Testament as "essentially Hebraic in its cultural background." Despite the New Testament authors' use of the Greek language, Schlorff argues, they do not engage in a "theological use of Hellenism."[46] This leads Schlorff to conclude that those who argue for a "theological use of the Qur'ān" (or anything in Islamic culture) are guilty of fostering syncretism.[47] Much of what fuels Schlorff's concern is related to his theological method and hermeneutics, both of which will be treated more fully in chapter five. For now it is important to recognize that the distinction Schlorff draws between Hebraic and Hellenistic culture/thought enables him to identify "correct" and "incorrect" sources for contextualizing the gospel. Yet part of the problem with his argument is that there is no hard and sharp distinction between that which is "Hebraic" and that which is "Hellenistic" in the New Testament. Exploration of this theme is well beyond the scope of the present work; however, this distinction has been used by some missiologists, like Schlorff, to develop arguments for or against using various aspects of a culture in the process of contextualization. In the study of the New Testament, the problem is a methodological one and has been thoroughly examined by Barr[48] and Hengel. Moreover, as Hengel points out, labeling sources as "Hebraic" or "Hellenistic" enables some scholars to demarcate boundaries of supposed legitimacy:

> The concern to attach clear labels has often given rise to polemical arguments, and still does so. The fact that here a preference for the predicate 'Old Testament/Jewish' often goes with a more

46. Schlorff, *Models*, 120.

47. Ibid., 120–23.

48. Barr, *Semantics of Biblical Language*.

> 'conservative' approach and a preference for all that is 'Hellenistic' goes with a more 'liberal' or 'critical' attitude has not helped to produce an objective discussion.[49]

Hengel notes that by the time of Jesus knowledge of the Greek language and the influence of Greek culture were both widespread. Most people living in Palestine during the first century were either bi-lingual or tri-lingual. The implications of this are clear. The supposition of a purely Hebraic culture or system of thought in contrast with a Hellenistic culture and system of thought is an artificial construct. Granted, there were clear distinctions in the theological systems of paganism and biblical faith, but the cultures and languages were intertwined to such an extent that isolating various elements in order to determine whether they were of Hebraic or Hellenistic origin is difficult if not impossible. Indeed, the way in which the New Testament writers interact with and make "theological use of Hellenism" is more complex than Schlorff assumes.

Regarding Acts 17, Schlorff offers three arguments that encapsulate the biblical objections that some evangelical scholars have against using the Qur'ān as a point of contact. First, Schlorff states that Paul's allusion to a text from Epimenides and his quote from Aratus are not sources that "claim to be a revelation, such as one of the [Greek] oracles. By contrast, the Qur'an claims to be the speech of God."[50] In other words, Paul quoted from a literary genre within the Athenian religious system that Schlorff contends cannot be construed as a genre of revelational epistemology.[51] The implication seems to be that had Paul quoted from a Greek oracle, then there would be some justification for Christians who cite sources of purported revelation when discussing or defending Christian doctrines.

Part of the problem with this line of argumentation is that it imposes upon the Athenians (and Muslims) a Christian understanding of revelation, authority, and meaning as derived from religious texts, in this case the Bible. Every religion or philosophy has sources that it considers authoritative. This is as true for those that postulate the existence of a transcendent being as it is for atheistic systems of belief. Some of these sources of authority are in the form of texts. Others are the opinions of people. Still others involve various emotional or spiritual experiences.

49. Hengel, *The "Hellenization" of Judaea*, 1–2.

50. Schlorff, *Models*, 120.

51. The distinction between various genres of revelational epistemology comes from Hesselgrave and Rommen, *Contextualization*, 128–43.

Whether the sources claim to be special revelation in a sense that accords with the Christian understanding of this category or are simply authoritative sources that people place their trust in, like "science" in secular western societies, matters little. Functionally, they serve a very similar purpose. They constitute an authority to which adherents appeal for clarification, direction, and instruction.

Christians must be careful that in their analysis of others' texts and traditions they do not commit what Winfried Corduan has termed the "Protestant fallacy." According to him, the Protestant fallacy entails "reading other Scriptures in the way in which Protestant Christians, in particular, read the Bible."[52] By emphasizing that Paul does not cite a source that claims to be revelation from God, Schlorff appears to assume that the Athenians and Muslims view the "oracles" and the Qur'ān, respectively, in a way that accords with the function and authority status the Bible has in Protestant Christianity. While it is true that, theoretically at least, the Bible is the sole source from which evangelical Christians derive their doctrines and practices (in accord with the Protestant understanding of *sola scriptura*), it is unclear whether the Athenians viewed the oracles as functioning in a parallel manner. More importantly, Muslims derive their beliefs and practices from sources other than just the Qur'ān. Part of the reason for this is that the Qur'ān is very limited in the amount of practical instruction it offers. Much of what Muslims view as integral to their faith, such as praying five times each day, derives not from the Qur'ān but from the *ḥadīth*. Schlorff seems to assume that the conceptualization of genres of revelational epistemology is constant across religious traditions. He also assumes that each one functions in a way analogous to how Christians or Muslims understand the nature of divine revelation in their traditions. But even if Paul had quoted from a Greek oracle, this would not have impacted his strategy. Paul's goal was to reposition and resignify the objects, ideas, and phrases he references within a framework that supported a biblical worldview and subverted the Athenians' worldview. And as noted previously, words and phrases are not inherently tied to their religious systems or texts and can thus be used to express biblical ideas when properly resignified.

Second, Schlorff's concern to distance Paul from citing any supposed source of revelation appears to be motivated by an underlying concern to assert that there is no other basis or foundation for belief in

52. Corduan, *Tapestry*, 56.

distinctive Christian doctrines other than the Bible.[53] Schlorff says that Paul does not quote the "Greek poets in support of distinctive Christian teaching, such as the inspiration of the Old and New Testaments, the deity of Christ, the Trinity, or the substitutionary atonement."[54] If he did, this would constitute a case where Paul made "theological use of Hellenism."[55] Therefore, quoting the Qur'ān in the context of explaining or defending these doctrines constitutes a case of "theological use of the Qur'ān."[56] Coleman demonstrates a similar concern. He argues that using the Qur'ān to corroborate or prove specially revealed doctrines poses an epistemological problem. It interjects an authority conflict in the believer or the nascent church since it appears that the Christian is basing his belief in the specially revealed doctrines of Christianity on the sacred text of another religious tradition.[57]

There are at least three problems with the way this issue is conceived. First, Schlorff displays a tendency to reduce special revelation to a list of core doctrines that are special, distinctive, or unique in the sense that no other faith or religious text affirms them. Granted, the doctrines Schlorff mentions are derived from Scripture and constitute an integral part of what makes Christianity distinctive. But his list is not exhaustive, nor can one limit the specialness of revelation to these doctrines. Schlorff appears to conceive of specialness and uniqueness in a way that precludes any other book or system of belief from affirming similar beliefs. If those texts do affirm such truths, Schlorff seems to believe that this would detract from their uniqueness or divine origin in Christianity. But this simply does not follow. The uniqueness and divine origin of the Trinity or Incarnation or any other doctrine in Christianity is not tied to the absence of similar beliefs among other people. In other words, specialness is not inherently related to whether or not people of other faith traditions have beliefs or hold to tenets that are congruent with those

53. While Schlorff is technically correct on this point, the problem is how he ties uniqueness to the absence of particular theological ideas in other religions. See the discussion below.

54. Schlorff, *Models*, 120–21.

55. Ibid.

56. Ibid.

57. Coleman, "Insider Movement Paradigm," 107–12. Both Schlorff and Coleman are concerned about creating authority conflicts in the nascent church. Obviously, this is undesirable, which is why it is best to limit one's use of the Qur'ān to apologetic discourse (see the guidelines section below).

affirmed in Christianity. They may or may not, but this is not connected to why Christians consider these doctrines special or unique. Put another way, if there are ideas or beliefs in another religion or sacred text that are congruent with the specially revealed doctrines derived from the Bible, this does not diminish the specialness, uniqueness, or divine origin of those doctrines in Christianity. Christians believe in these doctrines because they are revealed in Scripture not due to the absence of them in another religion.

A second and closely related problem is the fallacious conclusion that if the Qur'ān can be shown to affirm certain core tenets of the Christian faith, this implies that the Qur'ān is of divine origin. Schlorff puts it succinctly:

> The doctrines that they attempt to prove from the Qur'an—the divine authority of the Bible, the deity of Christ, the Trinity—are truths that, according to the Bible, are available to man only by divine revelation . . . . These are not ideas that man can arrive at naturally. This means that if the Qur'an supports these Bible doctrines, then, on biblical grounds, it (or at least the passages quoted) comes from God.[58]

But does this follow? Let us delay the question of whether or not the Qur'ān actually supports the doctrines Schlorff mentions (and the way in which many of the theologians I am investigating here suppose) and simply ask the question: if one could conclusively show the Qur'ān does support these doctrines, does it follow that it "comes from God?" Why would one conclude that the Qur'ān is "from God" simply because it shows agreement with the Bible? Does every document that agrees with the Bible "come from God?" This is like saying that any hymn, article, commentary, or work of systematic theology that agrees with these doctrines can be considered to be of divine origin.[59] Schlorff appears to be conflating the property of truth, which can rightly be applied to many things that are not of divine origin, with inspiration. Although inspired texts (i.e., the Bible) are by definition true, not all texts that are true are inspired, which leads us to the third problem.

58. Schlorff, *Models*, 131–32.

59 A better way of understanding whatever *biblical truth* (e.g., the virgin birth) one might find in the Qur'ān is to view it as derivative. After all, the Qur'ān postdates the Bible by several centuries.

It is fallacious to conclude that if some Christians believe that the Qur'ān and the Bible are in agreement in certain areas, they are tacitly elevating the Qur'ān to a source of divine authority. The appeal many of these Christians are making is not to the Qur'ān as a *basis* for belief in these doctrines. They are appealing to the *agreement* they find between the Qur'ān and Bible on these doctrines. The difference is subtle but profound. Christians would not believe in the doctrines some purport they are trying to prove from the Qur'ān if they did not originate in the Bible. Thus, in actuality, there is no evidence or basis in the Qur'ān to which Christians can appeal for adhering to those doctrines. Their appeal is to the conceptual agreement they believe exists between the Qur'ān and the Bible on a select number of topics. The reason demonstrating this can be powerful for the Muslim is because the Qur'ān is a source of religious authority for him, and he has been repeatedly told that the Christian's belief in doctrines like the Trinity and Incarnation is irrational and tantamount to *shirk*, "associating partners with God" (i.e., polytheism). So if the Qur'ān actually agrees with the Bible on certain points, contrary to what his tradition has taught him, then this can undercut the trust he places in the sources normative Islam appeals to in order to interpret the Qur'ān, such as the *ḥadīth* and the corpus of classical *tafsīr* literature. These sources are among the places where Muslim scholars developed their unique Islamic depiction of salvation history and their objections to doctrines like the Trinity and Incarnation. Thus, separating the Qur'ān from how the *mufassirūn* interpret it can be part of an effective apologetic strategy for Christians in Arabic-speaking milieus to employ in order to subvert the Islamic construal of salvation history.[60]

Third and finally, Schlorff sides with scholars like Ned Stonehouse[61] who argue that Paul's appeal to and use of the pagan poets is essentially an appeal to truths which are available to all via general revelation. For them, Paul uses these quotes to demonstrate that the poets and his audience have suppressed the truth about God that is readily available to everyone. But as Beale noted earlier, this is an oversimplification of what Paul is doing. It fails to appreciate the extent to which Paul alludes to pa-

60. This is not to say the Qur'ān, taken as a whole, is pro-Trinity or pro-Incarnation. It decidedly is not. However, there are questions about a number of individual verses that remain open and many Arab Christians reference them in their explanation and defense of Christian doctrines.

61. See Stonehouse, *Paul before the Areopagus*; cf. also Bahnsen, "The Encounter of Jerusalem with Athens."

gan religious ideas in the context of explicating God's special plan of salvation for all nations revealed in the Hebrew Bible. Furthermore, simply classifying the type of truth to which Paul appeals as general/special revelation does not help circumvent the perceived problem of referencing a source of someone else's religious authority in the context of explaining the gospel. In Acts 17, Paul is clearly proclaiming the gospel message as revealed in the Bible from creation in Genesis to the resurrection of Christ. The whole message is a part of special revelation. Thus, classifying some truths as belonging to general revelation and others as belonging to special revelation can be helpful, but it is important to remember that all truths advanced in Scripture are a part of special revelation.

GUIDELINES FOR USING THE QUR'ĀN AS A POINT OF CONTACT

In what follows I have modified and expanded Tennent's guidelines[62] for use with the Qur'ān. However, two caveats are necessary to mention before looking at the guidelines in detail. First, these are guidelines, not hard and strict rules. Nor are they exhaustive. There may be cases or instances where one or more of these guidelines will need modification. Second, I have used these guidelines to inform my selection and analysis of the qur'ānic points of contact presented in chapters three and four. However, the authors I investigate in those chapters do not adhere to these guidelines in any strict sense, but this does not detract from what we may learn from them. Overall, having a set of guidelines can assist Christians by setting some broad parameters for how they use the Qur'ān, but the guidelines can also assist in evaluating how other authors employ the Qur'ān in their apologetic theology.

The first guideline suggested by Tennent is that when referencing noncanonical sacred texts, like the Qur'ān, one should do so only in the context of defending or explaining the Christian faith. In other words, qur'ānic points of contact should be used solely in evangelistic contexts and apologetic discourse. Paul's reference to the quotes from pagan sources was in the context of his defense of the gospel on Mars Hill. And the texts investigated here are all representative of apologetic theology authored in the Arab-Muslim milieu. One implication of this is that liturgical use of qur'ānic texts in the context of one's worship of Christ in the church is strongly discouraged. The Bible alone is sufficient for nurturing

62. Tennent, *World Christianity*, 71–73.

the faith of God's people when they are gathered together. Moreover, it is the sole source from which God's people are to derive their core beliefs, examine their ways of life, and derive patterns for godly living.

Second, Tennent states that "non-Christian texts should be used only to provide a *corroborative witness* to a biblical message, rather than an independent testimony in isolation from the biblical witness."[63] One way of ensuring this is the case is to select qur'ānic texts on the basis of their linguistic and/or conceptual congruence with biblical ideas. Many verses in the Qur'ān reference biblical topoi in a way that assumes its readership knows and understands the beliefs, people, and events to which it is referring. It is advisable that Christians limit their use of the Qur'ān to such verses. The apologetic benefit of such an approach is that it can demonstrate the referential nature of the Qur'ān and show how the Bible (or Christian tradition) sheds light on some qur'ānic verses that are obscure or lacking in narrative formation. But it can also indicate that the ideas the Christian believes are not outside the realm of possibility. However, if one quotes the Qur'ān in isolation from one's discussion of ideas that originate in the Bible, it could appear that the Christian believes the Qur'ān to be a source of authority in and of itself. Let me be clear—taken as a whole, the Qur'ān subverts the message of redemption through Jesus Christ and therefore cannot be considered a source that nurtures faith in Christ, leads people to salvation, or results in the formation of a robust and well-grounded understanding of Christian faith and practice.

Having stated that, one of the goals in corroborating biblical testimony with select verses from the Qur'ān is to demonstrate areas of conceptual agreement. As noted earlier, the goal is neither to establish the Qur'ān as being from God nor to use the Qur'ān as evidence or a foundation for adhering to certain Christian doctrines. Again, Christians would not believe in the doctrines some purport they are trying to prove from the Qur'ān if they did not originate in the Bible, so there is in fact no evidence in the Qur'ān to which Christians can appeal for adhering to those doctrines.[64]

Another goal in this process is to clarify and understand the message of the Qur'ān on its own terms. Much of Muslim belief and objections to Christian doctrines derive not from the Qur'ān but from the classical

63. Ibid., 72–73, *italics* original.

64. Again, I am not stating that the Qur'ān actually agrees with all the positions some Christians say it does. That is an open question not directly treated in this work. My aim is to defend and illustrate positive apologetic uses of the Qur'ān.

tafsīr literature. Separating the Qur'ān from that literature is important for clarifying what the Qur'ān actually asserts and what it does not. For those residing outside the Arab-Muslim world, appreciating this fact may be difficult. But for Christians and Muslims residing in the world of Islam, the importance of this is self-evident and has numerous ramifications for all those living in the region.

Third, "any nonbiblical sacred text that is quoted should be lifted out of its original setting and clearly reoriented within a new *Christocentric setting*."[65] It is important to situate the qur'ānic verses one uses as points of contact in an interpretive framework with biblical horizons. Doing so must drive one to situate the doctrines one is explaining, and to which the Qur'ān references in an elliptical manner, back within the context of the grand biblical narrative that gave them birth. Christians must guard against reducing their presentations of the gospel to a mere attestation of belief in core doctrines like the Trinity and Incarnation. Abstracting these doctrines from the Bible's narrative reduces the Christian faith to a list of propositions that can appear detached from God's redemptive activity in the whole of creation and throughout history. As a corrective to this tendency, Christians must make sure that they tie any explanation of these doctrines to how they are revealed, developed, and explicated in the whole of the canon and throughout the course of redemptive history. In other words, they must employ *scriptural reasoning* and not mere rational argumentation. The apologetic aim should be to subvert the Islamic interpretation of salvation history that originates in the Qur'ān but is fully developed in extra-qur'ānic literature.

Part of the means Christians can use to achieve this end is utilizing qur'ānic passages in a way that agrees with the Bible's construal of salvation history centered on the death, burial, and resurrection of Christ. In many cases, select qur'ānic verses can be used to corroborate Christian teaching in this regard. Nevertheless, it is important to remain aware of the Qur'ān's critique of Christian doctrines that is linked to its distinct conception of prophetology and revelation that, at its heart, varies immensely from the biblical conception of those doctrines.[66] Furthermore, Christians must be careful that they do not imply too much in their Christian exegesis of the Qur'ān. Every verse in Qur'ān cannot be

65. Tennent, *World Christianitiy*, 72, *italics* original.

66. See further discussion in chapters three and five.

interpreted using a "Christological key."[67] It is thus strongly recommended that Christians limit their use of the Qur'ān to verses that demonstrate linguistic and conceptual congruence with biblical ideas. Some may argue, however, that this violates the intent of those verses and constitutes a case of prooftexting or eisegesis. It will be shown that the way the Arabic Christian case studies examined below interact with the Qur'ān is much more complex than mere prooftexting, though there are features in the Qur'ān that invite such an approach and it should not *de facto* (or *de jure*) be ruled out as illegitimate. I have more to say about that in chapter five. For now, it is important to analyze several examples from medieval and contemporary Arabic texts that illustrate positive uses of qur'ānic locutions in Christian apologetics. I begin with the medieval texts.

67. This is the approach of Basetti-Sani. He develops an allegorical hermeneutic for viewing the entire Qur'ān through a Christological lens. See Basetti-Sani, *The Koran in the Light of Christ*. The authors I am investigating use select verses in ways that agree with their Christian positions, but they are not offering a comprehensive interpretation of the whole Qur'ān.

3

Christian Exegesis and Apologetic Use of the Qur'ān in Select Medieval Arabic Texts

The goal of the next two chapters is to provide some representative examples of how Christian theologians in Arabic-speaking milieus have made positive use of qur'ānic points of contact historically (chapter three) and continue to do so today (chapter four). As a reminder, a point of contact is defined as the use of qur'ānic locutions (i.e., ideas, words, phrases, or texts) exhibiting linguistic and/or conceptual congruence with biblically conceived ideas in the context of communicating the gospel and explaining Christian doctrines. The analysis in these two chapters is not meant to be exhaustive but merely representative. It serves to illustrate how the selected authors make use of the Qur'ān in their apologetic theology.

Turning to the two medieval texts, my analysis of them is divided into three parts. First, I briefly present background information on the authors (where known) and the texts under investigation. This includes a brief description of the goals, aims, and content of both texts. Second, there is a brief discussion of the author's exegetical strategy vis-à-vis the Qur'ān. In some cases, the author's references may be allusive—he may weave qur'ānic material into his work through carefully chosen echoes of terms, phrases, or concepts. In other cases, the references are more explicit, being prefaced by statements such as, "and you will find in your Qur'ān," followed by a quote, phrase, or a conflation of qur'ānically inspired ideas. Third, in order to illustrate how each author employs qur'ānic points of contact in his apologetics, I have chosen to limit my analysis to three broad Christological themes: the divinity of Christ, the

Incarnation, and the crucifixion and resurrection. Using thematic analysis illustrates the influence of the Qur'ān on the shape and language of the theology authored in this milieu, and how Christians articulated their explanation and defense of Christian doctrines. I end the chapter with a summary of conclusions and make some observations regarding the use of the Qur'ān in the apologetic strategies of the two medieval treatises. I begin with the oldest of the texts, *On the Triune Nature of God.*

ON THE TRIUNE NATURE OF GOD

Background and Contents

In 1893 Margaret Dunlop Gibson accompanied a small team of scholars to St. Catherine's Monastery on Mount Sinai in search of ancient Christian texts. Altogether, Gibson would make four trips back to Mount Sinai, each time photographing various manuscripts to edit for publication. Among the first dozen books the team investigated upon their initial trip was an Arabic manuscript containing Acts, the seven general epistles, and a theological treatise. Gibson later edited the theological treatise and gave it the title, *On the Triune Nature of God* (*fī tathlīth Allāh al-wāḥid*).[1] Though anonymous, the author of the *Tathlīth* indicates that he is writing at a period 746 years after the founding or "establishment" of the Christian religion. Depending on how one interprets the author's understanding of when the Christian religion began (i.e., at the Incarnation or the Resurrection), this dates the text to a period around 755 or 788,[2] making it the oldest original apology for Christianity in Arabic.[3]

Dividing the *Tathlīth* into sections for analysis has presented a number of challenges to scholars. This is due in part to the lack of a complete critical edition of the text,[4] but it is also due to the author's style of com-

1. Gibson, ed., *'On the Triune Nature of God,'* 2–36 (English); 74–107 (Arabic). Hereafter: *Tathlīth.*

2. See Griffith, *Shadow*, 54, 89–90n47; Swanson, "Dating," 115–41; Swanson, "*Fī tathlīth Allāh al-wāḥid*," 331; Samir, "Earliest Arab Apology," 61–64. Gibson's edition of the text is missing roughly 13 pages, which were identified by Samir. He has included a number of them in his study of the manuscript, including the page whereupon the approximate date is given. See Samir, "Earliest Arab Apology," 101–5.

3. Griffith notes that there are two texts preserved in some papyrus fragments that may be older; however, scholars have yet to arrive at a definitive estimation regarding the date of those texts. See Griffith, *Shadow*, 53n28.

4. Swanson reports that Samir is preparing a new edition of the work that will be published with Swanson's full English translation (Swanson, "Apology," 40). In the

munication. Samir Khalil Samir[5] divides the text into an introduction and two parts, while Mark Swanson[6] divides the text into three chapters prefaced by an introductory prayer.[7] Swanson's study of the introductory prayer of the *Tathlīth* demonstrates that it is filled with qur'ānic allusions and echoes and is written in an elegant rhymed style (*saj'*) characteristic of the Qur'ān.[8] Chapter one covers the doctrine of the Trinity,[9] which is defined at the outset of the chapter as "God and his Word and his Spirit."[10] Included in this chapter are seven Trinitarian analogies based on things found in nature and the human constitution. The author uses these as accessible examples of diversity within unity.[11] Chapter two is focused on Christ and his work.[12] It opens with a recapitulation of salvation history that, according to Swanson, is framed in the pattern of the Qur'ān's punishment stories.[13] The third chapter[14] consists of thirty-four *testimonia* taken from the Old Testament that are used as a witness to the life of Christ and the veracity of Christian doctrines.[15] As stated, my analysis of the *Tathlīth* is limited to Christological themes taken from each chapter, but before proceeding it is important to gain a general understanding of how the author of this text exegetes and makes use of the Qur'ān in his theological writing.

"Apology," Swanson provides a short introduction to the *Tathlīth* and a partial English translation (ibid., 40–59).

5. Samir, "Earliest Arab Apology," 64–65.

6. Swanson, "*Fī tathlīth Allāh al-wāḥid*," 331.

7. *Tathlīth* 74:1–16. All of the page numbers refer to Gibson's Arabic edition of the *Tathlīth* aided by Samir's corrections and additions where pertinent. Translations of the text into English are my own unless noted otherwise. The format will be to give the page number of the *Tathlīth* in Gibson's Arabic edition followed by the line number.

8. Swanson, "Beyond Prooftexting," 305–8. For more on qur'ānic prosody, see Stewart, "*Saj'* in the Qur'an," 213–52.

9. *Tathlīth* 74–78.

10. Ibid., 74:22, *et passim*.

11. Ibid., 76:1–20; cf. also Samir's discussion in Samir, "Earliest Arab Apology," 70–72.

12. *Tathlīth* 78–85.

13. Swanson, "Beyond Prooftexting," 308–11. The notion of "punishment stories" or "punishment sequences" is treated by Watt and Bell, *Introduction to the Qur'ān*, 127–35; cf. also Reynolds, *Emergence*, 102–5. The construal of these sequences is rooted in the Qur'ān's particular prophetology. See the discussion below.

14. *Tathlīth* 85–107.

15. Swanson, "*Fī tathlīth Allāh al-wāḥid*," 331.

Exegesis of the Qur'ān

As noted in chapter one, when Christian theologians began authoring apologetic treatises in Arabic in the eighth century they made frequent reference to the Qur'ān. Their purpose in doing this was to defend their doctrines and practices and to refute Islam. In many cases, they achieved their apologetic goals by adopting a type of interpretive approach that made use of the plain and immediate meaning (*ẓāhir*) of select qur'ānic texts. Many of these texts exhibit linguistic and conceptual congruence with the very ideas Christians were seeking to defend,[16] and so it was only natural that as they adopted the Arabic language they would begin conceiving of and writing their theology in ways that echoed various qur'ānic locutions.

Over the course of time, it appears that each of the various Christian ecclesiastical communities came to a general consensus regarding the proper interpretation of the Qur'ān. This consensus was achieved through their common interpretation of a number of verses that, in their minds, point to the veracity of the Christian faith. In many instances, this consensus was based upon the legend of Baḥīrā, which was used to explain the origins of the Qur'ān and the reason as to why it appears (partially) to affirm certain Christian beliefs and practices.[17] Understanding this background helps elucidate why some Arabic-speaking Christians were uninhibited from making positive use of the Qur'ān in their apologetic theology. Additionally, given that this Christian consensus developed rather early, as is confirmed by the record of Muslim objections to it,[18] Christian critiques of the Qur'ān may have played a role in solidifying the methodology that Muslims eventually developed to interpret the Qur'ān in the century after the *Tathlīth* was written. Foremost in that process was the prescription—by scholars like al-Shāfi'ī (d. 820) —that the canonized sayings and reports attributed to Muḥammad in the *ḥadīth* are to be the first and most authoritative interpreters of the Qur'ān. But during the period in which the *Tathlīth* was authored, those methodologies had

16. If Lüling is correct, this might be attributable to the fact that about a third of the Qur'ān is based upon an earlier Christian strophic hymnody. See Lüling, *A Challenge to Islam for Reformation*.

17. Roggema explains how this developed in Roggema, *Sergius Baḥīrā*, 130–34.

18. Ibid., 133–34. Ibn Hishām refuted several early Christian interpretations of the Qur'ān, such as its use of the majesty of plural in their defenses of the Trinity (see below). His refutations illustrate how early and widespread the consensus apparently was that developed among the Christian communities regarding the origins of the Qur'ān.

yet to obtain widespread Muslim consensus since many of the purported sayings and reports of Muḥammad were still in the process of being canonized (and/or authored).[19] Thus, it is evident that one of the motivations Christians had in utilizing the Qur'ān in their apologetic theology, particularly during the first several centuries of Christian-Muslim interaction, was to influence how Muslims interpreted their scripture.

As mentioned, the introductory prayer of the *Tathlīth* is written in rhymed prose (*saj'*), similar to the style of the Qur'ān. An example of this is observable in the refrain, *kull shay'* ("everything" or "all things"). It is repeated some seven times in the first several lines and three times towards the end of the first section of the prayer.[20] This refrain is coupled with a number of words that form parallel ideas emphasizing God's knowledge of all things, his possession of all things, and, ultimately, his sovereignty over all things. Additionally, many of the turns of phrase in this prayer echo a word or concept found in the Qur'ān. For example, the author says of God: "Praise be to God, before whom was nothing, and who was before everything. There is nothing after him; he is heir of all things, and to him all things return."[21] In these three lines alone, Swanson identifies at least six qur'ānic echoes or phrases.[22] The wording of the final phrase, "and to him all things return [*wa ilayhi maṣīru kulli shay'*]," is echoed, in one form or another, in at least ten qur'ānic passages.[23] This is not to say that the author had each of these verses in mind when he composed what he did; nevertheless, there are terminological parallels throughout the introductory prayer that appear designed to engender rhetorical force for what the author aims to argue in the coming chapters.

These stylistic features are undoubtedly designed to resonate with Arabic-speaking Christians who were surrounded by the echoes of the Qur'ān in their daily lives, many of whom might be tempted by the Qur'ān's rhetorical force. But this style would also appeal to Arab Muslims who might venture to read this treatise in an attempt to understand

19. In addition to the work by Schacht mentioned earlier, Brown's introduction to the *ḥadīth* is helpful. See Brown, *Hadith*; cf. also Berg, *The Development of Exegesis in Early Islam*; Motzki, *Ḥadīth*.

20. Samir, "Earliest Arab Apology," 67.

21. *Tathlīth* 74:3–5.

22. Swanson, "Beyond Prooftexting," 305. Swanson lists Q 1:2; 15:23; 21:89; 28:58; 5:18; 24:42.

23. Cf., e.g., Q 2:285; 3:28; 5:18; 24:42; 31:14; 35:18; 40:3; 42:15; 60:4; 64:3.

the faith and doctrines of their more numerous Christian neighbors.[24] Upon doing so, they would immediately be met with an opening prayer that "could have equally been written by a Muslim."[25] The reason for this is that there is nothing explicitly "Christian" about the opening prayer. The author's style is fluid and his knowledge of the Qur'ān is impressive. As Swanson notes, "In the introduction to the *Tathlīth* we are dealing with a Christian author who has absorbed the Qur'ān's vocabulary and cadences of worship and praise, and without a hint of affection can make them his own."[26] Notwithstanding this fact, the author remains a Christian author. This becomes clear as he moves from the introductory prayer into his explanation of God's identity and his redemptive acts on behalf of humanity.

In his analysis of the intertextual relationship between the *Tathlīth* and the Qur'ān, Swanson has identified three strategies employed by the author in select parts of the treatise.[27] First, he notes that the introductory prayer is a "sacramental imitation" of the Qur'ān's rhymed prose style. Samir labels this prayer a "*fātiḥa*" since it serves a purpose similar to that of the opening *sūra* of the Qur'ān, *Sūrat al-Fātiḥa*.[28] Both are written in rhymed prose, but the *fātiḥa* of the *Tathlīth* aims to draw its readers into the worship of the God signified in the text—"God and his Word and his Spirit." It achieves this goal by utilizing familiar rhymes, cadences, and diction, many of which are patterned after or inspired by the Qur'ān. All of these literary devices are designed to elicit an emotional and spiritual response to God of the Bible. Second, Swanson points out that the numerous near-qur'ānic phrases found scattered throughout the *Tathlīth* are evidence of an "eclectic imitation" of its qur'ānic subtext. The author employs these phrases in order to strengthen the force of his discourse. But in doing so he pays little attention to the "semiotic universe of the

24. At the time the *Tathlīth* was authored, Christians would have still comprised the majority in Syria-Palestine and the Sinai, the likely provenance of this treatise. See chapter one.

25. Samir, "Earliest Arab Apology," 69.

26. Swanson, "Beyond Prooftexting," 307.

27. Swanson adopts an analytic framework used by Richard Hays for understanding Paul's use of Old Testament Scripture. Of the four strategies employed by Christian theologians for utilizing qur'ānic texts Swanson discusses, three of them are found in the *Tathlīth*. Thomas Greene originally suggested the framework as a way of analyzing Renaissance poetry. For an explanation, see Swanson, "Beyond Prooftexting," 314–19.

28. Samir, "Earliest Arab Apology," 66.

precursor."[29] Finally, Swanson says the author of the *Tathlīth* uses "heuristic imitation" by reworking the typical sequence of punishment stories one finds in the Qur'ān, as in Q 7 and Q 11. He does this in order to couch his presentation of the Bible's construal of salvation history in qur'ānic mold.

One other aspect of the *Tathlīth's* exegesis that bears mentioning is the author's explicit appeal to the Qur'ān as a corroborative witness to the truth of what he is conveying. Most of the instances of these phenomena are prefaced by the phrase, "and you (pl.) will find in the Qur'ān."[30] The first of these is found in the section presenting proofs of the Trinity. The author's appeal to the Qur'ān in this context is based on its use, much like the Hebrew Bible, of the first person plural when describing God's actions (i.e., the so-called, "plural of majesty"). This is an approach that was used from the earliest period of Arabic Christian apologetics, and, as Roggema notes, was critiqued by Ibn Hishām.[31] The other instances of an explicit appeal to the Qur'ān in the *Tathlīth* serve to demonstrate the author's belief that the verses and ideas he references exhibit linguistic and conceptual congruence with his own beliefs.

In summary, the author of the *Tathlīth* displays an intimate familiarity with the Arabic of the Qur'ān. His treatise is distinctly Christian, yet it is written in a way that would appeal to many Muslims. Samir provides a summary of the author's approach:

> [He] is impregnated with Qur'ānic culture. He does not live in a "Christian ghetto," nor does he use what some might call a "Christian Arabic" vocabulary or style, and much less a "Christian Arabic grammar." He shares with Muslims . . . the common Arabic culture, which carries many Qur'ānic words and expressions, and a certain style and even some Muslim thoughts . . . [H]e has brought into Arabic Christianity all that he could draw from the Islamic and Qur'ānic heritage, and he introduced it

29. Swanson, "Beyond Prooftexting," 316. Swanson also mentions in this regard texts that he says engage in "exploitative prooftexting." These are texts that pay "no attention to the original context of the Qur'ānic verses" and thus tear them "violently" from their context (p. 317).

30. Cf., e.g., *Tathlīth* 77:19; 77:24; 84:14; 88:5; 104:20.

31. Something similar is found in the Heidelberger papyrus fragment, Schott Reinhardt 438. See Roggema, *Sergius Baḥīrā*, 132–33; cf. also, Graf, "Christlich-Arabische Texte," 1–31. Ibn Hishām is credited with editing the most authoritative biography on Muḥammad attributed to Ibn Isḥāq (d. 768). See Ibn Hishām, *Sīrat al-Nabī*; Ibn Isḥāq, *The Life of Muḥammad*.

> into his theology. On the other hand, he has presented Christian theology to Muslims in a Muslim garment. He has strived to avoid all confusion (he is undoubtedly a Christian in his theology), or pan-religious thinking. He has avoided the temptation of syncretism. He really acculturated himself to the Qur'ānic and the Islamic tradition. While not rejecting the slightest part of his faith, he acquired for himself what he thought was good and useful and presented it to his Christian readers.[32]

In what follows, I have selected two broad areas wherein the author discusses three Christological themes—the divinity of Christ, the Incarnation, and the crucifixion and resurrection.

Christological Themes

Christians Worship "God and His Word and His Spirit"

From the outset of the *Tathlīth*, the author makes clear that the designation, "God and his Word and his Spirit," refers to the one true God; the God to whom all of humanity is expected to turn to be rescued from their sin. The author of the *Tathlīth* uses the combination of God's "Word and Spirit" throughout this treatise as a hendiadys for referring to the tri-unity of the one God. Normally, one would expect a Christian author to use the designation "Father, Son, and Holy Spirit" to refer to the different persons of the one triune God, and the author does do this; however, the hendiadys "Word and Spirit" permeates his Christological discourse. Together, these two names elucidate the identity and nature of the one God as well as the redemptive purpose behind his self-revealing in Christ. As the author states, "This is our faith and our testimony in God and his Word and his Spirit: He is the Father and the Son and the Holy Spirit. One God and one Lord. And in Christ he has saved humanity and rescued them."[33]

What makes the author's use of the combination "Word and Spirit" unique is that the terms are an explicit echo of the two Christological appellations found in Q 3:45 and Q 4:171 where Christ is identified as God's "Word" and "a Spirit from him." Despite the apparent conflation these titles evidence in their qur'ānic context between the second and third persons of the Trinity, the author's use of them in this treatise is in keeping with the earliest examples of Christian apologetic literature written

32. Samir, "Earliest Arab Apology," 109.

33. *Tathlīth* 78:20–21.

in response to Islam.[34] On the whole, the author of the *Tathlīth* uses the title "Word of God" to refer to Christ rather than the more contentious designation "Son of God." He does this in order to demonstrate an acceptable way both of conceptualizing and expressing his Christology in his Arabic-speaking milieu. Indeed, the author's use of "Word and Spirit" dominates his whole discussion of God's redemptive purposes in Christ on behalf of humanity.[35]

These appellations first appear in chapter one of the *Tathlīth* at the beginning of the discussion on the Trinity. The author states that God is worthy of worship since he alone is the creator of the heavens and earth and all that is in them. In a prayerful fashion, he addresses God, confessing that he has accomplished all of his creative acts "by your Word and your Spirit."[36] The author emphasizes that God's Word and his Spirit are fully divine by virtue of their participation in the Godhead's creative activity. Moreover, the God who makes himself known by his Word and his Spirit is the only God worthy of worship:

> For to you do we render service, our Lord and our God, in your Word and your Spirit. You, Oh God, by your Word, created the heavens and the earth and all that is in them, and by your Spirit you have given life to the host of angels. Thus do we praise you and extol you and glorify you in your creating Word [*bi-kalimatak al-khāliqa*] and in your holy and living Spirit—one God, one Lord, and one Creator. We make no division between God and his Word and his Spirit [*lā nufarriqu Allāha min kalimatihi wa rūḥihi*]. Nor do we worship any other god along with God in his Word and his Spirit. Indeed God has made clear [*bayyana*]

34. Roggema notes that the Jacobite church father, Jacob of Edessa (d. 708), is the only Eastern Christian who criticizes Muslims for not differentiating between the Word and Spirit. Most of the others, "chose not to focus on the awkwardness of this point, but rather to use Q 4:171 to their own advantage and to exploit the pair 'God's Word and His Spirit' in their apologetics vis-à-vis Islam as proof of the existence of three eternal hypostases of the Godhead." Roggema, *Sergius Baḥīrā*, 108–9. For an English translation of Jacob of Edessa's comments on Islam, see Hoyland, *Seeing Islam as Others Saw It*, 165–67.

35. It does not appear that the author of this treatise is particularly concerned with the qur'ānic conceptualization of Jesus as God's "Word." Instead, he seizes upon the obvious linguistic parallel this terminology presents for Christians who, upon hearing this term applied to Christ, would immediately identify it with the *logos* Christology of the New Testament. O'Shaughnessy has investigated the meaning of "Word" in its qur'ānic context and how the *mufassirūn* explained it in O'Shaughnessy, *Koranic Concept*, 15–31.

36. *Tathlīth* 74:17.

> his command and his light in the Torah, the Prophets, the Zabūr, and the Injīl—God and his Word and his Spirit is one God and one Lord.[37]

One aspect of the author's statement here deserves further comment. Prefacing the assertion that Christians "make no division between God and his Word and his Spirit" is a statement that the object of Christian worship is God's "creating Word." The point in making this assertion is to emphasize that God's Word is not created but creating (i.e., it is divine). And if it is divine it is eternal. By affirming this qur'ānic Christological appellation, the author aims to challenge his readers' understanding of the particular "Word" signified by this designation and push them to consider deeply the implications of their affirmation. Following the author's logic, those who affirm that Christ is God's Word are implying something unique about him that cannot be said of anyone else, whether a prophet or an apostle. This leads the author to his statement concerning the indivisibility of God's Word from him. Division or differentiation implies that God's Word is separable from him, which would render God's Word less than divine (i.e., not eternal). While the author is clearly asserting doctrinal content derived from the New Testament regarding Christ's identity as the eternal *logos* of God through whom all things were created,[38] his argument also reflects his awareness of the ongoing internecine debates among the *mutakallimūn* over the createdness of the Qur'ān and the status of God's attributes, particularly his "Word."

At the time of the *Tathlīth's* composition in the mid to late-eighth century, lines were being drawn in the debate over the ontological status of God's attributes. One trajectory of thought, which came to be represented by the Mu'tazilites, repudiated the notion that God's attributes were in any way comparable to human attributes or that they applied to him in any literal sense.[39] For them, this was tantamount to anthropomorphism (*tashbīh*). They explained the various descriptions of God "knowing," or "living," or "speaking," etc., using metaphorical interpretation (*ta'wīl*). Their concern was to protect the absolute unity and transcendence of God. The other trajectory, which came to be associated, broadly speaking, with the Ash'ārites and later Sunnī Islam, affirmed the reality and

37. Ibid., 75:5–8.

38. Cf. e.g., John 1:1–3, 10; Col 1:16; Heb 1:1–2.

39. Watt explores the early history of the Mu'tazilites and their opponents in Watt, *Formative Period*, 208–50.

eternality of the attributes. Their concern was to assert that the names and descriptions of God in the Qur'ān were substantive descriptions, even if they could not give a definitive answer as to how God knows, speaks, sits on a throne, etc. Eventually, this school of thought came to affirm seven essential attributes: knowledge, power, will, life, speech, hearing, and seeing.[40] As for the Qur'ān, these linguistic and philosophical debates issued in two stances regarding the book's status as God's "Word." The Muʿtazilites claimed it was created and not eternal since this implies a plurality within God. However, the followers of Ibn Ḥanbal (d. 855) and the later Ashʿārites asserted the eternality and uncreatedness of the Qur'ān since it represents God's eternal speech.[41]

From a Christian perspective, the debate over the status of God's attributes and the createdness of the Qur'ān left the door open for asserting the existence of a multiplicity within the Godhead. Moreover, identifying and emphasizing Christ as God's Word enabled Christians to assert his divinity as an inseparable aspect (or attribute) of God. And this is what the author of the *Tathlīth* does. By adopting this strategy—an early version of the so-called attribute apology—he could affirm Christ's divinity as the eternal *logos* of God. In ascribing to Christ various divine attributes and crediting him with actions attributable only to God, such as creation, miracles, etc., the author is ascribing to Christ that which is in keeping with his status as God's speech—the divine Word of God. And he could do this while making positive use of the Qur'ān's designation of Christ as God's Word.

By arguing in this manner, the author is subtly accusing those who deny the divinity of God's Word with holding that there was a time when God existed without his Word, something averse to both Christians and Muslims. But for this apologetic to be effective, "Christians needed the antithesis between the eternity and the createdness of God's Word in order to reconcile their views on Christology with the Qur'ān."[42] Stated another way, in order for the Christian author of the *Tathlīth* to use the Qur'ān's particular Christological locutions to affirm the divin-

40. Ibid., 287.

41. Cumming has explored al-Ashʿarī's conception of God's attributes and their relationship to his essence. Many of the parallels he identifies correspond to those noted both by the medieval Arab Christian authors examined here and the contemporary authors of the al-Kalima school examined in chapter four. See Cumming, "Ṣifāt Al-Dhāt," 111–46.

42. Becker, "Christian Polemic," 251.

ity of Christ, this antithesis was necessary. In using them, the author emphasizes the function of God's Word in creation, and hence his full divinity, while simultaneously declaring his belief in the unity of God—the God who reveals himself by his Word and his Spirit. Thus, the author of the *Tathlīth* formulates his Christology in a way that is in doctrinal alignment with what he must affirm as a Christian, but he achieves this particular articulation of his Christology using language and concepts understandable to his Muslim readers.

One other aspect of how the author uses the designation "God and his Word and Spirit" deserves further elaboration. Towards the end of the author's quote above there is a statement concerning the source wherein God has revealed knowledge of himself—knowledge of his Word and Spirit. He says, "God has made clear [*bayyana*] his command and his light in the Torah, the Prophets, the Zabūr, and the Injīl—God and his Word and his Spirit is one God and one Lord."[43] In the Qur'ān, there is an implicit assumption that its message is in continuity (or even conformity) with the content of previous revelations brought by "God and his apostles." And this extends to the message "brought" by Christ. For example:

> Q 2:136—Say you: We believe in God, and in that which has been sent down on us and sent down on Abraham, Ishmael, Isaac and Jacob, and the Tribes, and that which was given to Moses and Jesus and the Prophets, of their Lord; we make no division between any of them.
>
> Q 2:285—The messenger believes in what was sent down to him from his Lord, and the believers; each one believes in God and his angels, and in his books and his messengers; we make no division between any one of his messengers. They say, "We hear, and obey."
>
> Q 3:84 – Say: We believe in God, and that which has been sent down on us, and sent down on Abraham and Ishmael, Isaac and Jacob, and the Tribes, and in that which was given to Moses and Jesus, and the Prophets, of their Lord; we make no division between any of them, and to him we surrender.
>
> Q 4:150–52 – Those who disbelieve in God and his messengers and desire to make division between God and his messengers, and say, "We believe in part, and disbelieve in part," desiring to take between this and that a way. Those in truth are the unbelievers; and we have prepared for the unbelievers a humbling

43. *Tathlīth* 75:8.

chastisement. And those who believe in God and his messengers and make no division between any of them, those we shall surely give them their wages; God is all-forgiving, all-compassionate.

In making these assertions, the Qur'ān assumes that all prophets and apostles functioned in a similar way; they delivered God's message to their people and warned them to repent. The Qur'ān identifies the apostles as God's messengers and states clearly that to affirm their message ultimately is to affirm the messenger (i.e., God). Those who do not affirm these messengers and their message have, in essence, denied God and are reckoned unbelievers. Thus, for the author of the *Tathlīth*, those who venture to make a division between God and his Word—Christ—have separated themselves from God by denying that which has been revealed to them by the previous prophets in "the revealed books" (*al-kutub al-munzala*).[44] Hence, they are denying something that the Qur'ān itself affirms, at least in principle, in its denial of any division or differentiation between it and the previous revelation. In other words, the *Tathlīth* aims to build a case on scriptural grounds—using scriptural reasoning—that the Qur'ān's appeal to the Bible as a confirmation of its own message necessitates affirming that which is revealed therein concerning "God and his Word and his Spirit."[45]

It is helpful to note here that the combination, "God and his apostle" or "God and his apostles," is repeated on numerous occasions in the Qur'ān.[46] However, unlike the hendiadys of "Word and Spirit," which is used in the *Tathlīth* to signify identification and equality with God (the Father), the qur'ānic combination of "God and his apostle" is used to emphasize the source of divine authority. God has bestowed on his apostles (or "messengers," sing. *rasūl*, pl. *rusul*) his divine message. Moreover, as Willem Bijlefeld points out, an apostle acts both as his community's representative before God and God's representative to this community, though the emphasis in the Qur'ān is on the later. But the implications of this are clear according to Bijlefeld: "men are called to listen to, believe in, and obey God and His apostle."[47] The connection between obedience

44. *Tathlīth* 75:8–10.

45. The Qur'ān states that it comes to confirm that which came before it in verses like Q 3:50 and Q 5:46.

46. Cf., e.g., Q 2:279; 4:14, 136, *et passim*. Bijlefeld states that this combination appears over eighty times in the Qur'ān. Bijlefeld, "A Prophet and More Than a Prophet," 150–51.

47. Ibid.

to God and obedience to his apostle(s) can be seen in the following selection of qur'ānic texts:

> Q 4:136 – O believers, believe in God and his messenger and the book he has sent down on his messenger and the book which he sent down before. Whoso disbelieves in God and His angels and his books, and his messengers, and the last day, has surely gone astray into far error.
>
> Q 16:36—Indeed, we sent forth among every nation a messenger, saying: 'Serve you God, and eschew idols.' Then some of them God guided, and some were justly disposed to error.
>
> Q 24:54—Say: 'Obey God, and obey the messenger; then, if you turn away, only upon him rests what is laid on him, and upon you rests what is laid on you. If you obey him, you will be guided. It is only for the messenger to deliver the manifest message.'
>
> Q 58:13—Are you afraid, before your conspiring, to advance freewill offerings? If you do not do so, and God turns again unto you, then perform the prayer, and pay the alms, and obey God and his messenger. God is aware of the things you do.[48]

Obedience to God and his apostles, therefore, is expected and with it comes God's promise to vindicate them. If this were not the case and God's apostles were to be defeated, this would be tantamount to a victory over God, which is impossible. Prophets have been killed,[49] but no one can defeat or overthrow God's apostles. The "Apostle must triumph in order to manifest on earth the triumph of God."[50] Once again we see that the vindication of the apostles is ultimately a vindication of the message and the one who sent the apostles—God himself.

Returning to Christology, it is not surprising that this same combination, "God and his apostles," is present in one of the key Christological passages in the Qur'ān, Q 4:171a: "People of the Book, go not beyond the bounds in your religion, and say not as to God but the truth. The Messiah, Jesus son of Mary, was only the messenger of God, and his Word that he committed to Mary, and a Spirit from him. So believe in *God and*

48. Cf. also Q 4:59; 7:158; 9:80; 48:13; 49:15, *et passim*.

49. Bijlefeld notes that in the Qur'ān the words obey/obedience are used only in connection with *rasūl* and not in connection with *nabī*, which is one of the reasons he offers for a distinction between the two. Bijlefeld, "A Prophet and More than a Prophet," 152.

50. Ibid.

his messengers . . . ."[51] Towards the end of the first chapter of the *Tathlīth*, the author makes an explicit appeal to this verse's designation of Jesus as God's Word as a testimony to the truth of that which he is asserting concerning the divinity of God's Word and Spirit—the one God who is revealed in Christ. He states, "And you will find in the Qur'ān that God and his Word and his Spirit is one God and one Lord. He has commanded you to 'believe in God and his Word and the Holy Spirit.'"[52] Samir suggests that the substitution of "believe in God and *his Word*" in the *Tathlīth* for "believe in God and *his apostles*" in Q 4:171 may be a qur'ānic variant.[53] Regardless, the *Tathlīth* echoes this combination for the purpose of emphasizing the representative and authoritative role, in semi-qur'ānic mold, reserved for Christ in the *Tathlīth's* soteriological economy. Christ is depicted as one in a long line of apostles who faithfully presented God's message to his designated people and served as their representative before God. But he was not simply their representative. According to the *Tathlīth*, he was God in the flesh sent to save his particular community from their sins.

This raises the question concerning the people to whom God sent this particular apostle, Christ, who is God's Word. It is at this juncture

51. *Italics* added for emphasis. The two medieval texts I am investigating in this chapter are silent when it comes to the Qur'ān's apparent condemnation of the Trinity in Q 4:171b (cf. also Q 5:73). Theoretically, it is possible that they could have agreed with the Qur'ān in this regard had they construed the "three" mentioned there as a reference to tri-theism, something Christians would also condemn. However, neither of the texts I investigate here discuss this as a possible interpretation of Q 4:171b. It should be pointed out that this type of interpretation has a tendency to overlook the rhetorical strategy of the Qur'ān, which was clearly to critique Christian doctrines. Thus, any attempt at achieving a doctrinal synthesis between qur'ānic and biblical horizons must wrestle with this challenge. Moreover, there are good reasons to assume that the Qur'ān's critique of Christian doctrines is based on what the three ecclesiastical communities, the Jacobites, Melkites, and Nestorians actually believed, not supposed heretical groups. As Griffith notes, "[T]he Qur'ān's rhetoric of critique should not be mistakenly read as a somehow faulty report of what Christians believed or did in the time and place of its origins. Rather, the hypothetical assumption should be that the Qur'ān expresses itself in reaction to what its contemporary Christians believed and in reaction to the formulae in which they confessed their beliefs, the Qur'ān's own intention being to highlight what is wrong with them from an Islamic perspective, to critique and even correct them." Griffith, "Syriacisms," 100.

52. Cf., e.g., Q 2:87, 253; 16:102.

53. Samir, "Earliest Arab Apology," 73n54. Jeffery does not list any variants for this verse, but this does not render it impossible. Jeffery, *Materials.* For a more recent treatment of the issue of qur'ānic variants, see Small, *Textual Criticism.*

that the author of the *Tathlīth* departs from the Qur'ān's presumption concerning the particularity of Christ's mission:

> But in Christ he saved humanity and rescued them. And we will make this clear, if God wills, how God sent his Word and his light as a mercy and guidance to humanity; by him he bestowed his favor upon them. And why he came down from heaven to save Adam and his progeny [*ādam wa dhurrīyatahu*] from the Devil's darkness and misguidance [*ḍalālatihi*].[54]

In the Qur'ān's prophetology, each messenger is sent to a specific people; however, the *Tathlīth*, in concert with the grand biblical narrative, depicts Christ being sent to the whole of humanity in order to guide them and save them from their sin and "the Devil's darkness and misguidance." His mission was universal since the work he accomplished was on behalf of all humanity. This accounts for the absence in the *Tathlīth* of any mention of Muḥammad. The author shapes his Christology with features that mirror aspects of the Qur'ān's prophetology, but he emphasizes the fact that God's Word—Christ—is God's universal representative to all humanity and humanity's representative before God, not simply one particular ethno-linguistic group. This fact excludes any need for further prophets and apostles beyond Christ and his disciples. Moreover, Jesus is more than humanity's representative before God and to God—he is God himself who has come to rescue Adam's progeny from sin, thereby vindicating both God and humanity.

Christ is a "Mercy and Guidance," God Himself Veiled in Human Flesh

The quote above marks the end of the chapter on the Trinity and the beginning of the *Tathlīth's* chapter on salvation history. It opens with the author noting that "God and his Word and his Spirit" is God "the Father and the Son and the Holy Spirit, one God and one Lord."[55] The message the author aims to convey to his audience is that God sent his Word as a "mercy to the people" (*raḥmatan lil-nāsi*) and a "guidance" (*hudān*) to them.[56] The identification of Christ as a "mercy to the people" in the *Tathlīth* echoes God's reply to Mary in Q 19:20–21 at the Annunciation when she asked how it was possible for her to conceive a son since no

54. *Tathlīth* 78:21–25.

55. Ibid., 78:21–22.

56. Ibid., 78:23–24.

one had "touched her." In that passage, God replies that he has appointed Jesus "a sign to the people" (*ayatan lil-nāsi*) and a "mercy from him" (*raḥmatan minhu*). Though the *Tathlīth* echoes the Qur'ān's designation of Jesus as a "mercy," it does not identify him as a "sign to the people." Yet, its identification of Jesus as God's "guidance" (*hudā*) is obviously meant to echo the Qur'ān's repeated statement that God has promised to guide humanity in order to lead them "on the straight path" (Q 1:6). Indeed, the designation of God's Word being sent to humanity as a "mercy and guidance" forms yet another hendiadys that permeates the remainder of the treatise. And its use in the *Tathlīth* has clear implications: those who follow Christ and accept him will be saved (i.e., they will be guided to know the way of the straight path, which is the way of salvation).[57]

As mentioned previously, this chapter recapitulates the story of redemption from creation to Christ. But the focus of the presentation centers on the lives of the prophets beginning with Adam and extending to Noah, Abraham, Moses, and Lot.[58] Swanson notes in this regard that the author presents the story of salvation history in the format of the Qur'ān's punishment sequences.[59] At the heart of that presentation is the

57. Cf. Q 5:46–47 where the Qur'ān exhorts those who follow Jesus and the "guidance and light" that is in the *Injīl* (i.e., the qur'ānic conception of the message given to Jesus) to judge by that which God has revealed therein. This forms part of the background behind the *Tathlīth's* frequent reference to Christ as "God's light," demonstrating yet another place where a particular verse in the Qur'ān presents linguistic and conceptual congruence with biblical language and ideas that the author appropriates in his Christology (cf. John 1:4–5).

58. The Qur'ān's notion of prophethood parallels many aspects of biblical prophethood, but it also presents a number of stark divergences. Most Christians (and Jews) would not consider Adam or Lot prophets, though both are prophets in Islam. For more on Adam, see the discussion in Bijlefeld, "A Prophet and More Than a Prophet," 147; cf. also Tottoli's compilation and analysis of all the qur'ānic material on the biblical prophets in Tottoli, *Biblical Prophets*.

59. Swanson, "Beyond Prooftexting," 310–11. Reynolds provides a helpful paraphrase of the punishment sequence of Q 7. It demonstrates how the Muslim scripture portrays the role of the prophets in these punishment sequences. Noticable in this sequence are three basic features of the Qur'ān's prophetology: (1) the similarity in content of the prophet's message, (2) the role of the prophets as forewarners, and (3) the resultant consequences when the people reject the prophet and his message: "God sent Noah to his people. Noah called on them to acknowledge him as prophet and to believe in God. They rejected his message and God destroyed them with a flood (v. 64). God sent a prophet named Hud (not found in the Bible) to a nation named Ad. He called on them to acknowledge him as a prophet and to believe in God. They rejected his message and God destroyed them as well (v. 72; the Qur'an does not say how). God sent a prophet named Salih (also not found in the Bible) to a nation named Thamud.

author's emphasis on the fact that Adam's progeny (*dhurrīyat ādam*) inherited death as a result of their participation in Adam's sin: "And Adam transmitted disobedience and sin and death so that this continued among Adam's descendants, none of whom, whether prophet or otherwise, were able to save Adam's progeny from this disobedience and sin and death."[60] While obedience to "God and his apostles" is expected, ultimately, human obedience has its limits. It cannot cleanse humanity from the "disobedience and sin and death" they have inherited from Adam. Nor can it vindicate them and restore their position within the sphere of God's blessing and his honor. Indeed, Satan's strategy in dealing with Adam and Eve was, "to remove both of them [*yukhrijahumā*] from God's honor [*karāmat Allāh*]."[61] This prompted, therefore, in concert with the flow of redemptive history, a miraculous intervention by God himself on behalf of Adam's progeny. This intervention comes in the Incarnation:

> Indeed, God did not see fit that any human being should undertake the salvation of Adam's son and his progeny. Therefore, God undertook that, in his mercy, and saved them from the hands of the Devil and his misguidance [*iblīs wa ḍalālatihi*] in order that God be thanked and worshipped and praised, for his grace and largesse and favor upon them, and his mercy and salvation upon them . . . . And God made this and their salvation known to his creatures . . . . Thus God sent from his throne

---

Salih called on them to acknowledge him as a prophet and to believe in God. They rejected his message and God destroyed them with an earthquake (v. 78). God sent Lot to his people. Lot called on them to acknowledge him as a prophet and to believe in God. They rejected his message and God destroyed them in a 'rainstorm' (v. 84; presumably a rain of fire). God sent a prophet named Shu'ayb (not found in the Bible) to the nation of Midian. He called on them to acknowledge him as a prophet and to believe in God. They rejected his message and God destroyed them in an earthquake (v. 91). God sent Moses to Egypt. Moses called on them to acknowledge him as a prophet and to believe in God. They rejected his message and God struck the unbelieving people of Pharoah with plagues (v. 130) and then drowned the forces of Pharoah (v. 136) in the sea." Reynolds, *Emergence*, 103–5.

60. *Tathlīth* 79:11–14.

61. Ibid., 79:6, a possible echo of Q 2:36 though God's "honor" is not mentioned there. It is mentioned, however, at the beginning of the *Tathlīth* where the author quotes Isa 6:3 saying, "Holy, Holy, Holy is the Lord Almighty in Power [*al-'azīz*] by whose honor the heavens and earth were filled" (*Tathlīth* 74:21). This same phraseology is repeated in the section leading up to the section translated here and the author emphasizes Satan's role in gaining the upper hand over humanity (*Tathlīth* 82:16–17; Samir, "Earliest Arab Apology," 85). By setting the stage in this way, the author's presentation of salvation history proves a vindication of God's honor.

> his Word which is from himself, and saved Adam's progeny. He put on this weak, defeated man, [*fa-labisa hādhā al-insān al-ḍaʿf al-maqhūr*] from Mary the good, whom God elected over the women of the world,[62] and he veiled himself through her [*fa-iḥtajaba bihā*]. And he destroyed and conquered the Devil, by means of him, and overthrew him and left him weak and contemptible, not vaunting himself over Adam's progeny, and severely distressed when God defeated him by means of this man whom he had put on.[63]

Though much could be said about this passage, one aspect is of particular interest when considering the Qur'ān's influence on how Christians writing in Arabic conceptualized and articulated their Christology in light of the Qur'ān's critiques. It is the notion that the Incarnation was a type of self-veiling of God in human flesh—God revealing himself to humanity "from behind a veil." As Swanson notes, the author's use of this notion echoes Q 42:51 where God is depicted as speaking to humanity from behind a veil.[64] That verse states: "It belongs not to any mortal that God should speak to him, except by revelation, or from behind a veil, or that he should send a messenger and he reveal whatsoever he will, by his leave; surely he is all-high, all-wise." By adapting this notion and utilizing it in the context of explaining the Incarnation, the author has provided a "Qur'ānic way of thinking about the Incarnation."[65] Indeed, he ties the logic of the Incarnation to redemptive history and God's desire to vindicate Adam's progeny in the face of the "Devil's darkness and misguidance."[66] This deception removed humanity from the sphere of God's generosity and honor (*karāmat Allāh*); thus, God's plan is to vindicate his honor and restore human dignity.

62. Swanson identifies a direct quote from Q 3:42 in this passage. Swanson, "Beyond Prooftexting," 298.

63. Samir, "Earliest Arab Apology," 86–88. Part of this section is not present in Gibson but is found in Samir, thus I have adopted his translation here with slight modifications.

64. Swanson, "Beyond Prooftexting," 302. Commenting on the author's use of this notion, Samir states: "The word *ḥijāb* applies, in Oriental Christian theology, both to Christ and to the Virgin Mary . . . . It is interesting to note that, in the Oriental Churches, *ḥijāb* is concretely the Iconostatsis which separates the faithful from the sanctuary, the Holy of Holies (*quds al-aqdās*). Christ is mystically the *ḥijāb* which gives access to the Holy of Holies, to God; and the Virgin Mary, in a lesser degree, does the same by giving us access to Christ." Samir, "Earliest Arab Apology," 96.

65. Swanson, "Beyond Prooftexting," 302.

66. *Tathlīth* 78:25.

Two other places in the *Tathlīth* are pertinent for illustrating how the author uses the qur'ānic notion of "self-veiling" to explain God's incarnational action of "putting on human flesh." The first comes at the end of the second chapter, before the *Tathlīth's* discussion of the various *testimonia* in chapter three. It demonstrates something of the author's defense of his dyophysite Christology, which he ties to God's purpose in creation:

> Christ is the mediator between us and God; God from God and a man. No human is able to look towards God and live. Thus, God desired mercy for his creation and honor for them. Therefore, Christ was between us and God—God from God and a man; the judge of human deeds. For this reason, God veiled himself in a man who was without sin. In this way, he has shown us mercy in Christ and brought us near to him.[67]

The author notes that the motivation for God's self-veiling in the Incarnation originated in God's mercy and honor towards his creation. By availing himself of human flesh, God was able to judge sin and forgive humanity, thereby healing the breach in his honor wrought by human disobedience.

The final instance of God's putting on human flesh is mentioned in the third chapter. It occurs in the context of a messianic prophecy from Ps 2:8. In this passage, God speaks to David and tells him to request the nations as an inheritance and he will be granted his request. The reason for mentioning this verse in the *Tathlīth* appears to be related to the author's desire to show the universal scope of Christ's saving mission. In the course of establishing this fact, he echoes several Psalms where the universal mission of God is mentioned.[68] Culminating the author's discourse in this regard is a quote from Ps 110:1, a messianic prophecy quoted by Jesus in each of the Synoptic Gospels.[69] The author uses it to show that Christ, having been resurrected, is now sitting at the right hand of the Father and waiting for the time when all his enemies will be put under his feet. In the midst of stating this, the author glosses a familiar qur'ānic verse that Muslims usually refer to in order to dismiss Christ's crucifixion:

67. Ibid., 85:2–6.

68. He combines a number of ideas found in passages such as Pss 45:17; 48:10; and 72:17, among others. See *Tathlīth* 87:16—88:1.

69. Cf. Matt 22:44; Mark 12:36; Luke 20:42.

> Thus did Christ ascend to the heavens. He did not depart from there but sat to the right of the Father. And he has placed those who disobeyed him in a position under his feet and under the feet of those who have believed in Christ. Likewise, you will find in the Qur'ān: "I am putting you to death and raising you up to myself and purifying you from those who have not believed and making those who follow you above those who have not believed until the day of resurrection." Do not say that we believe in two gods or two lords. God forbid! God is one God and one Lord in his Word and his Spirit. But God has revealed to his servant and prophet David and clarified to him that Christ is God's Word and his light, which has been shown to humanity by his mercy. Indeed, he is God from God, even though he put on flesh. Thus, whoever obeys him has obeyed God, and whoever disobeys him God will put him under his feet so that humanity will know that God and his Christ are of the same throne and honor.[70]

The qur'ānic verse mentioned by the author is Q 3:55, which Muslims have traditionally used as a prooftext along with Q 4:157 to deny the crucifixion of Christ.[71] The author makes positive reference to this verse in the current context since it supports his contention that Christ died and ascended and is in heaven awaiting the time when God will judge those who disobey. In the author's mind, Christ's "putting on human flesh" to live, die, and be resurrected in order to save humanity in no way detracts from his divinity or the obedience and honor due him. Additionally, the author uses Q 3:55 to reinforce the idea that those who do not believe as the Christians do about Christ stand condemned. This explains the *Tathlīth's* response, after quoting Q 3:55, to the rhetorical question posed to Christ in Q 5:116–17, asking him if he told his followers to consider him and his mother "two gods" (*ilāhayn*). The author responds directly to this charge by situating his belief in the divinity of God's Word within the previous revelation—the Zabūr of David (i.e., the Psalms). The author is stating that those who obey Christ and recognize his deity are obeying God and rendering to him the honor he is due. The remainder of this treatise explores how the various *testimonia* taken from the Hebrew Bible testify to the veracity of Christian beliefs and practices.

70. *Tathlīth* 88:3–13.

71. For a discussion of the interpretive history of these two verses and the reason why they actually affirm the crucifixion, see Reynolds, "Muslim Jesus," 237–58; cf. also Ayoub, "Towards an Islamic Christology, II," 91–121.

THEODORE ABŪ QURRA'S DISPUTATION WITH THE MUSLIM MUTAKALLIMŪN IN THE MAJLIS OF AL-MA'MŪN

Background and Contents

While the *Tathlīth* is considered to be among the oldest Christian apologies authored in Arabic, Theodore Abū Qurra is the first named Christian theologian to compose original works of theology in that language.[72] Indeed, scholarship was the forte of this monk's response to Islam. Abū Qurra was born around 755 in Edessa, now the modern city of Şanliurfa in southeastern Turkey. At the time, Edessa was the center of Syriac Christianity, specifically Jacobite Monophysitism. Most of the details of Abū Qurra's life come from the Syriac chronicles of Michael the Syrian composed around 1240.[73] These reveal that Abū Qurra was a Chalcedonian bishop in the biblical city of Ḥarrān, located less than fifty kilometers to the southeast of Edessa, sometime during the last fifteen years of the eighth century. Abū Qurra was deposed from this position only to be reinstated later. Around 813 to 817 he went on an "apologetical pilgrimage" to Alexandria, Jerusalem, and Armenia, most likely in concert with the initiative of the Patriarch Thomas I of Jerusalem (r. ca. 807–20) to promote Chalcedonian orthodoxy among the Monophysites.[74] By 829 Abū Qurra reappears back in Ḥarrān once again as bishop. It is during this period that most scholars believe that Abū Qurra's debate took place in the court of the 'Abbāsid Caliph al-Ma'mūn (r. 813–33).[75] Textual evidence suggests he passed away sometime around 830.[76]

72. For his published Arabic works, see Constantine Bacha, *Mīyāmar*. For a translation of most of Abū Qurra's Arabic and Greek corpus, excluding the debate under examination here, see Lamoreau, *Theodore Abū Qurrah*. Nasry and Dick have both published critical editions of the Arabic text of Abū Qurra's debate. See Nasry, *Abū Qurrah wa al-Ma'mūn*; Dick, *Mujādalat Abī Qurra*. For the purposes of this study, I have relied upon Dick's edition and it is referred to throughout as *Mujādala*.

73. For a detailed examination of these documents and their relationship to the details of Abū Qurra's life, see Griffith, *Profile*, 15–34. Cf. also Bertaina, *Dialogues*, 212–13.

74. Griffith, *Profile*, 17, 30.

75. Griffith notes that al-Ma'mūn was known for his liberal policies towards minorities and his favor towards Abū Qurra. Due to his interest in theology and philosophy, al-Ma'mūn requested that Abū Qurra translate psuedo-Aristote's *De virtutibus animae* into Arabic, a testimony to the prolificacy of this scholar-monk (ibid., 25–26).

76. Lamoureaux is a skeptical about the sources used to ascertain these dates. He proposes Abū Qurra was born ca. 750 and died ca. 820. For his discussion, see Lamoureaux, *Abū Qurra*, xi–xvii.

Although there are questions regarding the historicity of the debate under investigation here,[77] "the very existence of debate reports testifies to Abū Qurra's fame in the Christian communities as an effective apologist and spokesman for the Christian cause."[78] Swanson even alludes to the existence of traditions suggesting that al-Ma'mūn converted to Christianity, possibly as a result of the arguments Abū Qurra put forth in defense of the Christian faith.[79]

The content of the debate itself covers several different themes. Bertaina summarizes them as follows:

> creation and circumcision, the old and new covenants, the divine status of the Word of God, the status of believers and 'submitters' (i.e., Muslims), the women promised to Muslim men in paradise, Jesus' humanity and divinity, his identity as Spirit and Word of God, the identity of the polytheists in the Qur'ān, the commendation of Christians in the Qur'ān, paradise and eternal life, the Incarnation, the hypostases of God, the Trinity, the human acts of Christ and his divine miracles, the accusation against Christians of polytheism, the voluntary passion of Christ, and the veneration of the Cross.[80]

As mentioned in chapter one, I am relying upon a critical edition of the Arabic text prepared by Dick. In that edition, the *Mujādala* has been divided into sixteen brief chapters. Each chapter consists of several questions or statements that are introduced either by Abū Qurra or one of his numerous interlocutors. Additionally, there are title headings in order to indicate something about the subject matter of the chapters. For purposes of contrast and comparison, I have chosen to examine the same three Christological themes and the associated qur'ānic verses examined previously in my treatment of the *Tathlīth*. With regard to the format, occasionally al-Ma'mūn introduces a topic for discussion or engages Abū Qurra in debate. Other times it is someone else. Towards the end of the

77. Griffith and Graf doubt that this text records an actual historical debate. Dick, Bertaina, and Nasry, on the other hand, argue that the work is a recollection of a historical debate. For more, see Dick, *Mujādala*, 35–40; Bertaina, "The Debate of Theodore Abū Qurra," 559; Bertaina, *Dialogues*, 213–14; Nasry, *The Caliph and the Bishop*, 85–123. Although the historicity of the debate is not necessarily pertinent for demonstrating the soundness of my thesis, I tend to agree with Dick, Bertaina, and Nasry and view the text as a recollection of an actual debate.

78. Griffith, *Profile*, 24.

79. Swanson, "The Christian al-Ma'mūn Tradition," 63–92.

80. Bertaina, "The Debate of Theodore Abū Qurra," 557.

debate, al-Ma'mūn is repeatedly depicted as turning to his fellow Muslims and asking (rhetorically), "Is there anyone left among you to debate Abū Qurra [*hal baqīya 'andakum man yunāẓir Abā Qurra*]?"[81] One is left with the impression that, as far as al-Ma'mūn is concerned, Abū Qurra is the victor.

Exegesis of the Qur'ān

Compared to his other Arabic works, Abū Qurra's use of qur'ānic passages in the *Mujādala* is quite widespread.[82] There is hardly a topic or issue that Abū Qurra addresses where he does not make some reference to a qur'ānic passage. Part of this is attributable to the venue and his audience. The *majlis* genre of Arabic Christian apologetic literature is often replete with qur'ānic references since it depicts a debate between a Christian and his Muslim interlocutors who base their repudiations of Christian doctrines on qur'ānic verses. Thus, it is not surprising to find the Christian controversialists making abundant references to the Muslim scripture both positive and negative.

Of great interest in this text is the manner in which Abū Qurra references the Qur'ān. Oftentimes he qualifies his use of qur'ānic references (or paraphrases) with the statement, or some variation thereof, "it is stated in your book," or "your Qur'ān says" or "your prophet says." But like the *Tathlīth*, Abū Qurra never mentions Muḥammad by name in the *Mujādala*, though he does make frequent reference to "your prophet" and what he is said to have proclaimed in the Qur'ān. Clearly, Abū Qurra cites the purported sayings of Muḥammad (in the Qur'ān, not the *ḥadīth*) in order to establish points of contact. For Abū Qurra, points of contact mean that he sees agreement between *some* of what the Qur'ān proclaims and his own Christian doctrines and teachings. However, it is also clear that he differs at times with the explicit teaching of the Qur'ān.

An example of this is found in chapter thirteen according to Dick's arrangement of the *Mujādala*. In that chapter, Abū Qurra deals with the question of which book (i.e., the Bible or Qur'ān) is distorted (*muḥarraf*). The question is raised by a man from Iraq (al-'Irāqī). He claims that Abū

81. *Mujādala*, 113, 114, 119.

82. Griffith discusses some of Abū Qurra's qur'ānic references in his tract on human freedom and his treatise on the veneration of icons in Griffith, "The Qur'ān in Arab Christian Texts," 218–20. Swanson discusses a number of them in his treatise on salvation in Swanson, "Beyond Prooftexting," 312–14. See also Bertaina's analysis of Abū Qurra's use of the Qur'ān in Bertaina, *Dialogues*, 217.

Qurra, and by extension all Christians, has distorted the Bible. In reply, Abū Qurra begins by noting that al-'Irāqī's claim in this regard contradicts the clear affirmation of the Qur'ān ("your book") and the Muslim prophet: "You deride your book and falsify the saying of your prophet where he says, 'Let the people of the Gospel judge by that which their Lord has revealed to them. For among them are priests and monks and they are not proud. They are the closest in love to those who have believed.'"[83] Abū Qurra conflates at least two verses here, most likely Q 5:47 or Q 5:68 and Q 5:82. But the point he makes is that the charge of scriptural distortion contradicts the clear teaching of the Qur'ān. He then turns to make the charge that it is the Qur'ān which in fact has been distorted: "If you [al-'Irāqī] knew the incontrovertible truth, you would know that your book is the one that has been distorted."[84] When asked how this is possible one of the examples Abū Qurra gives is the Qur'ān's pledge to give beautiful women—"wide-eyed *houris*" (*ḥūr al-'ayn*)[85]—in marriage to Muslim men in Paradise. Seizing on the morally objectionable nature of this, Abū Qurra asks,

> If it is as you say, regarding your believing women [*al-mu'mināt*], then who will their husbands be in the life to come if you have the *ḥūr al-'ayn* apart from them? You should not wish for your women a substitute [*badal*], whether in this life or in the life to come, if they are, as you say, Muslims and believers [*muslimāt wa mu'mināt*].[86]

Apparently, Abū Qurra found this depiction of the afterlife too carnal and sensual to be considered revelation from God and he criticizes the Qur'ān for containing such morally objectionable content. It is clear that in Abū Qurra's overall estimation there are things in the Qur'ān that affirm his own beliefs and he makes positive use of them. Yet there are also things that he finds objectionable, which he uses to demonstrate that the Qur'ān is a falsified Scripture.[87]

83. *Mujādala* 103.

84. Ibid.

85. Arberry's translation. Cf., Q 44:54; 52:20; 56:22. Luxenberg argues that this phrase actually refers to the "white, crystal-clear grapes of paradise" from the Syriac Christian tradition. See Luxenberg, *Syro-Aramaic Reading of the Koran*, 247–82. Some of Luxenberg's proposals have been criticized for reading everything in the Qur'ān "as if it were simply Syriac in a different script." Griffith, "Syriacisms," 99.

86. *Mujādala* 103.

87. Another example is Abū Qurra's criticism of Muḥammad's marriage to his

One other indicator concerning Abū Qurra's view of the Qur'ān is worth mentioning. It is found in a discussion of Christ's likeness to Adam, a topic to which I will return shortly. In this instance, a man named Abū al-Qāsim reckons Jesus' spirit (*rūḥ*) to that of Adam: "The spirit of Jesus Christ ['Īsā al-Masīḥ] is like the spirit which was in Adam. God said to it, 'be,' and it was."[88] In response to this comparison, Abū Qurra expresses astonishment that Abū al-Qāsim does not believe and accept that which God has revealed in the various sources of revelation. What is notable is that in referencing and listing those sources, Abū Qurra uses certain verbal designations to distinguish each of them. His appeal to them is rooted in his belief that each source provides a basis for affirming the eternality of God's Word, Jesus. However, he apparently does not consider each one divine revelation. This is demonstrable in the language he uses to describe them:

> You [Abū al-Qāsim] do not give credence to that which God revealed in the Torah [*lā bimā anzala fī al-Tawrāt tuṣaddaq*], and you do not give credence to that which is in the Zabūr, and you do not give credence to that which God revealed in the Injīl, and you do not give credence to that which was spoken by your book [lit. "your book spoke"; *wa lā bimā naṭaqa bihi kitābuka tuṣaddaq*]. I am astonished at your corrupt thinking, contemptible speech, vanity, and your denial of what God has said [*qawl Allāh*].[89]

The difference is subtle but significant. When referring to the Bible (i.e., the Torah, Zabūr, and the Gospel),[90] Abū Qurra uses the standard qur'ānic verb that can be understood as "revealed" or "sent down"

adopted son, Zayd's, wife (cf. Q 33:37). He states: "Zayd divorced his wife and he [Muḥammad] married her at the command of his Lord. You report this repugnance about your Prophet, pray it in your prayers, and ascribe it to the saying of God Almighty!" *Mujādala* 81.

88. Ibid., 105. Cf. Q 3:59.

89. Ibid., 106.

90. These three are the typical qur'ānic designations that collectively can be understood to refer to the canonical Bible. However, it is not at all clear that the Qur'ān is aware of the contents of the canonical Bible, including the four gospels, Paul's epistles, etc., nor does it appear to distinguish between apocryphal material and what Christians in the seventh century would have affirmed is canonical revelation. This later point can be illustrated by the Qur'ān's reference to apocryphal miracles (breathing into a clay bird and causing it to come to life) alongside canonical miracles (healing the blind, lepers, and raising the dead) in verses like Q 3:49.

(*anzala*).[91] But when referring to the Qur'ān, he stops short of using this verb and adopts *naṭaqa*, which simply means "to speak," and makes the Qur'ān ("book") the subject of the verb. This is significant since in self-referential discourse the Qur'ān refers to itself as being "revealed" or "sent down" by God and it does so by using the verb *anzala*. Abū Qurra adopts the Qur'ān's verbal revelational paradigm; however, he limits its use to sources that he considers divine and proper for determining right faith and practice (i.e., the Bible). These happen to be sources that the Qur'ān itself, in verses like Q 5:42–47, 10:94, etc., holds up as the standard by which Christians are to judge their beliefs. Yet Abū Qurra stops short of using the same language when he refers to the Qur'ān. Granted, Abū Qurra's statement at the end of the above quote that Abū al-Qāsim denies "what God has said" (*qawl Allāh*) could be construed as including the Qur'ān. But it is significant that there are no instances where Abū Qurra uses the verb *anzala* (or the passive form *unzila*) in the *Mujādala* when talking about the Muslim scripture.[92] This brief but telling exchange appears to indicate that Abū Qurra believes the Qur'ān to teach that the Bible is revealed by God and thus has ongoing significance for determining right beliefs and practices. But the absence of *anzala* in the context of referring to the origins of that which is recorded in the Qur'ān suggests that Abū Qurra does not affirm that the book is revealed or of divine origin, even though he makes positive use of several qur'ānic locutions.

Christological Themes

Christ is More Exalted than Adam

By and large the most widespread example of qur'ānic borrowing throughout the *Mujādala* is Abū Qurra's appropriation of the Qur'ān's identification of Jesus as God's "Word" and "Spirit" (Q 3:45; 4:171). Like the *Tathlīth*, Abū Qurra refers to Jesus as "God's Word and his Spirit" (or

91. Cf., e.g, Q 5:49, 59; cf. also Badawi and Haleem, *Arabic-English Dictionary*, 930.

92. One instance of a problematic appeal to the authority of the Qur'ān as "God's speech" occurs in chapter eleven, which includes a discussion of the Trinity. Abū Qurra appeals to the contents of the Qur'ān as an independent testimony as "the saying of God" for the truth of what he is asserting concerning the divinity of God's Word. In this instance, he accuses the Muslim, stating, "you falsify what God has said [*qawl Allāh*] in your book on the tongue of your prophet where he says that God created creation by his Word and his Spirit." *Mujādala* 95–96. However, he does not use the verb *anzala* in this instance, and he qualifies what he states by emphasizing this is the saying of "your book" and "your prophet."

"his Word and his Spirit") throughout the debate in order to emphasize the uniqueness and divinity of Christ. This phraseology is found at the beginning of the text on the lips of Abū Qurra,[93] but it is also found sporadically on the lips of his Muslim interlocutors.[94] Clearly, Abū Qurra couches his explication of Christology in these terms due to their echo in the Qur'ān. In his view, they provide points of positive contact that resonate with his Muslim audience. Indeed, Abū Qurra frames his whole discussion of Christology throughout the entire debate as an explanation of the identity of God's Word and his Spirit, who is none other than the object of Christian faith and adoration, Jesus Christ.[95]

Near the start of the debate, at the beginning of chapter two, a man identified as Muḥammad b. ʿAbd Allāh al-Hāshimī[96] charges that Christ (*al-Masīḥ*) is, "God's Word and his Spirit whom he sent [*baʿathhā*] to Maryam. His likeness to God is as the likeness of Adam whom God created from the dust and breathed in him from his Spirit."[97] Al-Hāshimī's comment is a paraphrastic conflation of several ideas found in Q 3:59, Q 4:171, and Q 32:9, but especially Q 3:59 where there is a comparison between Jesus and Adam. The qur'ānic passages he cites suggest that both Jesus and Adam are created beings. And this is the point that al-Hāshimī is making. Upon hearing the charge, Abū Qurra is at first silent, showing hesitation to defend his beliefs for fear of retribution. Al-Ma'mūn, however, reassures him that he can speak freely. Abū Qurra responds by noting that the similarity between Christ and Adam drawn by the Qur'ān is oftentimes confused since one assumes that they are made from similar substances. While the Qur'ān's emphasis is on how they are similar, Abū Qurra uses this as an opportunity to show how it is that Jesus differs from Adam.

93. *Mujādala* 66.

94. E.g., ibid., 67, 88; cf. also p. 80 where Abū Qurra asks if Ṣaʿṣʿa denies that Christ is the Spirit of God and his Word, which he does not.

95. Like the *Tathlīth*, Abū Qurra avoids any discussion of the apparent conflation presented here between the second and third persons of the Trinity in order to utilize the linguistic congruence he finds in these qur'ānic Christological appellations for his apologetic purposes. Indeed, on occasion Abū Qurra uses "Word" and "Spirit" to refer solely to Jesus and sometimes he uses them in reference to the second and third persons of the Trinity. My focus is on the former.

96. Nasry points out that apart from al-Ma'mūn the names of Abū Qurra's interlocutors are most likely fictitious. See his discussion in Nasry, *The Caliph and the Bishop*, 125.

97. *Mujādala* 67; cf. also p. 84.

In order to explain, Abū Qurra asks al-Hāshimī if Adam was created from a substance (*shay'*) that is describable (*yūṣaf*) and measurable (*yuqās*), and he agrees that he was. He also asks if al-Hāshimī would agree that the substance from which Adam was created is definable (*yuḥadd*). Al-Hāshimī says that it is. Abū Qurra then asks al-Hāshimī whether Christ was made from a created substance (*min shay'in huwa makhlūqun am lā?*). Al-Hāshimī responds by affirming that he was and identifies the substance as "the Word of God and his Spirit."[98] Upon identifying the substance from which Christ was made, Abū Qurra asks if the Word of God and his Spirit are "limitable [*yuḥadd*], adaptable [*tukayyif*], and describable [*tūṣaf*]," to which al-Hāshimī replies that it is not and adds that neither is it "perceivable [*wa la tudrak*]."[99] Upon making this confession, Abū Qurra asks al-Hāshimī whether God's Word is creating (*khāliqa*) or is created (*makhlūqa*). In other words, is the Word of God to be identified with the Creator or is it a created substance?

Abū Qurra's strategy in this regard reminds us of the *Tathlīth* where a similar argument was made. However, Abū Qurra is more sophisticated in the way he employs Greek categories in keeping with his affirmation of the Nicene Creed that Christ is ὁμοούσιος with God the Father. He appeals to the ontological implications of the Qur'ān's designation of Christ as God's Word and focuses his discussion on the nature and substance of that Word, thereby demonstrating how Christ is different from Adam but of the same substance as God. The implication of Abū Qurra's question is immediately clear to al-Hāshimī, and he responds by lowering his head and taking time to think. If he answers that God's Word is creating, he will be defeated since he will be conceding that the Word is in fact equal to the Creator and hence divine; however, al-Hāshimī is not ready to admit that God's Word was created. Abū Qurra ends this discussion by turning and addressing al-Ma'mūn and saying, "There is a difference between the one you see and the one you do not see, O Commander of the Faithful, [between] that one who is infinite whose greatness cannot be perceived and is indescribable."[100] Abū Qurra's strategy in this chapter sets the stage for the rest of the debate where he proceeds to defend his belief in the eternality and divinity of God's Word, Jesus Christ.

98. Ibid., 68.

99. Ibid.

100. Ibid.

Christ is the Divine Word in Human Flesh

Chapter six begins with al-Ma'mūn asking Sullām b. Mu'āwīya al-Hamzānī to appear before him to defend Islam. By his own confession, al-Ma'mūn is fearful "lest their minds deviate from the truth and they [those in his *majlis*] enter into his [Abū Qurra's] religion."[101] However, after al-Hamzānī's brief introduction wherein he derides Abū Qurra, al-Ma'mūn dismisses al-Hamzānī as an imbecile. He then tells Abū Qurra that he can go until they can bring someone worthy enough to debate him. Disturbed by the ineptness of the Muslim *mutakallimūn* brought to debate Abū Qurra, those present in the *majlis* request that al-Ma'mūn summon a man from al-Baṣra named Ṣa'ṣ 'a b. Khālid. The next day the stage is set and al-Ma'mūn tells Abū Qurra that he should not fear, for those present will only answer him "according to that which is better" (Q 29:46).[102]

Ṣa'ṣ 'a begins by asking Abū Qurra to clarify a verse from the Gospel of John that he believes demonstrates Jesus' affirmation of his own humanity and distinction from God. The verse he quotes is from John 20:17, "I am ascending to my Father and your Father, to my God and your God."[103] Martin Accad notes that this verse is the "most extensively used Gospel verse in the whole Islamic exegetical discourse of the second/eighth to the eighth/fourteenth centuries."[104] Muslims use it because on the face of it Jesus affirms his humanity by emphasizing the similarity between him and his disciples. However, Abū Qurra follows the long line of Church Fathers who use this verse to illustrate dyophysite (Chalcedonian) Christology. He responds by noting that if Jesus were *only* human he would not have been able to accomplish the miracles he did simply by the word of his mouth. Moreover, Abū Qurra does not deny that this verse affirms Jesus' humanity; however, he was not *merely* human. As Abū Qurra states: "He came to us fully human and fully divine. Thus he said to his disciples, 'my Father and your Father' in his divinity and 'my God' in his humanity."[105] Abū Qurra is stating that when Jesus refers to God as "my Father" he is indicating something about the uniqueness of his

101. Ibid., 75.

102. Ibid., 76.

103. This verse may be echoed in Q 43:64 where Jesus is depicted as saying, "Assuredly, God is my Lord and your Lord; therefore serve him; this is a straight path."

104. Accad, "Ultimate Proof-Text," 200.

105. *Mujādala* 76.

relationship to God.[106] God is his Father in a way that he is not the Father of the disciples. Likewise, when Jesus says "your God" to the disciples he is indicating something about the uniqueness of their relationship to God. God is their God in a way that he is not God to him. For Jesus, God is "his God" in a figurative sense (*'alā majāz al-kalām*).[107]

Upon clarifying this verse, Abū Qurra returns to the theme of miracles, which he referenced at the outset of his reply to Ṣa'ṣ 'a. He states that in order to test humanity and accomplish his will,

> He [God] sent his Word and his Spirit to the pure Virgin Mary. And she carried the light of the world who was from God and who appeared to humanity in human flesh [*mutajassidan*]. This was because human eyes could not behold him. Were it not for his being veiled in human flesh [*wa law lā iḥtijābuhu bi-dhālika al-jasad*], he would not have descended from his heaven to the earth, nor would he have mingled with humanity. Thus the Word of God took the form of a man but without sin [*fa-ṣārat kalimatu Allāhi shibih insānin bilā khaṭīya*]. He was God, able to do miracles, as your book testifies: "We sent to Mary from our Spirit and he appeared to her a perfect man." I mean by this that he (God) took the form of a man in the flesh.[108]

Abū Qurra's qur'ānic citation is taken from Q 19:17, one of two *sūras* that present qur'ānic versions of the nativity stories.[109] According to his interpretation, Christ's "appearing" to Mary in the flesh is taken to refer to the Incarnation, while his "perfection" refers to his sinless state (*fa-tamaththala lahā basharan sawīyan*). Abū Qurra clarifies this interpretation by noting that the reason God did this was because "human eyes could not behold him." Thus, he veiled himself in human flesh—appearing to Mary as a perfect man—in order to "mingle with humanity."

Abū Qurra's argument in this regard parallels the same idea we saw in the *Tathlīth* but without any development or explication of God's redemptive motivation for the Incarnation from the narrative of Scripture.

106. Though Abū Qurra states that God is Jesus' Father "in reality" (*bil-taḥqīq*), he is not, obviously, affirming any sort of physical lineage between them. However, later generations of Muslim theologians would critique Christians for the language they use to describe the "filial" relationship between God the Son and God the Father as implying physical lineage.

107. *Mujādala* 77.

108. Ibid.

109. Cf. Q 3:42, 45–47; 19:16–22.

And although Abū Qurra does not reference Q 42:51 here as a rationale for the Incarnation, once again we find it echoed in the notion that God chose to speak to humanity while "being veiled in human flesh." Elsewhere, in chapter ten, Abū Qurra mentions the notion of God's self-veiling in the context of answering an argument against the Incarnation on the basis that it limits the illimitable God. Abū Qurra objects to this argument because it prevents God from doing what he wills within the sphere of that which he created. Indeed, Abū Qurra argues, God cannot be contained or limited in any sense except by self-limitation: "If the creating Word and Spirit was meant for all that, how can anything or any place contain it or encompass it? And why would it not be possible for it to dwell in a creature of its creation, of its likeness, and be veiled in it?"[110]

One other instance where Abū Qurra quotes Q 19:17 is worth noting. In the final chapter of the *Mujādala*, in the context of replying to objections that he worships a God who was crucified by the Jews, Abū Qurra offers an explanation of how Christ's death and suffering affected his humanity but not his divinity. Within his argument, Abū Qurra references the notion that Christ is God's Word veiled in human flesh (*kalimat Allāh muḥtajaba bil-bashar*).[111] He ties this idea to his argument for how Christ could be God in the flesh and experience all that humans do, even death, without concluding that "God died" or that his divinity experienced the "pain of the cross, death, burial, hunger, thirst . . . ."[112] His basis for making this assertion is rooted in the idea that Christ has always been alive in the heavens until he made the choice to descend and "appear" to the Virgin Mary as a perfect man (Q 19:17).[113] Part of Abū Qurra's argument for asserting that Christ died and was raised is Q 3:55: "Indeed, God said: O 'Īsā, I am putting you to death and raising you up to myself and making those that follow you above those that have disbelieved in you until the Day of Judgment."[114] Abū Qurra glosses this qur'ānic text and uses it to defend his position on the resurrection and his stance that

110. *Mujādala* 91–92.

111. Ibid., 115.

112. Ibid.

113. Ibid., 116. The word translated by Arberry as "appear" in the Cairo text of Q 19:17 is *tamaththala*, which was cited by Abū Qurra earlier according to Dick's edition of the text. However, in this one instance, Dick (and Nasry, *Abū Qurrah wa al-Ma'mūn*, 242) records the verb *ishtamala*, which carries the connotation of being "enclosed in" or "enfolded in."

114. Ibid., 115.

"my God did not die" (*fa-ilāhī lam yamut*).[115] Upon appearing and accomplishing his work, Christ returned to where he was before and is now alive where he cannot experience death and judges both the living and the dead.

Christ is the Risen Savior

Abū Qurra's use of Q 3:55 in the context of his defense of the death and resurrection of Christ is unique since this is a verse to which Muslims oftentimes appeal for their belief that Christ did not die but was rescued by God and raised up to heaven where he waits his time to return. This topic is raised in chapter eight of the *Mujādala* where a man from al-Baṣra asks Abū Qurra, "Is not Christ your God?" to which, Abū Qurra responds, "Yes." Al-Baṣrī then says that if this is so, then "your God is dead." This prompts Abū Qurra to ask al-Baṣrī if he purports to believe that Christ died. After affirming that he does (apparently for the sake of presenting a consistent argument that Abū Qurra worships a dead God), Abū Qurra questions him regarding the present location of Christ. He asks, "Is Christ currently in heaven (*fī al-samā'*) or on the earth or in the grave?" At first al-Baṣrī responds, "I do not know except that Christ died," but after further questioning he says that Christ is "in paradise" (*fī al-janna*). Upon hearing his response, Abū Qurra asks when it was that Christ ascended to heaven or entered paradise. This time al-Baṣrī does not respond but asks Abū Qurra his view on the current location of Christ. "You tell me, is he in heaven?" Abū Qurra responds that he is and he refers to the testimony of the Qur'ān in this regard:

> Your book says in *sūrat al-nisā'*: "They did not kill him nor did they crucify him, rather God raised him up to himself." It also says, "Oh Jesus Son of Mary I am putting you to death and raising you to myself and purifying[116] you from those who do not believe in you. And I will set those who followed you above those who do not believe in you for you are the Judge of the World (*dayyān al-'ālamīn*)."[117]

115. Ibid.

116. In Dick's edition the word here is *muẓahharak*/*maẓharak*, which appears to be a transcription error. The word should be *muṭahharak* (cf. Nasry, *Abū Qurrah wa al-Ma'mūn*, 160; Nasry, however, misplaces the *shadda*).

117. Ibid., 84–85.

The first verse Abū Qurra quotes is a paraphrastic conflation of Q 4:157a and Q 4:158a. In selecting the parts of these two verses that he does, Abū Qurra avoids the difficult phrase, *wa lākin shubbiha lahum*, of verse 157. That phrase has been notoriously difficult for Muslim exegetes to explain, since, per the vocalization of the Cairo text, the verb is passive. This raises the question regarding the subject of the verb. What "appeared" or "seemed" to them? Was it the crucifixion or was it Jesus himself? As noted earlier, explanations abound; however, most Muslim commentators couple their understanding of Q 4:157–58 with Q 3:55 in order to assert that someone other than Jesus died and that God rescued Jesus from the plot of the Jews and raised him up to heaven.[118] But scholars have noted that when these verses are viewed within this *sūra's* broader rhetorical context—centered on rebuking the Jews for their perfidy and demonstrating God's control over life and death—it is clear that these verses affirm the death and resurrection of Christ.[119] And this appears to be the point Abū Qurra is making. He cites Q 4:157a and 158a along with Q 3:55, which emphasizes that God was in control of Jesus' death as well as his resurrection. Thus, those that follow him are above those who do not believe in him. By arranging the parts of these verses in the sequence that he does, Abū Qurra uses them to emphasize his point, which is that Jesus did die and that he was resurrected and is in heaven awaiting his appointed time to return as "Judge of the World" (*dayyān al-ʿālamin*).

One other place where Abū Qurra makes positive use of Q 3:55 and 4:157–58 is important to discuss. In this case, Abū Qurra's interlocutor, al-Dimashqī, glosses Q 4:157a and 158a in a way that parallels Abū Qurra's paraphrastic conflation of the same verses mentioned above, but he includes the phrase excised by Abū Qurra—*bal shubbiha lahum*.[120] Interestingly, al-Dimashqī uses these verses as a basis for his belief that Christ was not crucified, but he links his rejection of the crucifixion to the idea that this is "because he [Christ] is his [God's] Word and his Spirit."[121] In other words, Jesus was *not* crucified because he is God's Word and Spirit. Abū Qurra's reply indicates that despite his earlier removal of this phrase

118. Reynolds notes that the traditional interpretation of denying Jesus' crucifixion is motivated primarily by the particular eschatological concerns of Muslim exegetes. Reynolds, "Muslim Jesus," 240–51.

119. Ibid., 256.

120. The substitution here of *bal* for *lākin* is a variant appearing in at least two manuscripts of the *Mujādala*. Cf. Nasry, *Abū Qurrah wa al-Ma'mūn*, 170.

121. *Mujādala* 88.

in his quotation of Q 4:157a and 158a, he is aware of the Muslim argument in this regard. He responds by arguing that if the crucifixion was not real then Christ himself must not be real. Additionally, he appeals to Q 3:55 to demonstrate agreement between the truth of Christ's death, burial, and resurrection and what he finds in that verse: "Like the saying of your book and the witness of your prophet in *sūrat al-nisā,'* indeed he has ascended to the heavens. In this way he demonstrated in his essence that he is God from God."[122]

This final statement prompts a different interlocutor, al-Fārasī, to interject, asking what proof he can provide for this assertion. Abū Qurra asks if he agrees that Christ is God's Word and his Spirit, which he does. He then notes that if al-Fārasī purports to believe in God's Word and his Spirit, he cannot separate them from God. To do so would be tantamount to asserting they are created. Abū Qurra then links his argument to the logic some Muslim *mutakallimūn* were using to justify their belief in the eternality of the Qur'ān: "God's Word and his Spirit are, therefore, from him and inseparable from him. They are returning to him just like you say that the Qur'ān is the speech of God [*kalām Allāh*], revealed from above [*munzal*] and uncreated [*gayr makhlūq*] . . . ."[123] Abū Qurra's reference to the createdness of the Qur'ān parallels the same argument in the *Tathlīth.* But this is a surprising argument to make in the court of al-Ma'mūn. Towards the later part of his caliphate, al-Ma'mūn adopted the Mu'tazilite position on this issue and instituted a *miḥna* ("Inquisition") requiring all judges (*qāḍīs*) to adhere to a doctrinal statement affirming their belief in the createdness of the Qur'ān.[124] Abū Qurra's mention of this doctrine in the current context reveals his awareness of the debate and the conceptual congruence he found in it as a basis for defending his belief in the eternality and divinity of God's Word—Christ.

SUMMARY OF CONCLUSIONS

The purpose of investigating the *Tathlīth* and *Mujādala* has been to illustrate some of the ways that historically Arabic-speaking Christians made positive apologetic use of qur'ānic points of contact in their theological discourse. Each of the two treatises were authored in the context of Islam's growing social, religious, and political influence in the mid-eighth

122. Ibid.

123. Ibid.

124. Cf. Watt, *Formative Period*, 178–79.

to early ninth centuries. Both authors evidence an awareness of ongoing religious and philosophical debates and both couch their defenses of the faith in terms that would resonate with those engaged in such debates. And even if both texts were written with Christians primarily in mind, the authors were cognizant of the fact that what they wrote in Arabic would potentially be read by Muslims. Clearly, each text was written in the context of defending the Christian faith.

Oftentimes, the way these authors utilized the congruence they found in certain qur'ānic locutions was by weaving together paraphrastic conflations and glosses of qur'ānic verses so that they affirm their particular Christological positions. Three examples examined above are particularly illustrative this. Both authors made use of the Qur'ān's Christological appellations, "Word and Spirit," in Q 3:45 and Q 4:171a, and both reference Q 42:51 in the context of articulating their conceptions of the Incarnation. Additionally, both cite Q 4:157–58 in affirmation of their positions on the crucifixion and resurrection of Christ. In each case, when referencing these verses or alluding to them, the authors weaved them together into their discourse in a way that echoed the original but spoke the meaning each Christian author intended.

Another example of this can be seen in the stylistic and rhetorical conventions the author of the *Tathlīth* adopted in his introduction. The combined effect of *saj'* and the numerous qur'ānic locutions appear designed to elicit the same rhetorical and emotional effect one might have when listening to the Qur'ān. But the author's strategy is to draw his audience into the worship of the God signified in the Christian Scriptures—the one who created all things and made himself known by "his Word and his Spirit." Thus, the author has resignified the qur'ānic locutions and appellations he uses in order to affirm his belief in the God of the Bible.

In some cases, particularly in the *Mujādala*, one gets the impression that both authors believed the Qur'ān might have originally supported the Bible and its view on Christology but was subsequently corrupted. This would comport with the growing view at the time Abū Qurra wrote, a view apparently advocated by John of Damascus, that the Muslim prophet received his message from an errant monk (e.g., the Baḥīra legend). This is possibly what lies behind Abū Qurra's selective use of qur'ānic passages and his apparent affirmation that parts of the book are congruent with biblical revelation and parts of it are not. Indeed, both authors build much of their apologetic presentations on the implicit argument the Qur'ān itself makes, which is that the Bible (i.e., the *Tawrāt*, *Zabūr*, and the *Injīl*) is revealed by God and, hence, has ongoing relevance in determining right beliefs and practices.

Most of the qur'ānic verses used in the two texts analyzed above evidence an awareness and evaluation of Christian doctrines, whether positive or negative. Significantly, the authors made use of the positive aspects of qur'ānic verses that, in some cases, could simultaneously be interpreted as overt critiques of Christian beliefs. An example of this is their adoption of the Christological appellations derived from Q 4:171a. As noted earlier, Q 4:171b appears to contain a critique of the Trinity; yet, neither of the authors quoted this verse at length and both authors chose to make positive use of the qur'ānic locutions within this verse as a point of contact for constructing their arguments in defense of Christ's divinity. By resignifying these locutions, both authors utilized theological content derived from the New Testament to communicate their position on doctrines like Christ's preexistence, divinity, Incarnation, death and resurrection, but they did so using language derived from the Qur'ān. One conclusion that might be drawn from this is that in the minds of the Christian authors of these texts, their resignification of certain qur'ānic locutions is in actuality a reassertion of the original meaning these particular locutions had (and continue to have) within the semiotic universe of Christian theological discourse. In other words, the Christian arguments in defense of their doctrinal positions appear predicated on the idea that part of what is in the Qur'ān is itself a corruption of the original message brought by God's prophets and messengers, a message preserved in the Bible and Christianity.

One problematic feature of the *Mujādala* is that Abū Qurra limits his use of scriptural reasoning almost entirely to quotes from the Qur'ān. Moreover, he displays a tendency to quote from the Qur'ān as an independent testimony to the truth of what he asserts. Stylistically, he uses paraphrastic conflations and glosses of qur'ānic verses in order to construct locutions that serve his intended purposes; purposes that support the Christian understanding of Jesus' identity. But unlike the *Tathlīth*, the *Mujādala* is nearly void of references to the Bible. In fact, one of the only times there is a quote from the Bible comes on the lips of a Muslim (John 20:17). This is possibly due to the lack of a standardized Arabic translation at the time Abū Qurra was writing, but it is more likely attributable to the venue and genre as well as Abū Qurra's tendency to rationalize Christian doctrines versus rooting his arguments in scriptural reasoning. (The lack of a standardized edition did not stop the author of the *Tathlīth* from providing translations and quotes of scriptural verses.)[125] This rationalization frequently exhibits features that belie abstractionist and reductionist tendencies—practices that played into the hands of later generations of Muslim theologians who would reduce Christianity to the doctrines of the Trinity and Incarnation. Thus, despite Abū Qurra's adroitness at finding linguistic and conceptual congruence between qur'ānic ideas and biblically derived doctrines, he fails to redirect the congruence he finds back into a biblically grounded and enriched hermeneutical framework. He relies too heavily on rational argumentation and fails to illustrate how his doctrines are derived from biblical exegesis rooted in the triune God's redemptive acts on behalf of his creation through the course of salvation history.

This was not a problem, however, for the author of the *Tathlīth*. The *Tathlīth* structures its defense of the Trinity and Incarnation around the flow of redemptive history. The author understood that one of the strongest arguments he could put forward for the soundness of the doctrines he was defending was to root them in the Scriptures, both Old and New Testaments. Muslims frequently depicted their faith as a restoration of an original monotheism delivered to earlier prophets and apostles; something that Jews and Christians had corrupted. Muslims defended their position in this regard by arguing that their conceptualization of *tawḥīd* was in keeping with the faith of Adam, Noah, Abraham, Isaac, Jacob, Moses, and Jesus. To counter this claim, Christians frequently referenced Scripture as a testimony to the truth of Christian doctrines like the Trinity and Incarnation. This is particularly the case in the *Tathlīth*. Abū Qurra, however, appears to undermine this approach in two ways. First, he limits his use of scriptural reasoning to quotes from the Qur'ān, as mentioned earlier. Second, though not examined above, there are indications in the *Mujādala* that Abū Qurra adopts a supersessionist (or abrogationist) approach toward the *Tawrāt* that undermines any ongoing relevance for the Old Testament. Evidence for this can be found at the outset of the debate, in a discussion with al-Ma'mūn, where Abū Qurra cites five laws or pillars (*sharā'i'*) given to Israel that they were expected to keep. These included, "The Torah, circumcision, keeping the

125. In defense of Abū Qurra, it is important to point out that our selection of his works is limited to this one text and thus we cannot be too severe in criticizing him for a lack of scriptural reasoning. Indeed, as noted in chapter one, Samir considers Abū Qurra the example *par excellence* of Christians who utilized scriptural reasoning as an apologetic strategy.

Sabbath, sacrificing bulls and sheep, and prayer towards the *qibla* [i.e., Jerusalem]."[126] In place of these, Abū Qurra argues, Christ brought five new laws: "The Gospel in lieu of the Torah, Sunday in lieu of the Sabbath, baptism in lieu of circumcision, the Eucharist [*qurbān*] in lieu of sacrifices, and the East in lieu of the *qibla*."[127] This type of abrogationist approach to the Bible left him and others who employed it open to the charge by Muslims that just as Christianity had abrogated and replaced Judaism, so had Islam abrogated and replaced Christianity.[128] This type of thinking undermined the narrative unity that binds the entire Bible together. That narrative unity was better preserved in the *Tathlīth*. Abū Qurra's approach, moreover, seems to pave the way for the subversion of grand biblical narrative, or at least diminishes the power of the Bible to exert narrative control when telling the story of the prophets and apostles and God's redemptive intentions for humanity stretching from the Fall to the time of the Incarnation.

For Christians, God's actions on behalf of humanity culminate with the death, burial, and resurrection of Christ. There is a progressive movement within the grand biblical narrative that points towards Christ and his work on the cross. Emphasis in the Qur'ān, however, is always on the prophets' role in calling their people to believe in God, the people's subsequent rejection of this message, and God's condemnation of their people. Part of the reason for this appears to be in the Qur'ān's assumption that the basic content of each prophet's message was the same and that the Qur'ān's message, therefore, is in continuity with its precursors.[129] The author of the *Tathlīth*, however, uses the Qur'ān's pattern of prophetic punishment sequences but fills in the narrative details and shapes the theological gist of the stories to comport with the Bible's message of redemption through Christ. And he does this by utilizing qur'ānic language and turns of phrase to tell the message of salvation by "God and his Word and his Spirit."

Obviously, the Qur'ān's punishment sequences are an adaptation and revision of how these prophets are presented in biblical literature. A distinct understanding of the role of the prophets and the message they brought to their respective peoples marks the Qur'ān's revision in this

126. *Mujādala* 66.

127. Ibid.

128. Bertaina disagrees and says that Abū Qurra sees Christianity as a fulfillment of Judaism not an abrogation of Judaism. See Bertaina, *Dialogues*, 215–16.

129. Cf., e.g., Q 2:136.

regard, demonstrating the reductionist nature of the Qur'ān's prophetology. By reducing the prophets to communal representatives with a common message centered on *tawḥīd* and the conveyance of guidance to their people, the Qur'ān revises salvation history and redefines God's role in history and his redemptive intentions for humanity. Furthermore, by abstracting these prophets and their stories from the grand biblical narrative, the Qur'ān flattens the details surrounding the accounts of their lives. These details constitute the raw material of redemptive history—the record of God's redemptive actions on behalf of humanity culminating in the work of Christ.

This fact serves to illustrate the lack of narrative formation in the Qur'ān and how the author of the *Tathlīth* sought to use the Qur'ān's elliptical and allusive style for his own apologetic purposes. The *Tathlīth's* strategy is to reposition the qur'ānic echoes it references within the Bible's hermeneutical horizons thereby demonstrating, in a subtle but subversive manner, the referential and derivative nature of the Qur'ān's punishment stories. Their full significance can only be realized and understood when viewed within the flow of redemptive history; a history that culminates in Christ's life, death, burial, and resurrection. For the author of the *Tathlīth*, the qur'ānic locutions act to buttress the rhetorical force of what he wants to convey. By extracting words and phrases embedded within the Qur'ān's particular construal of the events cited, the author carefully and skillfully repositions them in a way that the rhetorical force of the original is utilized to assert the depiction of the events according to the author's construal of them—according to the Bible's story of salvation.

4

Christian Exegesis and Apologetic Use of the Qur'ān in Select Contemporary Arabic Texts

THE PURPOSE OF THIS chapter is to illustrate contemporary examples of positive apologetic uses of qur'ānic points of contact in the context of explaining the Bible and Christian doctrines. The examples come from two contemporary Arabic Bible commentaries published by the al-Kalima School. The commentaries are prefaced by a number of explanatory articles that are all anonymous. However, at least two of the leading contributors to the works are named, published scholars. Maẓhar al-Mallūḥī is among the editors and contributors to the first commentary, *A Sufi Reading of the Gospel of John*.[1] Mallūḥī is a self-ascribed Syrian Muslim follower of Christ and is the pioneer of al-Kalima's publishing efforts. In addition to working closely for many years with Frontiers, an evangelical missions agency,[2] Mallūḥī is a novelist who has published a number of books on his faith in Christ and addressed several sensitive socio-political issues in the Arab world.[3] Al-Hādī al-Jaṭlāwī is one of the editors of the other commentary, *The True Meaning of the Gospels and Acts*.[4] Jaṭlāwī is

1. Maẓhar al-Mallūḥī et al., eds., *Qirā'a Ṣūfīya*. Hereafter: *Sufi Reading*.

2. In the early 1990s, Mallūḥī was described as a "traveling evangelist" for Frontiers teams in the Middle East and the "Frontiers team leader in Cairo." See Livingstone, *Planting Churches in Muslim Cities*, 104, 143.

3. Cf., e.g., al-Mallūḥī, *Laḥẓat Mawt*; al-Mallūḥī, *Al-Layl al-Ṭawīl*; al-Mallūḥī, *Ḍā'i'a fī al-Madīna*; al-Mallūḥī, *Al-Rāḥil*. Mallūḥī is also the editor of two other Bible commentaries: al-Mallūḥī et al., eds., *Qirā'a Sharqīya*; al-Mallūḥī, *Nash'at al-'Ālam wa al-Basharīya*.

4. al-Jaṭlāwī et al., eds., *Al-Ma'nā al-Ṣaḥīḥ*. Hereafter: *True Meaning*.

Tunisian scholar who has published works in the field of literary style and Qur'ān interpretation.[5] Given that the commentaries and articles are joint works by anonymous scholars within the al-Kalima School, authorship of them in this chapter will be attributed collectively to "al-Kalima." The focus in this chapter is on several of the articles prefacing the biblical text and the composite picture they present of al-Kalima's use of the Qur'ān. But before examining this topic, it is important to outline in broad terms al-Kalima's translation philosophy and approach to hermeneutics.

THE THEOLOGICAL HERMENEUTICS OF THE AL-KALIMA SCHOOL

رُبّيتُ على أن المسيحية تمثّل الاستعمار و الصليبية، و لقد استخدم الغرب رسالة المسيحية و أساء إليها، و لكن حين قرأتُ كتاب **قراءة صوفية لإنجيل يوحنا** وجدتُ كم أن هذا الغرب بعيداً عن رسالة المسيح، كما وجدتُ أن لي جذوراً و روابط أكثر في رسالة المسيح من الإنسان الغربي.

> I was raised believing that Christianity represents imperialism and the Crusades and that the West has used the message of Christianity and besmirched it. However, when I read *A Sufi Reading of the Gospel of John* I discovered how far the West is from the message of Christ. I also discovered that I have roots and more connections to the message of Christ than the westerner.[6]

In an article at the beginning the *True Meaning*, al-Kalima provide the rationale for why they have come forward with their particular "reading" (*qirā'a*) of the New Testament.[7] They note that when Arabic-speaking Christians began translating the Bible in the ninth century they used an

5. Cf., e.g., al-Jaṭlāwī, *Madkhal ilā al-Uslūbīya*; al-Jaṭlāwī, *Qaḍāyā al-Lugha fī Kutub al-Tafsīr*. One other scholar who contributed a foreward to the *Sufi Reading* is important to mention, namely Riḍwān al-Sayyid. Al-Sayyid is a Lebanese Muslim scholar and leading editor of the journal, *Al-Ijtihād*. He is also a professor of Islamic studies at the Lebanese University and has published widely in the area of Arab and Islamic political and religious thought. Cf., e.g., al-Sayyid, *Mafāhīm al-Jamā'āt fī al-Islām*; al-Sayyid, *Al-Islām al-Mu'āṣir*.

6. Comments by Sheikh Muṣṭafā al-Jabārī in Mallūḥī et al., *Sufi Reading*, 6. All translations from the two commentaries are my own.

7. Jaṭlāwī et al., "Limādhā Hādhihi al-Qirā'a" in *True Meaning*, 4–6. In the *Sufi Reading*, al-Kalima adopt the Jesuit translation of the Gospel of John for the biblical text with the parenthetical addition of 'Īsā after each occurrence of Yasū' ("Jesus"). The biblical text of the Gospels and Acts presented in the *True Meaning* constitutes a new translation initiated by al-Kalima.

Arabic *lingua franca* that was understood by all speakers of the language regardless of religious affiliation. This included commonalities in greetings, religious vocabulary, and expressions.[8] However, over time, and due to a variety of political, religious, and socio-economic factors, Christian communities became isolated. Their participation in the broader culture waned as did their influence on the language of that culture. As a result, a gap formed between members of the same nation (i.e., the Arab nation) that continued to widen with the passage of time. Within a few centuries, Christians began speaking an Arabic that, though understood by their Muslim neighbors, varied greatly in terms of the connotation and significance of key terms. Eventually, Christian vocabulary and expressions began to disappear from Muslim publications (and vice versa). Today this gap remains and it impacts the degree to which Muslims comprehend the Bible. When reading one of the commonly available translations today, many Arab Muslims struggle to understand the meaning of key expressions and words. Thus, with the publication of the *True Meaning*, al-Kalima are embarking on a new translation of the Scriptures into Arabic that aims to preserve "a word-for-word translation of the inspired Greek text," but uses parenthetical comments and other means to clarify such things as the kinship language used in expressions and titles like the "Son of God."[9]

Al-Kalima state that their translation and the articles they have produced in the *True Meaning* are guided by four goals. The first goal is that the current "reading" seeks to convey the "meaning and significance" (*al-ma'nā wa al-dalāla*) behind the written word. They state: "This reading does not attempt to freeze the idea in words but give the words space and flexibility in order that it might enable the reader to understand that the written sentence is not the end of the matter. We present

8. One example al-Kalima offer of a shared linguistic and cultural heritage among Arabic-speaking Christians and Muslims is the ca. 9th c. Arabic translation of the Gospel of Matthew. Prefacing the gospel is the well-known qur'ānic invocation, "In the name of God, most compassionate, most merciful," which appears at the behest of 113 of the Qur'ān's 114 *sūras*. A facsimile of the Arabic manuscript appears in *True Meaning*, 33.

9. For more on al-Kalima's translation philosophy and how it impacts their treatment of titles like *Ibn Allāh* (i.e., "Son of God"), see al-Kalima Translation Committee, "A Response to Jay Smith," 19. An in-depth treatment over how to translate such titles like this in Bible translations in Muslim contexts is beyond the scope of the present work; however, Carson has addressed some of the issues in *Jesus the Son of God*, 73–109.

the meaning that is hidden behind the word but it is not the final word."[10] Though fixed in terms of the inscripturated words of the inspired biblical text, for al-Kalima, the applications one derives from the Bible extend beyond the fixed text to impact people in all times and places, including Arabic-speaking Muslims. This leads to their second goal, which is to make the current reading "contemporary" (i.e., "relevant" or "meaningful"). Al-Kalima aim to accomplish this by "framing the word so that it accords with the culture, time, and place . . . ."[11] The idea is that the current reading will act as a "bridge to connect between what was written two thousand years ago to today's culture and events [in the Middle East]."[12] The third goal is to illuminate issues surrounding the cultural and theological background of the events one encounters in the New Testament. This is accomplished through several introductory articles treating a number of theological issues that have traditionally hindered Muslim readers from fully comprehending the Bible. Additionally, there are copious explanatory notes that accompany their rendering of the four Gospels and the Book of Acts. These are designed to provide information on the cultural, religious, and political backgrounds of the New Testament, which are unfamiliar to Muslim readers. The fourth and final goal is that the words and terminology they use in their reading will be "neutral" in the sense that they will be understood and accepted by all speakers of Arabic "without feeling any sense of foreignness [*gharāba*]."[13] Although these goals are stated explicitly in the *True Meaning* and applied to their new translation of the four Gospels and Acts, it is apparent that they constitute a guiding philosophy that is generally applicable to both of the al-Kalima commentaries. Each is designed with the explicit aim of offering a contextually sensitive reading and explanation of the Bible for Arabic-speaking Muslims.

One other prominent feature that characterizes the *Sufi Reading* is important to clarify. The notion of a "Ṣūfī" reading of any part of the New Testament might at first glance seem to be anachronistic or an interpretive fallacy. But al-Kalima have adopted this interpretive motif in order to challenge their readership to consider deeply the meaning of the

10. Jaṭlāwī et al., "Limādhā Hādhihi al-Qirā'a," in *True Meaning*, 5.

11. Ibid., 6.

12. Ibid.

13. Ibid.

metaphors, symbols, and language that are unique to the Gospel of John.[14] Their belief is that John's Gospel has within it a number of ideas related to Christ's life, work, and teaching that parallel aspects of Ṣūfī thought and that can be used to communicate the gospel. Al-Kalima's connection between Ṣūfī thought and the Gospel of John in this regard should not come as a surprise. Many scholars believe that the Bible, Christian doctrines, and Christian spirituality (in particular, monasticism) played an influential role in the development of what is known as Ṣūfism or Islamic mysticism.[15] This is particularly the case when one considers the life, thought, and writings of such mystics as al-Ḥallāj (d. 922).[16] Al-Kalima's goal is to show that a careful reading of the Gospel of John reveals that several of the ideas one finds there are in concert with the deepest longings of many Muslim mystics. Indeed, the Gospel of John helps shed light on those ideas and al-Kalima assert that Christ himself aims to satisfy their longings.

As mentioned, several articles from the *Sufi Reading* and the *True Meaning* have been selected and are examined in this chapter to illustrate al-Kalima's use of qur'ānic points of contact in the context of discussing select Christological themes. The themes I investigate correspond to those investigated previously in the medieval texts. They include the divinity of Christ, the Incarnation, and the crucifixion and resurrection. The divinity of Christ and the Incarnation are treated together in what I have labeled al-Kalima's *logos*-apology. The final theme, the crucifixion and resurrection, is treated separately. Before proceeding, however, two caveats are in order. First, because the articles al-Kalima have composed do not address directly the Christological themes under investigation, I have selected a number of articles that touch on them in an attempt at forming a composite picture of how al-Kalima utilize qur'ānic locutions in the context of discussing them. Yet, it is important to understand that al-Kalima do not reference the Qur'ān in each and every treatment or discussion of these doctrines. Indeed, the examples I have selected

14. For more, see the first article in the *Sufi Reading*, which provides an explanation of al-Kalima's particular approach to this Gospel. Mallūḥī et al., "Al-Ramūz al-Ṣufiya," in *Sufi Reading*, 17–34.

15. For a general introduction to Ṣūfī thought, see Arberry, *Sufism*; Nicholson, *Mystics of Islam*; Schimmel, *Mystical Dimensions*. Most scholars identify al-Qushayrī (d. 1074) and his work, *al-Risāla al-Qushayrīya*, as the most influential work in Arabic on Ṣūfism. For an English translation, see al-Qushayrī, *Principles of Sufism*.

16. For more on his thought and the account of his crucifixion, see Arberry, *Sufism*, 56–60.

were chosen *because* they include positive uses of qur'ānic locutions in the context of discussing these themes. But this should not be construed as the sole approach al-Kalima use when elucidating the Bible's teaching on these doctrines. Nevertheless, al-Kalima are aware of the linguistic and conceptual congruence that exists between certain biblical ideas and select qur'ānic texts, or, at least, they are anticipating the preunderstandings that many of their readers will bring to their reading of the Scriptures. Their strategy, therefore, is to use that congruence to redirect their readers back into the Bible's world of discourse. Second, although I have limited my investigation to positive uses of qur'ānic points of contact in line with the stated purpose of this book, this does not mean the commentaries are absent of *potentially* problematic uses of the Qur'ān, as defined by the guidelines established in chapter two. However, evaluating these is beyond the scope of the present investigation.

AL-KALIMA'S EMPLOYMENT OF THE LOGOS-APOLOGY TO EXPLAIN THE DIVINITY OF CHRIST AND INCARNATION

We begin with a discussion of what I have labeled al-Kalima's "*logos*-apology." The *logos*-apology is a Christo-centric defense of biblical faith that centers on Christ, his Incarnation, and his identity as the eternal Word of God. Al-Kalima argue that Christ's identity as God's Word is affirmed in both the Bible and the Qur'ān. The articles in the commentaries that touch on this theme display a high level of agreement on this point. Thus, it is important to ascertain the flow of al-Kalima's argument in this regard. Having stated that, the argument I have labeled the *logos*-apology is not present in any one, stand-alone article in either of the two commentaries. My description of it is based on a composite reading of how the commentaries utilize qur'ānic points of contact in the context of discussing these particular Christological themes. In order to trace the flow of al-Kalima's argument, I have divided my presentation of the *logos*-apology into three parts: (1) an exploration of al-Kalima's *logos*-centric religious epistemology, (2) the eternality and uncreatedness of God's speech (i.e., his eternal *kalām* or "Word"), and (3) the identification of 'Īsā ibn Maryam ("Jesus the Son of Mary") as the embodiment of God's eternal, uncreated Word. As will be seen, the *logos*-apology displays a number of features that parallel the medieval attribute apology and its defense of Christ's divinity in a context shaped by the Qur'ān's critique of Christian doctrines; particularly, the Trinity and Incarnation.

Al-Kalima's Logos-Centric Epistemology

Al-Kalima believe that God created an intelligible universe by his Word. And they note that this belief is congruent with Q 30:25 where the heavens and the earth are said to stand (or "to be established") by his command (*amr*): "And of his signs is that the heaven and earth stand firm by his command . . . ." Al-Kalima identify God's "command" as being synonymous with God's "Word."[17] The implication of this is that everything in the universe is contingent upon God's Word for its existence. God spoke and all things were instantaneously brought into being: "God has created all things by his speech. For this reason the Almighty says to something, 'be,' and 'it is.'"[18] This statement echoes similar statements in the Qur'ān where God says to things, "be," (*kun*), and all things simply "come into being" (*fa-yakūn*).[19]

Importantly, God's creating Word happens to be the same Word by which he has graciously chosen to communicate with humanity. God's Word to humanity constitutes his revelation to them; revelation which has been providentially preserved by God's apostles. And since the message those apostles recorded contains the very Word of God, al-Kalima argue, it is deemed incorruptible.[20] But it is not only incorruptible; it is understandable. God's Word forms the basis upon which humanity establishes their knowledge of him. The reason this is possible is because God created people in a manner that accords with *some* of his attributes.[21]

17. Mallūḥī et al., "Kalām Allāh," in *Sufi Reading*, 41–42.

18. Ibid., 41–43.

19. E.g., Q 2:117; 3:47, 59; 6:73; 16:40; 19:35; 36:82; 40:68.

20. In the *True Meaning*, there are three articles that discuss the notion of revelation (*waḥī*) and compare, contrast, and correct the prevailing ideas about biblical revelation and its supposed corruption among contemporary Muslims. In one of the articles, numerous *mufassirūn* are quoted to demonstrate that though many of the earliest Qur'ān commentators charged Jews and Christians with interpretive corruption (*taḥriīf ma'nawī*), the notion of textual corruption developed rather late in Islamic thought and at the behest of Ibn Ḥazm (d. 1064) in Spain. The article argues that while someone may accuse Jews and Christians of misinterpreting the Bible, all Muslims must abandon the accusation of textual corruption. It ends with several photos of ancient Greek and Arabic manuscripts that are used to attest to the textual integrity of the Bible. Jaṭlāwī et al., "Taḥrīf al-Waḥī al-Ilāhī," in *True Meaning*, 15–33.

21. Al-Kalima do not explicitly delineate a list of communicable attributes versus

Not surprisingly, therefore, human similitude with God enables men and women, as distinct from other created beings, to have a relationship with him:

> In Genesis, the first Book of the Bible, we read that God created humanity in order to express his glorious attributes. Thus God said, "Let us make man that he might declare who we are and declare our attributes . . . . So God made man to express who he is—to make God known. He created them male and female" (Gen 1:26–27). The meaning of this is that humanity carries some of the Creator's attributes. And though humanity differs from him in many significant ways, e.g., in greatness and perpetuity, man's participation with God in some of his attributes makes us able to know God and to enter into a personal relationship with him.[22]

One "attribute" in particular enables humankind to encounter God and obtain true knowledge of him—God's speech or his Word. For al-Kalima, 'Īsā ibn Maryam is that Word; he is the apex of divine communication to humanity. It is through him that humankind encounters God and obtains true knowledge of him. Indeed, Christ is the goal of God's revelation to humanity in the Bible:

> All of the Bible's books point to the person of our master 'Īsā in his essence [*bi-ṣifatihi*] as the clearest and most complete manifestation of God Almighty's attributes. Thus, if we truly love knowing God, let us look to our master 'Īsā. And if we truly desire to know our master 'Īsā, let us read the books of the Bible, for they contain the revelation through which we meet the living Messiah and begin with him our journey of knowing God personally.[23]

This brief discussion demonstrates that the religious epistemology of al-Kalima is thoroughly Christo- or *logos*-centric—if one understands who Christ is he will understand who God is. Christ is the fullest revelation of God's attributes (*ṣifāt*). These epistemological parameters provide an important point of departure for al-Kalima's explanation of Jesus' divinity and his Incarnation in the *logos*-apology.

---

incommunicable; however, it is clear they make this distinction implicitly.

22. Jaṭlāwī et al., "Mafhūm al-Waḥī" in *True Meaning*, 8.

23. Ibid., 10.

The Eternal Kalām of God

In the *Sufi Reading*, in an article entitled, "The Speech [*kalām*] of God between Islam and Christianity," al-Kalima comment on the use of the Greek locution *logos* (λὸγος) in the prologue to the Gospel of John. They mention that in Arabic *logos* can be rendered either "word" (*kalima*) or "speech" (*kalām*). And, in accord with the teaching of both the Bible and the Qur'ān, God's Word is the means by which he spoke all things into being, as mentioned previously. Importantly, God's speech is not "something that is created or originated in time. Rather, God's speech is an eternal attribute [*ṣifa*] existing in God. God has created all things by his speech. For this reason the Almighty says to something, 'be,' and it is."[24] Therefore, for al-Kalima, God's Word is divine since it is an aspect of his very essence. The article goes on to assert that the eternality of God's Word is something upon which both the Bible and Qur'ān (i.e., both Christians and Muslims) agree:

> And this agrees exactly with the text of the Noble Gospel as found in John 1:1–3: "In the beginning was the Word, and the Word was with God, and the Word was God . . . ." This demonstrates that God's speech [*kalām*] is uncreated and that it is an eternal reality [*ḥaqiqa qadīma*] ever existing in God. In one sense he is "with God," and in another he "is God." Thus, everything that God created has been created by the means of his speech. This is a truth upon which Muslims and Christians both agree.[25]

Elsewhere in the *Sufi Reading*, in an article entitled, "Miracles and Signs," God's Word is said to be inseparable from his being, indicating that it is appropriate to attribute to God's Word all that is attributable to God himself: "The Word of God is not an entity separable from God, for no one disputes that there is but one God. The Word of God refers us to God and is from God. By it, God speaks. . . . It is not possible to separate God from his creating Word [*fa-lā yumkinu faṣlu Allāhi 'an kalimatihi al-khallāqa*]."[26]

Al-Kalima's line of argumentation in this regard parallels how the medieval authors examined in chapter three used the ninth century debate over the createdness of the Qur'ān and the argument regarding God's

24. Mallūḥī et al., "Kalām Allāh," in *Sufi Reading*, 41.

25. Ibid.

26. Mallūḥī et al., "Mu'jizāt wa 'Alāmāt," in *Sufi Reading*, 94–95.

Word as an eternal attribute existing in God—the attribute apology—to defend the Trinity and, by extension, assert Christ's divinity. Indeed, they make this parallel explicit in an article on Christ's death. In that article they note that God's "Word" or "Wisdom" is described as a person—Christ—who is said to be eternal "in the same way in which some Muslims describe the existence of the Qur'ān prior to its being revealed."[27]

Building on this idea elsewhere, al-Kalima argue that the intellectual heirs of Ibn Ḥanbal and al-Ashʿarī (i.e., the Sunnīs) are correct in affirming the reality of God's attributes. They regard this as "proper Islamic doctrine," since it accords with al-Kalima's position regarding God's speech:

> This is a truth that Islam affirms with regard to God's speech, even though the Muʿtazilites denied it, claiming that the Noble Qur'ān is created. They also denied that God's speech is an eternal reality existing in God's essence [*ḥaqiqatun azalīyatun qā'imatun bi-dhāti Allāhi*]. Moreover, they denied all the other eternally existing attributes in God like his life and his power. In their saying that God's speech is created, they claim that his Word is without reality and meaningless—that God speaks by himself and not by a Word existent within him. . . . Abū al-Ḥasan al-Ashʿarī (d. AH 325/AD 935) clearly summarized proper Islamic doctrine regarding this issue in his book *Ibāna ʿan Uṣūl al-Dīyāna*,[28] demonstrating its foundation in the Noble Qur'ān. He says, "indeed the speech of God Almighty is an eternal attribute in the being of God [*inna kalāma Allāhi taʿālā ṣifatun qadīmatun lam yazil qā'iman bi-dhātihi*].[29]

Al-Kalima's affirmation of the Ashʿarite position on the attributes enables them to assert a measure of multiplicity within the Godhead in a way that corresponds to the medieval Arabic Christian treatments of the same issue examined earlier. Al-Kalima's adoption and distinct articulation of this position serves to buffet the argument they are making to their predominantly Sunnī Muslim audience regarding the Bible's teaching on Christ's identity. Al-Kalima seize upon the accepted Sunnī view, inherited from al-Ashʿarī, to claim that the view they advocate regarding

27. Mallūḥī et al., "Mawt Sayyidnā ʿĪsā al-Masīḥ," in *Sufi Reading*, 99. The author of this article states on p. 101 that he is also the author of the previously cited article, "Muʿjizāt wa ʿAlāmāt."

28. For a discussion of the problems surrounding this work's attribution to al-Ashʿarī see Watt, *Formative Period*, 303–7.

29. Mallūḥī et al., "Kalām Allāh," in *Sufi Reading*, 41–42.

the eternality of God's speech [i.e., Christ] is conceptually congruent with what Muslims themselves assert regarding God's Word:

> In this way we see that both the Qur'ān and the Noble Gospel report that God's speech is eternal, uncreated, and exists in God's being [*qā'imun bi-dhāti Allāhi*]. Both books report that all things were created by God's Word, and both books report that 'Īsā al-Masīḥ is the Word of God which was manifest at birth from the Virgin Mary, may God be pleased with her, in order to give hope and repentance to the world.[30]

For many Muslims, this raises the question of what is meant in the Bible and Christian discourse when Jesus is described simultaneously as the "Word of God" and the "Son of God." In article on this topic, al-Kalima use the analogy of the Arabic idiom *bint shafa* (lit. "lip-daughter") to explain what is meant when Jesus is called the "Son of God" and "Word of God":

> In Arabic the expression "lip-daughter" refers to every word spoken by someone. . . . Obviously, this does not mean that someone's lips took a female companion [*ittakhadhtā ṣāḥibatan*][31] and birthed a daughter, which is his word. Rather, the point is that every word uttered by someone is like his symbolic daughter in that it springs forth from him. It expresses his person. . . . Similarly, we find our master 'Īsā, his peace be upon us, uses the expression "Son of God" and other similar expressions to indicate that he is "the one who eternally springs forth from God like a word springs forth from a speaker" [*dhālika al-nābi'u azalīyan min Allāhi mithilmā tanba'u al-kalimatu min al-mutakallim*]. . . . Everything God has created, he has done so by his Word. Therefore, when one honors God's Word, he honors the very being of God.[32]

Al-Kalima employ this analogy in order to support the idea that the use of figurative language, even when speaking about God, is legitimate. Their strategy in this regard is similar to the strategy of the Nestorian

30. Ibid., 43.

31. There is an echo here of Q 6:101; 72:3.

32. Mallūḥī et al., "Ma'nā 'Ibārat Ibn Allāh," in *Sufi Reading*, 36–40. This same article appears in the *True Meaning* with some slight changes. For example, in the last sentence of the article in the *Sufi Reading*, the phrase, "he who has seen me has seen the Father," a reference to John 14:9, is expanded in the *True Meaning* and interpreted in this way: "he who has seen me has seen the revelation [*tajallī*] of God in flesh," *True Meaning*, 67.

theologian, 'Ammār al-Baṣrī, mentioned in chapter one. Like al-Baṣrī, al-Kalima's goal is to dispel the notion that the physical aspects of human generation obtain when the Bible or Christians speak about God as "Father" and Jesus as his "Son." In another place, al-Kalima make their rejection of this notion explicit by referencing Q 112, a well-known *sūra* used by Muslims to emphasize God's oneness:

> The notion of the "Son" has continually been subject to misunderstanding. God's "fatherhood" on the one hand and the "sonship" of 'Īsā al-Masīḥ on the other were never meant to be construed as meaning "fatherhood" and "sonship" in a physical sense for this assumes somewhere the existence of a mother. Thus, from this perspective, God is "only one God, eternal, who has not begotten nor has he been begotten and none is equal to him."[33]

Al-Kalima's next step is to identify the person of Īsā ibn Maryam as the embodiment of God's eternal, uncreated Word.

'Īsā al-Masīḥ: God's Eternal, Uncreated, and Incarnate Word

"Is it possible . . . for God to send his Word to us in a form that reveals God's nature to us within the confines of our human capacity to understand? Is it possible for God to send his Word in the form of a man?"[34] These are questions that are addressed in the *Sufi Reading* in an article entitled, "The Revelation [*tajallī*] of Divine Wisdom." In that article, al-Kalima state the following regarding the "coming down [*nuzūl*] of God's Word to the earth":

> How is humanity to know God, the Great and Almighty, and to communicate with him unless he reveals himself to him? Is it possible . . . for God to send his Word to us in a form that reveals God's nature to us within the confines of our human capacity to understand? Is it possible for God to send his Word in the form of a man? "And remember when the angels said: O Mary! Lo! God gives you glad tidings of a Word from him, whose name is the Messiah, Jesus, son of Mary, illustrious in the world and the hereafter, and one of those brought near unto God."[35] "The Messiah, Jesus son of Mary, was a messenger of

33. Mallūḥī et al., "Mawt Sayyidnā 'Īsā," in *Sufi Reading*, 101.
34. Mallūḥī et al., "Tajallī al-Ḥikma," in *Sufi Reading*, 59.
35. Q 3:45.

> God, and his Word which he conveyed unto Mary, and a Spirit from him."[36] Thus, the merciful—out of the bounty of his mercy toward us—cast his Word, or his wisdom, into the womb of the young maiden Mary, and became flesh. He was born, grew, and matured. His life revealed the heavenly wisdom . . . . Therefore, the Messiah (PBUH) embodied for us the wisdom of God and has enlightened us regarding his noble attributes in accord with our limited, human understanding.[37]

Central to al-Kalima's articulation of Jesus's divinity and Incarnation in the *logos*-apology is the qur'ānic designation of Jesus as God's Word. This connection, or point of contact, in the Qur'ān provides al-Kalima with the linguistic and conceptual congruence they need to explain their position. Indeed, this elucidates the reason for their frequent citation of the two qur'ānic passages, Q 3:45 and Q 4:171, in the context of discussing Christology. These are the same two verses cited frequently in the medieval texts. And like the medieval texts, they are used throughout al-Kalima's publications to establish conceptual congruence for explaining, understanding, and accepting the Bible's teaching that Jesus is the eternal, divine, and uncreated Word of God. Accepting this ostensibly paves the way for accepting the Incarnation.

But does al-Kalima's interpretation of Q 3:45 and Q 4:171 contradict the traditional Muslim interpretation of the Qur'ān that Jesus was created *by God's Word* in a similar way to other beings? Traditionalist *mufassirūn*, like Ibn Kathīr, typically use Q 3:45 to establish that Jesus is a created being. Countering that position and Ibn Kathīr's interpretation of it, al-Kalima state:

> We find that the scholars [*'ulamā'*] frequently exercise independent judgment [*yajtahidūn*] in their interpretation [*tā'wīl*] of what the "Word" means when accompanying the name of

36. Q 4:171.

37. Mallūḥī et al., "Tajallī al-Ḥikma," in *Sufi Reading*, 59–60. Al-Kalima scholars appear to be aware of the limits of human reason and the noetic effects of sin. The truths they affirm are, for them, first and foremost, revealed truths that can be explained through scriptural reasoning. They are not overly occupied with "proving" their beliefs through philosophical arguments. This brings to mind the comments of Thomas Aquinas who, in the context of writing a treatise for Christians engaged in missionary activity among Muslims, wrote: "First of all I wish to warn you that in disputations with unbelievers about articles of the Faith, you should not try to prove the Faith by necessary reasons. This would belittle the sublimity of the Faith, whose truth exceeds not only human minds but also those of angels; we believe in them only because they are revealed by God." Aquinas, "De rationibus fidei," 736.

> our master the Messiah or referring to him [in the Qur'ān]. Ibn Kathīr says the following in his interpretation of Q 3:45: "'When the angels said: O Mary! Lo! God gives you glad tidings of a Word from him . . .,' God informed Mary of a son whose existence would be by a Word from God; i.e., God would say to him, 'be,' and he would 'be.' This makes the 'Word' synonymous with God's act of creation—'be, and it is' [*kun fa-yakūn*]. Therefore, the meaning of the verse is that the Messiah himself is not the Word but is created by means of the Word, 'be, and it is' [*kun fa-yakūn*]." But this is inconsistent with Q 4:171 which says that the Messiah is, "his Word conveyed to Mary and a Spirit from him." Here the understanding of the Word is linked to the name of our master the Messiah, making him . . . synonymous with the act of creation itself, something which accords with the Gospel according to John, but is not favored by the majority of Muslim *mufassirūn*.[38]

Clearly, al-Kalima scholars situate the divine and eternal Word of God in the person of 'Īsā al-Masīḥ. As God's Word, Christ is the means by which God spoke all things into existence. Moreover, he is God's Word conveyed to Mary and indeed to all of humanity. And the way God accomplished this "conveyance" of his Word to Mary was through the Incarnation, as attested in the New Testament. To a certain extent, this answers the *how* and *why* questions surrounding the logic of the Incarnation. God's eternal Word, Jesus the Messiah, appeared in human flesh for the sake of redeeming a people who are estranged from him: "The Noble Gospel confirms that the speech of God [*kalām Allāh*] was revealed [*tajallā*] to us as a human . . . in the body of the Messiah, to him be the glory."[39]

Elsewhere, al-Kalima elucidate further on the redemptive rationale behind the Incarnation. In so doing, they articulate a dyophysite understanding of the relationship between Christ's human and divine natures and how this relates to his suffering in the flesh:

> The divinity is not affected by suffering. But we say that our master 'Īsā al-Masīḥ was a real man and, at the same time, he is the eternal Word of God—one person with two natures, two natures in one person. So when we speak about suffering, we are not referring to the dignity of the divine being which is unaffected by pain, rather we refer to the weakness of that humanity

38. Mallūḥī et al., "Muqaddima li-Injīl Yūḥannā," in *Sufi Reading*, 174.

39. Mallūḥī et al., "Kalām Allāh," in *Sufi Reading*, 42–43.

> by which he was clothed [*tasarbala bi-hā*]. The Incarnation of God's Word does not involve a diminution [*khifḍ*] of divinity, but rather there is an elevation [*raf'a*] of humanity.[40]

Although al-Kalima explain the rationale for the Incarnation through use of scriptural reasoning (i.e., through the frequent citation of biblical passages), they also corroborate their belief through qur'ānic verses; verses that are interpreted in a way that puts distance between the Qur'ān and the corpus of classical *tafsīr* literature used by the majority of Muslims to interpret it. They use these locutions as points of contact in order to establish linguistic and conceptual congruence on the matters they address. By adopting this approach, al-Kalima are subtly drawing their readers into the world of the Bible's discourse on the nature of God and the message of salvation through Christ.

A question that might present itself to Muslim minds at this juncture pertains to the issue of whether or not Jesus urged others to view him as "another God." Al-Kalima's response is worth quoting. They state:

> The Noble Gospel informs us that our master 'Īsā al-Masīḥ is not only God's Word, but it also tells us that all things were created in him (John 1:1–4) . . . . The central idea in the Noble Gospel is that our master 'Īsā al-Masīḥ embodies [*yujassad*] God and possesses his authority in the world . . . . Behind all the interpretations and speculations regarding 'Īsā al-Masīḥ, the truth becomes clear. When people were standing in front of our master 'Īsā al-Masīḥ, they were really standing before God . . . . It was not a matter of Jesus' occupying the center, but rather God himself taking the place of that center. This is because our master 'Īsā al-Masīḥ was always pointing to God. He never announced that he is the life, light, or truth apart from God. Rather, he declared that he is the reflection [*in'ikās*] and embodiment [*tajsīd*] of God's nature so that he who looked at him was looking at God.[41]

Thus, Jesus did not present himself as an "another God." However, for al-Kalima, he is rightly identified with the Almighty since he is the embodiment of God's Word.

Al-Kalima's affirmation of the divinity of Jesus and the reality of the Incarnation raises a question regarding the divinity of the Spirit and, indeed, whether al-Kalima embrace belief in the Trinity. At the beginning

40. Jaṭlāwī et al., "Ḥulūl Kalimat Allāh," in *True Meaning*, 137.

41. Māllūḥī et al., "Mu'jizāt wa 'Alāmāt," in *Sufi Reading*, 94–95.

of an article on the Spirit of God, a definition of God is given: "The Books of the heavenly religions teach us that God is one God, existent by himself [*kā'inun bi-dhātihi*], living by his own Spirit [*ḥayyun bi-rūḥihi*], and speaking by his own Word [*nāṭiqun bi-kalimatihi*]."[42] The article goes on to dispel any notion that the Spirit is a created being or to be identified with Gabriel, a common belief among most Muslims. On the contrary, the Spirit is to be equated with God himself, "*fa-hīya dhātu Allāh*."[43] This idea is then coupled with al-Kalima's interpretation of Q 4:171 that Jesus is God's "Word" and "a Spirit from him":

> Additionally . . . the Qur'ān's expression, "his Word conveyed to Mary and a Spirit from him,"[44] is distinguished from other qur'ānic expressions. It defines the essence [*dhāt*] of the Messiah as a Spirit from the Almighty which proceeds [*ṣādira*] from him, not by creation but by procession [*ṣudūr*]. This is demonstrated by the succession of the two names, "Word," and "a Spirit from him." He is a Spirit from the Almighty, proceeding from him. The procession of the Word is from the communicative essence of God by his intra-personal communication. And seeing that there is no origination [*ḥudūth*] in God, his Word, which is in his essence, is unoriginated, or the Spirit from him is unoriginated.[45]

Later in the article, there is a discussion regarding Jesus' statement in John 14:16 that he would send a "helper" (i.e., the *paraclete*; παράκλητος). Muslims have long appealed to this verse as a prophecy about the coming of "Aḥmad," (i.e., Muḥammad). However, they accuse Christians of substituting the Greek word περίκλυτος ("praised one"), which is equated with "Aḥmad" in Q 61:6, with παράκλητος ("helper"), the word found in the Greek New Testament.[46] The article notes that in addition to the absence of any manuscript evidence for such a substitution, the descriptions Christ gives of the Spirit simply cannot be applied to "a man who would come six centuries after Christ," a subtle but firm denial that this verse refers to Muḥammad.[47]

42. This definition accords well with the trinitarian understanding of God as articulated in the medieval attribute apology.

43. Jaṭlāwī et al., "Rūḥ Allāh," in *True Meaning*, 68–69.

44. Q 4:171.

45. Jaṭlāwī et al., "Rūḥ Allāh," in *True Meaning*, 72.

46. Accad traces the historical development of this apologetic argument in, "Muḥammad's Advent," 228–35.

47. Jaṭlāwī et al., "Rūḥ Allāh," in *True Meaning*, 75.

At least two things become clear from al-Kalima's discussion in this section regarding the Spirit. First, God's Spirit works in a way that is distinct from Christ; nevertheless, he is intimately related to Christ's sanctifying work in the human heart.[48] Second, al-Kalima ascribe personhood to the Spirit. This is evident from a statement in defense of the integrity of the New Testament manuscript tradition, in particular John 14:16: "Nothing is found in all the [Greek] manuscripts except the word παράκλητος, which means the helper [*al-mu'īn*] or the mediator [*al-shafi'*] or the defender [*al-mudāfi'*]. He is the person who is called to help another or is a close friend."[49] Among the conclusions we can draw from this article is that al-Kalima are attempting to articulate accurately what the Scriptures say and teach about God, Christ, and the Holy Spirit, without using the explicit categories and language of Trinitarian theology. Undoubtedly, their motivation in this regard is to keep their explanations of Christian doctrines from being construed as "foreign" to Arabic-speaking Muslims.

THE CRUCIFIXION AND RESURRECTION OF CHRIST

Turning to the theme of Christ's death, burial, and resurrection, it is notable that throughout both of al-Kalima's commentaries the reality of these events is generally assumed. Unlike the *Tathlīth* and *Mujādala*, which interpreted verses like Q 3:55 and Q 4:157 in a way that upheld their position on Christ's crucifixion and resurrection, the contemporary texts are more comfortable operating from a position that asserts these events are true as depicted in the New Testament. This is notable given the continued denial of these doctrines today within most quarters of normative Islam. Notwithstanding this general approach to Christ's crucifixion and resurrection, al-Kalima do make some subtle references to the Qur'ān within the context of their discussion of this Christological theme.

Within the *Sufi Reading*, for instance, there is an article that highlights eight "symbols" (*rumūz*) from the Gospel of John that have significance for Ṣūfis. The eight include: "the beginning," "life," "light," "love," "the lamb," "wine," "water," and "bread."[50] In their discussion of the fifth of these symbols, "the lamb," al-Kalima note that the image of the lamb

48. This topic is covered in detail in ibid., 73–74.

49. Ibid., 75. There is a transliteration error in the reproduction of the Greek that I have corrected.

50. Mallūḥī et al., "Rumūz," in *Sufi Reading*, 17–34.

is among the most prevalent in Christian spirituality. The reason for this is "because of its deep connection to the substitutionary death which our master the Messiah underwent for the redemption of humanity."[51] They point out that John ties the events surrounding Christ's death directly to the events of the Passover and the deliverance of the Children of Israel from the bondage of slavery in Egypt. Al-Kalima note that John is not concerned as some of the other Gospel accounts are with the details surrounding the crucifixion. Evidence of this can be seen in the fact that he excludes any mentioned of Jesus' participating with the disciples in the Passover meal. Al-Kalima interpret the absence of these details as a significant indicator that John's focus is on Christ himself as the "Passover Lamb, the Great Sacrifice [*al-dhibḥ al-ʿaẓīm*]." In other words, John's emphasis is more theological in nature, versus being solely concerned with the historical details surrounding the crucifixion.

Taking their cue from John and his theological concerns, al-Kalima echo the language of Q 37:107 in characterizing Christ's sacrificial death on the cross as "the Great Sacrifice."[52] Their choice of this qur'ānic language is intentional since this verse appears in one of the qur'ānic accounts of Abraham's sacrifice of his son. In verse 102 of *sūra* 37, Abraham has a dream wherein he sacrifices his son. The son, not mentioned by name in the Qur'ān,[53] says that his father should be obedient and comply with God's command. Doing so, Abraham is promptly stopped (by God) and is told he has fulfilled what is required of him. Upon intervening to keep Abraham from killing his son, God announces, "And we have redeemed him by a great sacrifice [*wa fadaynāhu bi-dhibḥin ʿaẓīm*]" (Q 37:107).[54]

In its qur'ānic context, this statement is void of any redemptive significance. Those who are aware of these events as depicted in Genesis, however, immediately understand their significance (within the Bible's horizon of meaning, of course). However, in the Qur'ān's account of this event, there is an allusive echoing of words tied to events that were (originally) set within a context that more fully explained the terms. For those

51. Ibid., 25.

52. Arberry translates "great sacrifice" as a "mighty sacrifice."

53. Interestingly, the Qur'ān does not mention the name of the son in this immediate context as being Ishmael. Isaac is mentioned, however, in the verses just subsequent to this event, a possible indication that in the Qur'ān's mind the son was Isaac not Ishmael. See Q 37:102–13.

54. My translation.

aware of the importance tied to sacrifice and forgiveness within the biblical economy, words and concepts like "redemption" (as in: *fadaynāhu*) and "sacrifice" (*dhibḥ*) carry immense significance when tied to the redemptive narrative within which they are explicated. In the Qur'ān's construal of these events, the lack of narrative formation effectively rends these words from that context resulting in a loss of meaning and significance. Within its qur'ānic context, the statement about being redeemed by a great sacrifice is used to point to the reward Abraham and his son received due to their obedience: "Thus do we reward those who do right" (Q 37:110).[55] Aware of the Qur'ān's allusive reference to the events of Abraham and its resignification of these key redemptive terms, al-Kalima use the language of Q 37:107 to point to the work of Christ as the "great sacrifice" for all of humanity. Explicitly, they link Christ's identity as the "great sacrifice" to the words of John the Baptist in John 1:29, who upon looking at Jesus states, "Behold the lamb of God who takes away the sin of the world." In making this connection, al-Kalima are drawing upon the linguistic and conceptual congruence they find in a qur'ānic locution to explain the significance of Christ's sacrificial death as construed within the Bible's soteriological economy.

In order to establish further conceptual congruence, al-Kalima evaluate Christ's sacrificial death in the light of similar ideas found in the thought of Ṣūfī mystics like al-Ḥallāj. They also point out parallels between the Passover and ʿĪd al-Aḍḥā, the Muslim holiday devoted to commemorating Abraham's near sacrifice of Ishmael. Al-Kalima use these links in order to establish conceptual congruence for accepting the truth of Christ's sacrificial death on behalf of humanity. This is something that, according to al-Kalima, is not as foreign as many Muslim scholars sometimes make it appear.

Christ's death and resurrection are mentioned in a number of other places in the *Sufi Reading*. Indeed, there is a whole article devoted to the topic.[56] Yet, the crucifixion is discussed in that article without making positive use of the Qur'ān. In a different place, the crucifixion is described as being the greatest sign of victory, but only if one has the eyes of faith to see the events as intended by God—as God's victory over sin and death.[57] Other places in the commentary mention Christ's death and/or

55. My translation.

56. See n27 above.

57. Mallūḥī et al., "Muʿjizāt wa ʿAlāmāt," in *Sufi Reading*, 97.

resurrection,[58] but there are no further references to this Christological theme in the *Sufi Reading* that utilize qur'ānic points of contact.

When we turn to the *True Meaning*, we find a similar usage of Q 37:107 to that found in the *Sufi Reading*. In an article entitled, "The Understanding of Ransom, 'Redemption,'"[59] al-Kalima provide a brief description of the lexical meaning of the word "ransom/redemption" along with its usage in Judaism, Islam, and the Gospels. A connection is made between the notion of sacrifice affirmed in Q 37:107 and the much richer understanding of substitutionary death found in the Gospels; specifically, in the life and death of Christ.

This idea is continued in another article entitled, "Our Master 'Īsā Himself Came to be the Complete Sacrifice," where another reference to Q 37:107 is made. However, this article provides more detail than the previous article in its description of what Christ achieved by dying on the cross. Indeed, this article states clearly that acceptance of Christ's work on behalf of humanity is the only way one can be reconciled with God:

> Our master 'Īsā's death on the cross fulfilled the perfect offering [*al-qurbān al-akmal*] required for the purification of humanity from all impurities because it was the only way *for humanity* to approach God. It was, as has been said, the fulfillment of every legal code [*iktimālu kulli sharī 'atin*].[60] It was, in other words, the perfection of and satisfaction of all ceremonial cleansings and offerings.[61]

In another article in the *True Meaning*, there is a discussion about Christ's "meekness" (*wadā 'a*). Emphasis is placed on his gentle-hearted nature and humility in facing all that he did on behalf of humanity. At one point in the article, mention is made of Christ's sufferings and death. Al-Kalima note that each of the gospel authors record the details surrounding the crucifixion. They also point out that the Qur'ān itself is aware of Christ's sufferings and crucifixion, despite the lack of detail it gives of these events. Indeed, al-Kalima state that the mention in Q 5:112–14 of a "table," "festival," and "sign" are all veiled references to the Passover meal and the Lord's Supper:

58. Among the places Christ's death is discussed in the *Sufi Reading* are: p. 113, 121, 127–30, 147, and 179.

59. Jaṭlāwī et al., "Mafhūm al-Fidya," in *True Meaning*, 81–83.

60. This is a subtle reference to Matt 5:17.

61. Jaṭlāwī et al., "Jā'a Sayyidunā 'Īsā li-yakūn Nafsahu al-Dhabīḥata al-Kāmila," in *True Meaning*, 125. *Italicized* words added for clarity.

> Such was and remains the meekness that brought Christ to Gethsemane where he experienced suffering as depicted in the four gospels. Even though the whole story in all its detail is absent from the qur'ānic text, it is noteworthy that the Qur'ān is actually well aware of it, as it is of the 'table' that Christ brought down to his apostles (or helpers) in compliance with what they were asking. It is through this table that they remember his passion, and so it becomes a "feast" and "sign" for all generations to come (see *sūrat al-mā'ida* 112–114). It is a sacramental practice that is perpetuated in the Lord's Supper celebrated by Christians.[62]

The article goes on to mention that Christ's "resurrection" (*tarfī'*) would not have been possible were it not for the victory achieved at the cross. Neither event, in fact, would have been possible had Christ "evaded all danger by the works of his special power, or by unleashing a revolt, or by abdicating his mission, or by keenly evading the final crisis before it reached its climax."[63] Thus, the crucifixion did take place, and it did so in accord with the grace of God.

It is important to mention one other place where qur'ānic verses are cited in the context of discussing Christ's crucifixion and resurrection. In an article referenced earlier on the Holy Spirit, there is a discussion concerning the role of the Spirit at key events in the life of Christ: "in his birth, calling, miracles, and his resurrection from death."[64] Al-Kalima discuss each of these topics briefly and emphasize the Spirit's role in supporting and confirming Christ in each event. For instance, at the time of Christ's birth, al-Kalima note that the Spirit came upon Mary and "planted the seed in her womb that became an fetus and then a child."[65] Matthew's account is cited to illustrate this since it reports that before Joseph and Mary came together, "she was found to be with child from the Holy Spirit" (Matt 1:18).

After establishing these details from the New Testament birth narratives, al-Kalima point out that the Qur'ān also supports this construal of events related to Christ's life: "And the Qur'ān confirms this by mentioning that God Almighty sent his Spirit to Mary who 'appeared to her

62. Jaṭlāwī et al., "Wadā'at al-Masīḥ," in *True Meaning*, 134. I would like to thank Ibrahim Arafat for his assistance in understanding this passage.

63. Ibid.

64. Jaṭlāwī et al., "Rūḥ Allāh," in *True Meaning*, 70.

65. Ibid.

as a perfect man [Q 19:17],' 'and he breathed into her from his Spirit [Q 21:91; 66:12],' thus 'Īsā was the 'Word of God and a Spirit from him' [Q 4:171]." Each of these qur'ānic verses is weaved together in a paraphrastic conflation similar in style to the conflations of qur'ānic verses used in the medieval texts. The point in citing them is to demonstrate conceptual congruence on the matters being discussed; in particular, to draw a close link between God's Spirit and key events in Christ's life and ministry. Specifically, al-Kalima mention the Spirit's role in anointing Christ at the outset of his public ministry after being tested in the wilderness (Luke 4:1); the Spirit's role in each of the miracles he performed (Matt 12:28); and finally, al-Kalima note that Christ's resurrection was a work of God's Spirit: "As for his resurrection from the dead, God's Spirit raised up the Messiah 'Īsā from death *and made him* victorious over the grave, defeating the thorn of death."[66] Upon establishing the Spirit's role in these events, al-Kalima echo a phrase that appears twice in the Qur'ān in connection with Jesus. In Q 2:87 and Q 2:253 a phrase is used to emphasize that Christ was confirmed by the Holy Spirit in the many "signs" or miracles he performed: "And we confirmed him [Jesus] with the Holy Spirit [*wa ayyadnāhu bi-rūḥ al-qudus*]." Al-Kalima use this qur'ānic phrase to emphasize the Spirit's support and confirmation of Christ in his birth, commissioning, miracles, death, and resurrection. And for al-Kalima, the conclusion one should draw from all this is clear: Christ is "more exalted than any mere creation."[67] Indeed, he is deserving of human praise and worship.

SUMMARY OF CONCLUSIONS

It is important to make two brief observations about some of the differences between the historical and religious locations of the medieval texts and the modern ones. First, both of the medieval texts were authored well before many of Islam's most authoritative Qur'ān commentators and theologians were born. Although political, philosophical, and theological disputations were ongoing at the time of their composition in the eighth and early ninth centuries, many methodological procedures and processes related to interpreting the Qur'ān, such as the canonization of the *ḥadīth*, the development of *aḥkām* for delineating issues within Islamic jurisprudence, etc. (elements that are now part and parcel of normative Islam), had yet to be fully systematized.

66. Ibid.; emphasis added.

67. Ibid.

By contrast, the contemporary texts have been authored under very different circumstances. Muslim consensus on most issues has been reached and there are specific extra-qur'ānic authorities and lines of argumentation to which those engaged in theological debates appeal. Thus it is not surprising that many Muslims consider the discussion of certain theological matters closed and all answers finalized. Examples of the issues that generally fall into this category include the corruption of the Bible, the divinity of Christ, the Incarnation, the Trinity, and the denial of Jesus' vicarious death, burial, and resurrection. The Muslim exegetical and theological tradition has treated and rejected the biblical teaching on these issues and most Muslims take their conclusions as final. Hence, any apologetic strategy adopted by Christians that would challenge these conclusions must begin by challenging the link between those sources and the Qur'ān. Together, they contain the theological infrastructure undergirding the Muslim construal of salvation history. It is not surprising, therefore, to find al-Kalima scholars and theologians treating numerous issues from this body of literature that impede Muslims from understanding the Bible and Christian doctrines—issues that shape Muslim preunderstandings. They accomplish this by offering a thoughtful and relevant engagement with the interpretive presuppositions derived from both qur'ānic and extra-qur'ānic sources alike.

Likewise, in their explanations of the Bible and Christian doctrines, much of the terminology al-Kalima use has been adapted for their Arab-Muslim audience. Generally, their approach is non-philosophical. Traditional terminology like "Trinity," "hypostases," and "substance," rarely appears in their works. They do however make reference to the fact that Jesus is the physical "incarnation" or embodiment of God's eternal Word and that he "emanates" or "proceeds" (*yaṣdur*) from the very being of God.

It is notable that in discussing Christ's divinity and Incarnation, al-Kalima are highly devoted to scriptural reasoning. Additionally, they do not attempt to explain the *how* of the Incarnation, as the medieval texts did, by adopting the veiling motif of Q 42:51.[68] They are more comfortable rooting their belief in Christ as God's eternal, uncreated Word, embodied in the person of Jesus the Messiah, since this is in keeping with

68. Al-Kalima do mention God's "Wisdom," a reference to Christ in his pre-incarnational state, being "veiled from us" (*muḥtajiba ʿannā*) in an article on the Incarnation. However, upon being sent to humanity and embodied, they refer to Christ as God's "Word." See Mallūḥī et al., "Tajallī al-Ḥikma," in *Sufi Reading*, 57.

God's redemptive intentions for humanity. They assert this despite the absence of a comprehensive treatment of the story of redemption like that present in the *Tathlīth*. Al-Kalima's approach, rather, is to establish conceptual congruence by rooting the logic of Christ's divinity (and subsequent Incarnation) in a version of the attribute apology that shares many similarities to the approach of the medieval authors. Their adaptation of this approach—what I have called the *logos*-apology—implies Christ's divinity and explains the Incarnation of God's Word who was "conveyed to Mary" as the means by which God has revealed himself to humanity. It is the logical extension of God's speaking his creation into existence by his Word and then physically speaking to humanity by that same Word in order to redeem them from the destructive influence of sin and Satan's deception.

With regard to the positive use of qur'ānic locutions, al-Kalima make use of them selectively on the matters they address. And although they do not state this explicitly, their approach appears aimed to bring the Qur'ān's oftentimes elliptical discourse about Christ within the Bible's horizons. These horizons, they contend, better explain the significance of the locutions one finds in the particular passages they cite. Al-Kalima assert this while simultaneously challenging the traditional interpretation of these verses that most Muslims are accustomed to hearing.

In quoting the Qur'ān, most of the references are set apart by quotation marks or highlighting, or the use of special parenthetical marks common in Islamic publications. Additionally, all quotations of the Qur'ān are from the 1924 Cairo edition, despite the recognition of qur'ānic variants (or "readings").[69] There are occasional echoes of qur'ānic language and diction, but unlike the introduction of the *Tathlīth*, there is no attempt to mimic the Qur'ān's rhymed prose style. Muslims would immediately identify this as an attempt at imitating something that in their minds is inimitable. Unlike the medieval texts, however, there are fewer paraphrastic conflations of qur'ānic texts. There are occasional echoes of qur'ānic language, as we saw with the reference to the "great sacrifice" in Q 37:107, but most references to the Qur'ān are made explicit.

69. See Jaṭlāwī et al., "Muqaddima," in *True Meaning*, 2.

5

Theologizing in Arab-Muslim Milieus

THIS FINAL CHAPTER REFLECTS on some of the implications this book has for theological method in Arab-Muslim milieus. In particular, it critiques two aspects of Sam Schlorff's Betrothal Model: his concept of theological starting points and his hermeneutics. At the outset, however, it is important to reassert that I am not prescribing the use of qur'ānic points of contact in *all* gospel-oriented discussions with Arabic-speaking Muslims, whether written or otherwise. My focus has been to demonstrate that on biblical, historical, and theological grounds there is justification for those who do so within certain boundaries.

Having stated that, if Christians residing in the world of Islam are to address the array of worldview issues that impede Muslims from properly assessing (and accepting) the gospel, qur'ānic points of contact will undoubtedly factor into their theological discourse and shape their apologetic response to Islam moving forward. The question is not *if* but *how*. This position, of course, presumes that Arab-Muslim milieus are valid contexts within which the gospel is to be contextualized. It also presumes that qur'ānic frames of reference (both linguistic and conceptual) shape how Muslims interpret the biblical message. Dealing with that reality will continue to occupy Christians residing in the Arab world for the foreseeable future. Indeed, this issue must be addressed if the contextual theology produced in the Arab world is to remain faithful *and* meaningful.

Unfortunately, many who criticize the use of qur'ānic points of contact seemingly delegitimize Arab-Muslim cultures as valid arenas for gospel-contextualization. Some of the more extreme critiques in this regard even go so far as to delegitimize the Arabic language.[1] While Schlorff does not go this far, he does contend that nothing within Muslim cultures can be used to contextualize the gospel message. Though there is much about Schlorff's Betrothal Model of contextualization that is commendable, there are two key areas where his method faces problems—his conceptualization of theological starting points and his hermeneutics. However, undergirding these methodological problems, I would argue, is a broader problem with his understanding of the scope and nature of the gospel message. Therefore, this chapter begins with a discussion of God's redemptive intentions in the gospel and the implications this has for all human contexts but particularly Arab-Muslim contexts.

THE GRAND BIBLICAL NARRATIVE AND THEOLOGICAL TRANSLATABILITY

The Story of Redemption and Human Contexts

History, the biblical text, and the very nature of Christian faith demonstrate that what is deemed "Christian" is not bound to one sacred language, culture, human context or location. Indeed, each language, every culture, and all geographic locations are considered legitimate mediums and venues for communicating the gospel of the kingdom and creating Christian communities. From the perspective of biblical theology, this reality issues from the nature of the redemptive story narrated in the Bible from Genesis to Revelation. The scope of that story is nothing less than the whole of the cosmos (Gen 1:1; Col 1:19–20) and it encompasses every tribe and language and people and nation on the face of the planet (Gen 10; Rev 5:9, 7:9). God's redemptive intentions for humanity and for all of creation form the foundation of God's mission—the *missio Dei*. Moreover, God's mission provides the hermeneutical lens through which God's people are to interpret not only the Bible but also the entire flow of cosmic history and their place within it.[2]

God's redemptive intentions for humanity are made explicit with the call of Abraham in Gen 12:3. God promises to bless Abraham and make him and his "seed" the source of blessing for "all families of the earth."[3] These are the same families whom God judged, dispersed, and

1. Cf., ch. 1, n102.

2. For more, see Wright, *The Mission of God*.

3. Cf. also Gen 18:18; 22:18; 26:18; 28:18; Gal 3:8–9, 14, 16, 29. Bauckham argues that the calling of Abraham in Genesis 12 must be seen against the backdrop of God's

whose languages he confused at the tower of Babel in Gen 11.[4] God's mission is to bless humanity through Abraham by creating *a people* from among *all peoples* of the earth who will be known by his name and will be redeemed for the praise of his glory. God's intention for his people is that they dwell with him forever in a renewed heaven and on a renewed earth (Isa 65:17; 66:22; Rev 21:1–5).

Fast-forwarding through redemptive history, God's promise to Abraham comes to fruition in his seed, Jesus, "the Son of David, the Son of Abraham" (Matt 1:1). After Jesus died on the cross as a ransom for humanity (Matt 20:28; Mark 10:45; 1 Tim 2:6) and rose again victorious over sin and death, he commissioned his followers to fulfill God's original creation command to "multiply and fill the earth" (Gen 1:28). The way Jesus envisioned his disciples accomplishing this mission was by going to the uttermost parts of the earth and "making disciples of all *ethnolinguistic* groups" (Matt 28:19; Acts 1:8).[5] The Spirit further validates Jesus' mission in Acts 2:6–11 by empowering his disciples to spread the gospel of the kingdom with boldness until he returns as the triumphant king.

The Spirit's validation of God's mission in Acts 2 is notable for the fact that the diversity of languages spoken at Pentecost reflects God's intention for the gospel to traverse all cultural and linguistic boundaries. The eschatological fulfillment of this is seen in Rev 5:9 and 7:9 where a multitude from every tribe and language and people and nation are

---

dealings with the whole of humanity in the preceding chapters. For instance, the list of 70 nations in Genesis 10, with seven and derivatives thereof being symbolic of completion or comprehensiveness, represents all of humanity. God's choice of Abraham, therefore, must be seen in light of this; he is chosen for the purpose of redeeming a people for himself from among "all the families of the earth." See Bauckham, *Bible and Mission*, 57–61.

4. Reflecting on whether Babel was a "bad thing" or not, Carson notes: "If a bad thing, then presumably the unity of language before Babel was a good thing—yet it was this unity that enabled the people to attempt the massive rebellion symbolized by Babel. If that unity was so bad, then perhaps the diversity itself is a good thing. At the very least, even though the imposition of the diversity of languages was a rebuke and a restraint, it is not transparently clear whether the multiplicity of languages *in itself* was a good or bad thing. . . . [W]e human beings can corrupt the unity and turn it into rebellion, and we can corrupt the diversity and turn it into war. One cannot fail to remark, however, that at Pentecost God did not give the gift of one language, a kind of restoration of the pre-Babel situation; rather, he gave the gift of many languages, so that one message could be heard in all the relevant languages [including Arabic], thus preserving the diversity." Carson, *Christ and Culture*, 74, *italics* original.

5. See Robinson's explanation of the connection between the Great Commission and Gen 1:28 in "The Gospel and Evangelism," 82.

united in their worship of the one who sits on the throne and the Lamb who was slain for their redemption. D. A. Carson notes that this vision gives us "no reason to think that the glorious unity we will enjoy in the new heaven and new earth does not embrace the equally glorious diversity of race and nation *and language*."[6]

One important implication we can draw from this affirmation of cultural and linguistic diversity—stretching from God's choice of Abraham to be a blessing to all peoples, to the birth of the church at Pentecost, and into the eschaton—is that God views each language and every culture as valid conduits for communicating the gospel message and planting churches.[7] Both the scope and goal of mission, therefore, presume that the gospel message—from Genesis to Revelation—will be translated and diffused across all cultural, linguistic, and conceptual boundaries. Indeed, the ability to adapt and diffuse itself across such boundaries is indicative of the inherent translatability of the Christian faith and is tied to its success in taking root among the various ethnolinguistic groups around the globe.

Theological Translatability in Christianity and Islam

Lamin Sanneh, a convert from Islam to Christianity, notes that the inherent translatability of Christian faith stands in stark contrast to the

6. Carson, *Christ and Culture*, 74–75; emphasis original.

7. This does not mean that *everything* within a particular culture is equally valid or equally redeemable for communicating the gospel or living as faithful members of God's kingdom. Yet, culture is a God-ordained reality, which implies that it is structurally good. However, each culture is also created and populated by fallen humans. Therefore, each culture will, in its unique way, be tainted by human idolatry. For this reason, each community must reflect on their culture in light of Scripture in order to work through what kingdom faithfulness looks like in their particular time and place. As Sanneh notes, "All cultural forms that distinguish and define human life and experience are in principle worthy of bearing the truth of Christianity, and by that attraction their true value is revealed. Another way to say this is that no one cultural expression of the religion is exclusive for expressing the fullness of the gospel. Christianity, we recall, is without a revealed language or a founding original culture. The universal, omnipotent God can dispense with a universal, omnipotent culture. It explains why in the Christian movement there was often a grassroots reaction to the imposition of a foreign mandate, with the vernacular time-fuse undermining permanent domination. Christians first crossed this intercultural threshold with the Jewish heritage of Jesus. Christians henceforth pursued mission through multiple cultural idioms, convinced that no language was exempt from God's salvific work." Sanneh, *Translating the Message*, 74. For more on culture's structural goodness and its misdirection resulting from the fall, see Bartholomew and Goheen, *Living at the Crossroads*, 127–45.

inherent untranslatability of Islam.[8] Over time, normative Islam came to hold that the Qur'ān was untranslatable due to the nature of its inimitable language—the doctrine of *'ijāz al-qur'ān*.[9] Many Muslims believe the Qur'ān to be an instantiation and perfect replication of the eternal "Preserved Tablet" (*al-lūḥ al-maḥfūẓ*) kept in heaven to prevent corruption. This notion of a pristine form of revelation manifests itself in the base impulse of normative Islam, which is dictation. According to the standard Muslim narrative, Gabriel dictated God's revelation to Muḥammad, which he then dictated to his followers who memorized it, recorded it on palm branches, bones, papyrus, and other materials so as to preserve it.[10] Upon codification and canonization, it became incumbent upon subsequent generations of Muslims to dictate the religion—to dictate the Qur'ān—to new generations. One implication of this is that the quintessential Islamic notion of "religion" (sing. *dīn*, pl. *adyān*) is a system attended by identifiable and fixed religious, socio-cultural, and linguistic forms.[11] This explains why attempts to translate the Qur'ān or to accommodate the religion to changing cultural situations are viewed in many quarters of normative Islam as acts of innovation (*bid'a*; "heresy"). Replication of the Islamic ideal is the goal.[12]

In contrast to this, Andrew Walls notes, "The Christian Scriptures . . . are open to translation; nay, the great Act on which Christian faith

8. Sanneh, *Translating the Message*, 252–62. This does not mean that there is no cultural or linguistic diversity within Islam, for there is. But the sacralization of both the Arabic language and Arab culture in Islam and the preference for them over other vernaculars and cultural expressions has no parallel in Christianity despite the early "heresy of the three languages" [cf. Moreau et al., *Introducing World Missions*, 107–9].

9. See von Grunebaum, "I'djāz," 1018. For an explanation of this doctrine in its classical form and how it continues to influence (and impede) all literary approaches to the Qur'ān in the Middle East, see Abu-Zayd, "The Dilemma of the Literary Approach to the Qur'an," 8–47.

10. See Gilliot, "Creation of a Fixed Text," 41–57; cf. also Motzki, "Alternative Accounts of the Qur'ān's Formation," in the same volume.

11. This is, of course, a description of normative Sunnī Islam. Most who hold this position feel their vision of the religion and its relationship to all aspects of society represents the "purest" and hence "truest" form of their religion. For an example of this position, see Quṭb, *Khaṣā'iṣ al-Taṣawwur al-Islāmī wa Muqawwimātihi*; Qutb, *Basic Principles of the Islamic Worldview*.

12. Sanneh gives the example of an Indian Imam who sought to use his native Hindi in ritual prayers. When his co-religionists heard about it they issued a *fatwā* denouncing him as "an infidel, an atheist, and a wanderer from the truth." Sanneh, *Translating the Message*, 253.

rests, the Word becoming flesh and pitching tent among us, is itself an act of translation."[13] Walls identifies two principles underlying the ostensible plasticity of the Christian faith and how this manifests itself in its transmission among people groups. The first is the "indigenizing principle," which refers to the process whereby the Christian faith takes root in a culture at such a depth that it becomes indigenous to that culture; it becomes a central part of their identity. This happens partly because, in Christ, God accepts us as we are and where we are. As Walls states, "He does not wait to tidy up our ideas any more than He waits to tidy up our behavior before He accepts us as sinners into His family."[14] Walls points out that this reality has led "to one unvarying feature in Christian history: the desire to 'indigenize.'"[15]

Indigenization invariably issues forth in domestication, which entails the gospel's close connection to (and transformation of) the worldviews, vernaculars, social structures, etc. of the peoples among whom it has taken root. Much of the variety that marks Christian communities around the globe stems from this instinctively Christian desire for indigenization. This principle also accounts for the tendency (and danger) on the part of some Christians—in areas where the faith has been wildly successful in capturing the hearts and minds of large segments of a particular society—to so domesticize the faith that they view their understanding and expression of it as normative for everyone regardless of time, location, or culture.

In tension with the indigenizing principle but equally found in the gospel is the "pilgrim principle." This refers to the transformation of human societies and cultures into the image of what God wants. Walls aptly notes:

> Not only does God in Christ take people as they are: He takes them in order to transform them into what he wants them to be. Along with the indigenizing principle which makes his faith a place to feel at home, the Christian inherits the pilgrim principle, which whispers to him that he has no abiding city and warns him that to be faithful to Christ will put him out of step with his society; for that society never existed, in East or West, ancient time or modern, which could absorb the word of Christ painlessly into its system. Jesus within Jewish culture, Paul

13. Walls, *Missionary Movement*, 23.

14. Ibid., 7.

15. Ibid.

> within Hellenistic culture, take it for granted that there will be rubs and frictions—not from the adoption of a new culture, but from the transformation of the mind towards that of Christ.[16]

Transformation of the mind towards Christ is not limited to the private or personal dimension of one's life. It is public and communal in scope and aim. Human languages, socio-cultural structures, politics, education, in short, all things are in view when a people seeks to live in conformity with God's intention for them in Christ. Unlike the utopian idealism of normative Islam, however, there is no set pattern for how this looks in each particular culture, and it remains an ongoing process until Christ returns to usher in the fullness of his kingdom.

Yet even with coming fullness of the kingdom cultural and linguistic diversity will be preserved.[17] One conclusion we can draw from this is that God views all cultures and every language as inherently redeemable and worthy of embodying *and* articulating the message of redemption in Christ. Methodologically, this fact should drive us to adopt a position of neutrality or, as Clark puts it, "cultural relativism," towards other cultures. This does not mean that *all* of a culture's various forms, religious or otherwise, are neutral or meaning-free and thus can be adopted for use in contextualization. As Hiebert notes, "Not all cultural practices can be used to communicate the message of the gospel."[18] What it does mean, however, is that our default position should be to regard every culture as a valid arena for gospel-contextualization. Clark explains:

> Cultural relativism means taking cultural particulars seriously, from a relatively neutral viewpoint. It means abandoning ethnocentrism. It means willingly viewing all cultures both sympathetically (especially other cultures) and critically (especially one's own). As a methodological commitment, cultural relativism mitigates the tendency to condemn other cultures and coronate one's own.[19]

16. Ibid., 8.

17. Cf. Rev 5:9; 7:9; 21:24–26. Reflecting on Isa 60:5 and Rev 21:26, Mouw argues that "pagan treasures" will appear in the New Jerusalem, a possible indicator of the extent to which God intends the gospel to bring concrete socio-cultural and religious transformation among the nations. See Mouw, *When the Kings Come Marching in*, 24.

18. Hiebert, "Form and Meaning," 106.

19. Clark, *To Know and Love God*, 100–101. Clark notes that cultural relativism "does not entail ethical relativism." See his discussion on p. 100.

In sum, these two principles—the indigenous principle and the pilgrim principle—are at the heart of the gospel and they act both to affirm and transform each person and every culture where the gospel takes root and where the church is planted. Doing this faithfully is the challenge for all those who claim the name of Christ.

Faithful Embodiment of the Gospel of the Kingdom

From a missiological perspective, at least two characteristics distinguish the success of a people's faithful embodiment of these two principles. First, those who embrace the gospel must realize that they are essential to its continued propagation, both inside their birth culture and beyond it. The lifeblood of Christian faith and its base impulse, in contrast to Islam, is translation and diffusion not dictation and replication. As Walls notes, "If the acts of cultural translation by which the Christians of any community make their faith substantial within that community cease—if . . . the Word ceases to be made flesh within that community—the Christian group within that community is likely to lose, not just its effectiveness, but its powers of resistance."[20]

Second, theological fidelity is guided by the extent to which believers from all tribes and languages and peoples and nations are able to "incorporate the history of Israel and God's people and to treat it as one's own."[21] Appropriation of the faith of God's people by another people, regardless of context or culture, is contingent upon their adherence to the baseline, non-negotiables of biblical theology. But intellectual assent is not the sole criterion. A people must appropriate these non-negotiables at such a depth that they impart to them a biblical understanding of cosmic history and a transcultural grid for evaluating how the story of the gospel relates to and challenges both their worldview and the worldviews of those around them.[22] They must see that these non-negotiables constitute the bedrock of what Vanhoozer lables a *canonic* and *Christological* principle. This principle trumps all other contextual or cultural concerns. As Vanhoozer states, "the Spirit speaking in Scripture about what God

20. Walls, *Cross-Cultural Process*, 13.

21. Walls, *Missionary Movement*, 9.

22. For a detailed examination of how worldview transformation takes place, see Hiebert, *Transforming Worldviews*.

was/is doing in the history of Israel and climactically in Jesus Christ is the supreme rule for Christian faith, life and understanding."[23]

Carson has termed the non-negotiables of biblical theology the "great turning points of redemptive history."[24] Denial, reinterpretation, or revision of any of these turning points puts those who do this outside the camp of historic Christianity and outside the camp of those whose faith is truly "Abrahamic" (cf. Gal 3:29). But as Carson notes, the major tenets of the faith and their organic relationship to the overarching grand narrative of Scripture are more than a mere litmus test for orthodoxy. They provide a template—a "canon-stipulated vision"—through which believers of every generation, time, and place are to evaluate and relate their faith to their particular culture.[25] The aim in this process is to achieve what Vanhoozer has labeled "theodramatic correspondence." He explains:

> Theology is faith seeking understanding, and we have genuine understanding only when we are able to situate properly our particular contexts within the larger theodrama. Theodramatic correspondence is thus tied to theodramatic coherence . . . . In the final analysis, however, no single method can guarantee such correspondence or coherence. On the contrary, discerning how to embody the gospel in new contexts requires not methodical

23. Vanhoozer, "One Rule," 109. Prior to articulating this canonic principle, Vanhoozer spends considerable time developing the idea that all theology is inescapably contextual. Realizing this fact leads to three methodological commonalities between various majority world theologies: "Formally, the turn to context involves (1) a hermeneutical principle: an attention to lived experience, especially that of the poor, as the *medium* in which biblical interpretation takes place; (2) a critical principle: an analysis of social structures and a praxis oriented to liberating transformation; and (3) a cultural principle: an attempt to make use of indigenous categories in order to convert people to Christ without destroying their memories or cultural identities" (p. 98). Vanhoozer notes, however, that each of these must remain subservient to the overriding concerns and agendas issuing from the canonic principle.

24. Carson, *Christ and Culture*, 43 *et passim*.

25. As Carson notes: "[It] is not just that the dismissal of such realities as creation, fall, incarnation, Jesus' death and resurrection, the coming of the Spirit, and the final judgment and consummation, places one outside the Christian camp, but that it is important to think through the *positive* bearing of these realities on the topic. To put the matter more personally: on the one hand, however loyal one judges oneself to be to Jesus, it is difficult to see how such loyalty is a mark of *Christian* thought if the Jesus so invoked is so domesticated and selectively constructed that he bears little relation to the Bible. But on the other hand, there is a need to spell out the bearing these epochal events on how we *should* think about the relations between Christ and culture" (Carson, *Christ and Culture*, 43–44; emphasis original).

> procedures but sanctified persons, persons whose minds and hearts and imaginations are captive to the Word.[26]

This assumes that those who embrace Christ, regardless of their ethnic, cultural or religious background, will hold a high view regarding the truthfulness of the Bible and its depiction of reality—in all that it describes, claims, teaches, and affirms. It alone is the "ultimate locus of transcultural authority," not the various interpretations of it.[27] But again the expectation is not merely a propositional attestation of faith in the trustworthiness of the Bible. Inevitably, the Bible's depiction of reality—as defined by the great turning points of salvation history—must challenge and shape the existing categories and the core tenets of the worldviews and the belief systems of all those who profess faith in Christ. The Bible must be unleashed to challenge the words, concepts, and categories a people use to describe themselves and how they relate to the world around them. Language is particularly important in this regard:

> A culture's preferred way of viewing and engaging the world is embedded in its language. The categories of a language—the connotations and the semantic range of its terms—pass along far more than a description of reality. They pass on sets of concepts, attitudes, and values. They provide the mental structures of art, technology, law, and social function. They embody a society's plausibility structures, its mental frameworks or conceptual grid within which certain kinds of ideas seem obvious and others unthinkable. Culture is a conversation between a people

26. Vanhoozer, "One Rule," 124. Vanhoozer goes on to state: "What ultimately gets translated, contextualized, or performed from culture to culture, then, is theodrama: the pattern of evangelical—gospel-centered—speech and action. How do we recognize theodramatic fidelity from one context to another? The operative term is *direction.* Doctrinal formulations must lead people in different contexts in the same basic direction, namely, in the way of truth and life as these are defined by the story of God's words and deeds that culminate in Jesus Christ. Theology that can do that is 'warranted wisdom'; theology that is warranted because it tells the truth and wise because it leads to shalom . . . . Truth and justice and the righteousness of Jesus Christ are the universal elements in the good news that must be embraced and embodied in and by every local church. The task of theology is to train speakers and doers of the Word, people who can render in contextually appropriate forms the poiesis and praxis, the truth and justice, of God or, in terms of the proposal set forth herein, people who can improvise the gospel of Jesus Christ" (p. 124).

27. Ibid., 112. Cf. also Clark, *To Know and Love God*, 120. Obviously, this is a statement of principle; an assertion of *sola scriptura.* In practice, we cannot help but interpret Scripture, yet not all interpretations are equal in terms of accuracy and truthfulness in reflecting the teachings of Scripture.

> and their environment, a conversation they cannot escape even if they critique it.[28]

Thus, if a true and thorough appropriation of the faith history of God's people is to take place and if the gospel is to be translated and communicated intelligibly to all people groups, like Arab Muslims, a transfer of biblical ideas and categories into their vernaculars is necessary. And this is where the challenges lie. For on a linguistic and conceptual level, numerous historical, cultural, philosophical, and religious factors, including literary frames of reference, shape the vernaculars of human languages and the connotations and the semantic ranges of a people's words. One of the places these frames of reference originate (or are preserved and continue to exert influence) is in the religious texts of the birth religions of those who come to faith in Christ.

THEOLOGICAL METHOD IN ARAB-MUSLIM MILIEUS: A RESPONSE TO SAM SCHLORFF'S BETROTHAL MODEL

Theological Starting Points

The previous discussion regarding the scope and nature of the redemptive story and the validity of each human context is important to keep in mind when evaluating models of contextual theology, particularly Schlorff's Betrothal Model.[29] At the heart of that model is Schlorff's understanding of theological/contextual starting points. By theological starting point, Schlorff means "the sources, whether theological or cultural, that will be used in the contextualization of the gospel and the church."[30] His emphasis on choosing the right sources to contextualize the gospel is important since, as he states, "The choice of starting point controls the hermeneutical method that will be used for interpreting the biblical message within the receptor culture."[31]

Framing his method in this way leads Schlorff to pose a central question that guides his approach to contextualization. He asks, "May

28. Clark, *To Know and Love God*, 100.

29. For more on the various models of contextual theology, see Schreiter, *Constructing Local Theologies*; Bevans, *Models of Contextual Theology*; Flemming, *Contextualization in the New Testament*; Moreau, *Contextualization in World Missions*. Both Schreiter and Bevans are Catholic scholars while Flemming and Moreau are evangelicals.

30. Schlorff, *Models*, 115.

31. Ibid.

anything in the Qur'an or Islam be used as a starting point for the contextualization of the gospel and church?"[32] In Schlorff's estimation, there are valid sources for contextualizing the gospel and invalid ones. After considering his central question, Schlorff concludes that there is no biblical precedent for using "the receptor culture as [a] starting point for the contextualization either of theology or of the church."[33] As a result, "[One] cannot use the Qur'an as a source of truth for proclaiming the gospel or try to fill Muslim forms with Christian meanings."[34] Therefore, the only valid theological starting point for Schlorff is Scripture.

Schlorff's understanding of theological staring points has been influenced by the thought of the Dutch missiologist, J. H. Bavinck. Bavinck points out that on numerous occasions in Christian history various scholars and theologians have upheld Christianity as a fulfillment or realization of certain aspects of other religions or philosophies. Those who have advocated such positions have generally argued that these religions, philosophies, or their religious books contain "moments of truth" or deposits of revelation (variously labeled general or special) that one can appeal to when proclaiming Christ. Bavinck discusses notable examples of this from church history, including Clement of Alexandria who argued that Greek philosophy played a role in bringing Greeks to Christ analogous to the role played by the Law in bringing Jews to Christ.[35] Yet Bavinck rejects this idea:

> It is understandable that such efforts have been made, but from the point of view of Scripture, to seek such a point of contact is erroneous. All such endeavors mistakenly suppose that somewhere within non-Christian religions, perhaps in a hidden nook or cranny, there lie hidden moments of truth, and that it is to these that one should join his own argument. It is, of course,

32. Ibid., 116.

33. Ibid., 122.

34. Ibid., 149. Questions surrounding the utilization of Muslim forms (i.e., ritual prayer, Ramadan, etc.) in contextualizing the gospel is a controversial topic not treated in this book.

35. Coleman rightly criticizes advocates of the Insider Movement Paradigm who argue that the Qur'ān plays a role analogous to that of the Old Testament in bringing Muslims to Christ. Those who advocate ideas of this sort are simply out of touch with the narrative unity that binds the 66 books of the Bible together and the story of redemption stretching from Genesis to Revelation told therein. The Qur'ān plays no role in this story and cannot be viewed as a substitute for the Hebrew Bible. See Coleman, "Insider Movement Paradigm," 131–34.

> admitted that it is subsequently necessary to eliminate many errors, but it is still thought possible to find a point of contact from which one can climb up to the truth of Jesus Christ. . . All such efforts and outlooks are to be rejected as improper and illegitimate.[36]

Commenting on Bavinck's rejection of this approach, Schlorff adds, "The fundamental problem with using the religious thought of a culture as a theological starting point is that it fails to take into account the devastating effects of repression and substitution on that culture."[37] Unfortunately, Schlorff fails to provide any means of ascertaining those elements that are considered purely "religious" or "theological" and those that are cultural. Neither does he discuss the extent to which his own culture and assumptions are repressed and affected by sin. But the bottom line is that, methodologically, Schlorff rejects using receptor cultures as a source for contextualizing the gospel.[38]

36. Bavinck, *Science of Missions*, 135. Quoted in Schlorff, *Models*, 122.

37. Schlorff, *Models*, 122.

38. To be clear, at the end of his chapter on contextual/theological starting points, Schlorff admits that the receptor culture does play a role in contextualization. He even goes so far to state, "There are still legitimate ways the Qur'an may be used effectively to communicate the gospel to Muslims" (p. 123). It is at this stage that he introduces his notion of "communicational starting points." He says that some of the Qur'ān/Islam's "linguistic and cultural forms may be usable as sign vehicles for the biblical message" (p. 123). This is possibly a reference back to his discussion in chapter three of his book about qur'ānic language. However, Schlorff fails to expound on what he means by this or explain the difference between contextual/theological starting points and communicational starting points. There is a great deal of tension, if not outright contradiction, in Schlorff's thought on this point. And it is reflective of the same tension and/or contradiction found in Bavinck, who also spends a great deal of time rejecting any use of the receptor culture to contextualize the gospel only to conclude that one cannot avoid making contact with people where they are [cf. Bavinck, *Science of Missions*, 140]. Both attempt to distinguish between theological starting points ("points of contact" in Bavinck's parlance) and communicational starting points ("points of attack" for Bavink). But the problem with both scholars' thought on this point is that each presumes that all the various ideas, beliefs, practices, etc. that constitute "culture" are easily classified as either "religious/theological" and/or "cultural" categories. They label the former as an invalid source for contextualization while the later category is deemed potentially valid. There are three problems here. First, this categorical distinction is rooted in a false dichotomy that is prevalent in the thought of many western theologians that pits the "sacred" (religious/theological) against the "secular" (cultural). Second, this approach makes the western missionary the arbiter of what is labeled "sacred" and what is labeled "secular." And finally, both appear to equate the forms religious beliefs/practices have with their meaning as if these are fixed for all people in all times and places [cf. Hiebert, "Form and Meaning," 102–3]. Schlorff, following

If we assume that God intends for the gospel to be embodied in every culture, then Arab-Muslim cultures are just as valid as any milieu for gospel-contextualization. But why then does Schlorff reject using culture as a "starting point" for theology? Indeed, can the gospel be freed from all cultural accretions and is this the actual goal of faithful contextualization?

Linear Theology and the Locus of Responsibility in Contextualization

It is important to note that Schlorff's sensitivity to those who allow their cultural or religious context to determine the *agenda for theology* is reasonable. Clark points out that in mainline and liberal models of contextualization context determines the agenda of theology: "This means that liberation, feminist theology, ethnic theology, poverty, religious pluralism, and praxis become the recurring themes of mainline/liberal versions of contextualization. These versions of contextualization follow an agenda that mandates a starting point for theology . . . ."[39] The result of this is that one's cultural context controls the interpretive grid for understanding the Scriptures.[40] Vanhoozer notes the problem with this stating, we must "get beyond a situation in which each local or regional branch of the church inhabits its own HUT (Homogenous Unity Theology)."[41] In other words, "Location should never become the essential characteristic of Christian theology."[42] Clearly, this type of an approach fails to preserve Scripture's role as ultimate determiner of one's theological agenda.

Bavinck, then rules that beliefs/practices that are deemed "religious/theological" are illegitimate for gospel-contextualization. Even if we preserve the distinction between religious/theological and cultural (which I think we should), what is the mechanism Schlorff is using to determine whether a thought, belief, or practice is strictly religious, strictly cultural, or a combination of the two? His confusion on these matters is why sanctified locals, ultimately, must be responsible for the contextualization of the gospel in their own culture. See further discussion below.

39. Clark, *To Know and Love God*, 103.

40. Ibid., 111.

41. Vanhoozer, "One Rule," 99–100.

42. Ibid., 106. Vanhoozer notes: "Theology is always contextual. Yet we should resist the ethnification of theology if this means reinforcing parochialism or fostering a hermeneutics of advocacy on behalf of a particular interest group only. Nonetheless, ethnic theologies make a positive contribution to the catholic church insofar as their particular cultural vantage point gives them insights into Scripture that we would otherwise miss. It is therefore important to see ethnic theologies as local instantiations of the faith of the church universal, where 'Universal' stands not for something supracultural but for something multicultural, namely, catholic faith" (p. 107).

Yet we must remain cognizant of the fact that everyone's cultural and religious context shapes the preunderstandings that they bring to the text of Scripture. As Vanhoozer notes elsewhere,

> If twentieth-century hermeneutics has anything to teach us, it is that our readings and interpretations of texts are never neutral—as though we could simply step out of our skins: our place, our time, our culture, our social situation—nor exhaustive, as though we could escape our finitude. It follows that Scripture is always read from within a certain interpretive tradition.[43]

Nobody approaches the Bible with a *tabula rasa*, nor do they formulate their views of Christ or understanding of the gospel in isolation from their other beliefs about the nature of God and the world around them. Nevertheless, Christians must guard against allowing their "culturally derived agendas" to dominate their theology.[44] In order to do this, Clark summarizes how evangelicals should conceive of the relationship between context and theology:

> In sum, we who are evangelicals should do several things. (1) We should recognize the reality of cultural influence on all theological interpretation. (2) We must purposefully adopt a self-critical stance toward any and all cultures. (3) Yet we should assert the need for theology to achieve cultural relevance. And (4) while doing so, we must yield to the priority of Scripture over any and all cultural assumptions.[45]

Clark goes on to note that theologians commonly make two mistakes in this process. The first one is "to pretend that cultural or philosophical preunderstanding does not exist or is relatively unimportant. This is where too much evangelical theology has failed in the past."[46] The second mistake is one that mainline/liberals commit, which is "to so delight in cultural and philosophical assumptions that they set in concrete the entire agenda for theology."[47]

As it pertains to Schlorff, his desire to assert the primacy of Scripture in all contextualizing is correct. However, he fallaciously assumes

43. Vanhoozer, *Drama of Doctrine*, 27.

44. Clark, *To Know and Love God*, 110.

45. Ibid. This is where the al-Kalima School would do well to monitor its theological agenda.

46. Ibid.

47. Ibid.

that all faithful theologizing (i.e., all evangelical theologizing/contextualizing) takes place in a linear (and binary) fashion. Either one begins with Scripture or one begins with culture. While all evangelicals assert the primacy of Scripture, there is a problem when the relationship between Scripture and the hermeneutical community is viewed as operating in a linear fashion. According to Schlorff, this linear orientation is one-directional—from Scripture to culture. Yet, in order to conceive of theology in this way, he presumes that we can decode Scripture so as to ascertain a set of deculturalized or supracultural principles that we then encode in another context.[48] Robert Schreiter has labeled this approach to theology the "translation model" which, simply put, involves freeing the Christian message from "its previous cultural accretions. In doing so, the data of revelation are allowed to stand freely and be prepared for a second step of the procedure, namely, translation into a new situation."[49] Moreover, this view assumes "that contextualization happens only or primarily in the encoding stage."[50] But as Clark succinctly points out, "Humans cannot duplicate a supracultural, God's-eye view-point. Theologians who think they are expressing theological principles at a purely transcultural level mislead only those who are members of their own culture."[51] Again, the Bible alone is the locus of transcultural authority.

What is needed is a way of conceptualizing and doing theology that reflects all that Christians bring to the Scriptures from their contexts and how it is that God, through his Word and by his Spirit, aims to transform them. Clark's dialogical model better reflects these realities and the complex interplay that should mark the Christian community's reflection on Scripture and their context:

1. From within the culture, with its own values, beliefs, practices, and dilemmas, Christians raise questions and issues.
2. Christians offer initial responses to these questions by relating them to themes and texts from the biblical teachings. They will begin with what they know of Scripture. Their concern will lead them to explore and interpret unfamiliar biblical passages. (Here they use the tools of biblical studies to direct their grasp of the Bible's message.

48. Clark classifies this view of contextualization as a naïve form of principlizing. See ibid., 94.

49. Schreiter, *Constructing Local Theologies*, 6–9.

50. Clark, *To Know and Love God*, 112.

51. Ibid., 94.

They will not get absolute readings of the Bible, but will gradually gain increasingly clear, well-justified understandings of the relevant texts.)

3. As this process goes on, Christians seek to obey what the Bible teaches on the question at issue. They look for new applications of God's Word to their lives and contexts. They cultivate sensitivity to the voice of the Spirit in all things. The reading of Scripture does not just lead to, but also requires as its presupposition, an open heart toward God.
4. They permit the Bible to judge the cultural viewpoint from which questions arise. They ask whether Scripture deals with the issues, but from different perspectives or categories. They ask whether the Bible challenges their questions instead of answering them.
5. Out of this initial attempt to relate biblical teaching to cultural issues in a spirit of humble obedience, Christians allow certain themes for a culturally relevant theology—a contextual theology—to emerge. They begin to formulate their theological framework.
6. Christians in one culture discuss their findings with theologians in another culture, either in time or in space. Maybe the "other culture" is a *distant era of time*. Theologians from the past who struggled with parallel questions might have wisdom to offer. Maybe the "other culture" is a *far-off place*. Theologians from the other side of the world who grapple with similar issues could suggest ways to interpret the Bible more faithfully or resolve the questions more authentically.
7. But Christians return to the Bible (and again, Scripture is understood with increasing clarity through the tools of biblical studies) to evaluate the emerging theology and continue the dialogical cycle.[52]

Clark notes that that there is an "all-at-onceness" to this process and that "feedback loops abound."[53] What is important is that this model preserves both the primacy of Scripture and emphasizes that ultimate responsibility for theologizing lies with the local church. Schlorff's approach, on the other hand, presumes that the transmitter's conception *and* articulation of the faith must be preserved so as to avoid syncretism. And the way to do this, in his view, is to avoid making "theological use" of

52. Ibid., 114.

53. Ibid.

Arab-Muslim cultures in translating and interpreting the faith. Schlorff's position fails to recognize both the complexity of culture as well as contextual nature of all theologizing.[54]

Hermeneutics

As noted in chapter one, Schlorff argues that the two hermeneutical methods traditionally employed by Protestant missionaries for referencing the Qur'ān in Muslim contexts, the prooftexting method and the "new hermeneutic," are syncretistic.[55] The first method aims to read Christian meanings into select qur'ānic passages while the second method "envisages a two-way synthesis where both the Qur'an and the Bible are opened up to meanings from the other."[56] Schlorff objects to the use of both methods on three grounds. First, these methods remove the passages from their qur'ānic contexts. Second, they cut the texts off from their original meaning, offering sectarian interpretations of key verses. And third, such methods introduce an authority conflict into the young church.[57]

The solution, according to Schlorff, is to engage in an analytic method of Qur'ān interpretation that is consistent with how one interprets the Bible. This method is guided by three principles. First, the meaning of a text is determined by analyzing the original language. This entails investigating how various terms are used within the context of the Qur'ān's original language system and cultural context. The result, Schlorff states, is that "Qur'anic language may not be interpreted in terms of what one might think similar biblical language might have meant. It cannot be filled with Christian content."[58]

Second, Schlorff says that all interpretation of the Qur'ān must begin with the presuppositions of the believing community—the Muslim community. For Schlorff, this means "that we take the presuppositions of the Muslim community as the starting point to understanding the Qur'an's meaning, and, therefore, basic to our use of the Qur'an in presenting the

54. Schlorff's theological method exhibits features critiqued by Clark as naïve principalizing and appears to be undergirded by a naïve realist epistemology. See Hiebert, "Form and Meaning," 102–3.

55. Cf. also his discussion in Schlorff, "The Hermeneutical Crisis," 143–51.

56. Schlorff, *Models*, 126.

57. I address the third of Schlorff's critiques about there being an authority conflict in chapter two.

58. Schlorff, *Models*, 133.

gospel."[59] Indeed, "This should be considered the *sine qua non* of our use of the Qur'an in communicating the gospel to Muslims."[60]

The third principle is that the believing community of the book is central to its interpretation. Practically, this means that Christians must interpret the Qur'ān in a manner that accords with the corpus of classical Muslim *tafsīr* literature. Schlorff argues that Christians must "respect the primacy of the Islamic tradition of Qur'anic interpretation" if we expect Muslims to "respect the primacy of Christian tradition of biblical interpretation."[61] Schlorff believes that his approach will enable Christians to avoid the syncretizing tendencies endemic to the prooftexting method and the new hermeneutic.

It is important to note that Schlorff's approach is aimed at influencing how missionaries originating from outside the Muslim world use the Qur'ān. The approach of this book, however, has been to investigate how followers of Christ originating from and/or residing in the Arab-Muslim world use the Qur'ān. Despite this distinction, it is clear that Schlorff believes his analytic method is normative for all those working among Muslims. With that in mind, there are at least three problems with Schlorff's assumptions about the Qur'ān that feed into his critique of those that make positive apologetic use of the Muslim scripture. First, Schlorff presumes that the meaning one derives from the language and context of various qur'ānic passages is ascertainable in a way that parallels other types of literature. But scholars have shown that this is anything but clear. Second, he assumes that the Muslim community's understanding of the Qur'ān's meaning has been accurately preserved in the corpus of classical *tafsīr* literature. However, any approach to the Qur'ān, whether Christian or otherwise, must come to terms with the Qur'ān's literary relationship to biblical literature. This is something that most Muslims today deny, which keeps them from understanding the Qur'ān on its own terms. Finally, Schlorff says that when interpreting the Qur'ān, Christians must begin with Muslim presuppositions about their book. In and of itself this is not problematic. Every Christian must understand those presuppositions, particularly since they shape how Muslims read and understand the Bible. Although Schlorff recognizes that Christians will not, ultimately, share the presuppositions Muslims have about their scripture, he fails to

59. Ibid., 135.

60. Ibid.

61. Ibid., 136.

discuss how it is that Christians residing in the Arab world are to account for the Qur'ān. In particular, he offers no guidance for how Christians are to respond theologically to the Qur'ān's subversive reinterpretation of two key doctrines: revelation and prophetology. In what follows, I will address each of Schlorff's three assumptions about the Qur'ān separately.

Language, Context, and Meaning in the Qur'ān

Muslim and western scholars alike have long noted that the Qur'ān contains frequent ellipses and many ambiguous features that complicate how one interprets the text. When reading the Qur'ān, one is frequently confronted by obscure vocabulary[62] and syntactic ambiguities that leave one questioning certain parts of speech—such as the proper subject(s) of certain sentences, the object(s) of some verbs, the proper antecedent(s) of various pronouns, etc. This is particularly the case when one questions the accepted vocalization of the text associated with the 1924 Cairo edition. That edition lacks a critical apparatus containing all the possible variant readings (*qirā'āt*) from the ancient Qur'ān codices, manuscripts, and early Muslim works treating this topic.[63] Additionally, there are the mysterious letters (*al-muqaṭṭa'āt*) that open 29 of the Qur'ān's 114 *sūras*. These continue to puzzle many scholars.[64] Added to this is the allusive

62. Despite Jeffery's classification of much of the Qur'ān's vocabulary as "foreign" in *The Foreign Vocabulary of the Qur'an*, it is difficult to determine the level of "foreignness" this vocabulary exhibits since, as Reynolds notes, "we have no pre-Qur'ānic Arabic literature, if any ever existed. This means . . . that we cannot generally claim that the Qur'ān itself has borrowed foreign vocabulary, having no way to know whether this vocabulary entered into Arabic long before." Reynolds, *Biblical Subtext*, 36.

63. For a historical overview of issues related to various Qur'ān codices, punctuation, and the fixing of the Qur'ān's text, see Leemhuis, "From Palm Leaves to the Internet," 145–61. Reynolds notes that the choice in 1924 by Egyptian scholars in Cairo of the Ḥafṣ 'an 'āṣim *qirā'a* ("reading") as the textus receptus of the Qur'ān was a choice not based on textual criticism but religious doctrine. This text is what most Muslims refer to today as the "'Uthmānic codex." However, this version of the Qur'ān has no critical apparatus listing the "seven canonical variants" established by Ibn Mujāhid (d. 936). But even if it did Reynolds points out that referring to these variants as "canonical" is a declaration rooted not in textual criticism but in the Muslim doctrine of canonicity. See Reynolds, "Qur'ānic Studies and its Controversies," 1–3.

64. Bellamy argues that these are abbreviations of the *basmalla*, but his theory is not widely accepted among scholars. See Bellamy, "The Mysterious Letters of the Koran," 267–85. The problem with these letters is that none of the classical exegetes have an explanation for them. Moreover, Muslim confusion over them demonstrates, in part, the amount of distance that exists between the classical *mufassirūn* and the text of the Qur'ān. Reynolds explains: "These letters seem to play an important role in the

manner in which the Qur'ān refers to biblical and/or historical events and personalities. The Qur'ān assumes that its audience understands these allusions, but due to its lack of narrative formation, later generations of Muslim scholars had to rely upon extra-qur'ānic sources in order to explain them. All of these features persist in spite of the Qur'ān's repeated assertion that its verses or "signs" (*ayāt*) constitute a "clear book."[65] Indeed, the lack of narrative formation and the odd sequencing in many of the Qur'ān's accounts make it difficult to rely solely upon linguistic or contextual factors for determining the Qur'ān's meaning. Nasr Abu-Zayd explains:

> First of all, the Qur'an deliberately ignores mentioning not only the time and place of the historical incidents in its stories, but also some of the characters. Second, in dealing with some historical stories the Qur'an selects some events and omits others. Third, the chronological arrangement of the events is violated. Fourth, the Qur'an sometimes relates certain actions to some characters and sometimes relates the same actions to different characters. Fifth, when the story is repeated in another chapter of the Qur'an, the dialogue related to the same character is not the same as in the first case. Sixth, the Qur'an sometimes adds to the story some incidents that are supposed to happen chronologically afterward.[66]

These features have long been the source of much discussion and disagreement regarding the Qur'ān's meaning and how best to interpret the text. What is clear is that the Qur'ān's original meaning cannot be ascertained from its context as easily as Schlorff presumes. Moreover, the above discussion demonstrates some of the reasons why scholars, like Wansbrough and Reynolds, have advocated the use of literary methods

organization of the Qur'ān. For example, every consonantal form in the Arabic alphabet is represented at least once by these letters, while no form is used for more than one letter. Meanwhile, Sūras that begin with the same or similar letters are grouped together, even when that grouping means violating the larger ordering principle of the Qur'ān (from longer to shorter Sūras). Yet the classical *mufassirūn* do not know any of this. They do not demonstrate any memory of the role these letters played in the Qur'ān's organization. Instead their commentary reflects both confusion and creative speculation." Reynolds, *Biblical Subtext*, 19.

65. Cf. e.g., Q 12:1; 15:1; 26:2; 27:1 *et passim*.

66. Abu-Zayd, "Literary Approach," 26.

for understanding the Qur'ān. In particular, Reynolds advocates reading the Qur'ān through the lens of biblical literature.[67]

Reading the Qur'ān through the Lens of Biblical Literature

In order to explain the Qur'ān, one of the methods many early *mufassirūn* employed was to turn to the established narratives of the "People of the Book" (*ahl al-kitāb*), i.e., Jews and Christians. Indeed, relying upon Jewish and Christian narrative material in early works like Wahb b. Munabbih's (d. ca. 730) *Qiṣaṣ al-Anbiyā'* ("Stories of the Prophets") was considered a legitimate practice. As Roberto Tottoli states, "His [Wahb's] fame is direct evidence that during the first century of Islam there was nothing particularly controversial associated with people consulting [*sic*] Jewish and Christian texts, and that on the contrary, to have read these texts was regarded favorably and helped to boost the reputation of the student of the lives of the prophets."[68] Tottoli notes that Wahb's work would influence later generations of scholars who in turn had a tremendous influence on the burgeoning notion of Islamic of prophetology that was developed more fully in the biographical literature (*sīra*) on Muḥammad's life.[69]

However, with the passage of time, Muslim scholars came to repudiate the use of Jewish and Christian material to interpret the Qur'ān.[70] This development was related in part to Muslim interaction with Jews and Christians in a sectarian milieu and the impact this had on the process of Muslim self-definition. A key component in that self-definition was the

67. Reynolds defines biblical literature as including the Bible but he also includes pseudepigraphical works and some Rabbinic works. See Reynolds, *Biblical Subtext*, 37–38. In this book, Reynolds presents 13 case studies that demonstrate how interpreting the Qur'ān in the manner he advocates provides a much clearer understanding of its message than do the explanations of the same passages provided by the classical *mufassirūn*.

68. Tottoli, *Biblical Prophets*, 140–41.

69. Commenting on Wahb b. Munabbih's role in this regard, Tottoli states: "The work of Wahb had a decisive influence upon the genre of the stories of the prophets. Even prior to the systematisation undertaken by Ibn Isḥāq he was able to produce a text dedicated to the topic, relying upon traditions of various provenances. The details and the stories not mentioned in the Qur'ān are identified by making recourse to the traditions of clear Jewish and Christian origin, with the addition of certain particulars that are typically Arabian or Islamicised." Ibid.

70. Indeed, later Muslim scholars began to interpret the Bible in light of the Qur'ān and *ḥadīth*. For an example of this, see Ṭūfī, *Muslim Exegesis of the Bible*.

growing consensus among many Muslims that Jews and Christians had tampered with and falsified the Bible since both communities continually denied Muḥammad's prophethood.

By the time of Ibn Kathīr in the fourteenth century, the use of Jewish and Christian material to interpret the Qur'ān was deemed well outside the acceptable boundaries of what Muslim scholars could access in order to fill out the lack of narrative detail in the Qur'ān.[71] Ibn Kathīr labeled this narrative material derived from the Bible and other non-canonical works "*isrā'īlīyāt*."[72] Relying on it enabled early exegetes to situate the people and events alluded to in the Qur'ān within the mold of biblical religion. Doing this provided continuity (and legitimacy) between the "new" revelation brought by Muḥammad and the previous revelation held by Jews and Christians. Interpreters who utilized this material believed it was helpful in establishing links and points of contact with the previous community and their revelation, all the while forging a new and distinct identity. Yet once this identity was forged, Muslims dispensed with the previous materials. Jane McAuliffe explains:

> In a process of evolving self-definition, the Muslim scholarly community began consciously to mark narrative material as "within" or "beyond" those boundaries that it claimed for itself. Debates about the reliability of stories associated with the Jews or Christians, whether biblical or extrabiblical, drove some Muslim scholars to question the utility of their inclusion within Islamic literature, broadly conceived, even for purposes of popular religious oratory and moral exhortation.[73]

On the whole, the *mufassirūn* became circumspect in their reliance upon any sources other than those deemed "in bounds" to elucidate the meaning of the Qur'ān. Eventually, Muslim scholars linked a number of passages in the Qur'ān to what they termed "occasions of revelation" (*asbāb al-nuzūl*). These helped explain the ambiguities they faced in the text of the Qur'ān and rooted many of the events in history. The Islamic sources that developed were, for the most part, constrained to "reports" (*akhbār*) or "sayings" (*aḥādīth*) attributed to Muḥammad. This material

71. One notable exception to this general pattern is al-Biqā'ī (d. 1480) who advocated using the Bible as a prooftext for interpreting the Qur'ān. See Saleh, "A Fifteenth-Century Muslim Hebraist," 629–54.

72. For a discussion of the historical background on the use of this term see Tottoli, "The Origin and Use of the Term Isrā'īliyyāt," 193–210.

73. McAuliffe, "Prediction" 108.

was recorded in the biographical works (*sīra*) that were authored beginning in the eighth century and in the *ḥadīth* collections, which began to be canonized in the late ninth century.

Western scholars of Islam, including Christian scholars with polemical motives, oftentimes assume the historical reliability of the traditional Muslim sources. Indeed, they rely upon these both to describe the emergence of the Qur'ān and to interpret it. In the West, Theodor Nöldeke (d. 1930) followed the medieval Muslim method of linking various passages in the Qur'ān with events from the most authoritative biography (*sīra*) of Muḥammad, that of Ibn Isḥāq (d. 768).[74] He also followed them in arranging the various *sūras* of the Qur'ān to accord with the Meccan and Medinan periods of Muḥammad's prophetic career. Doing this provided a chronological structure that other western scholars have since built upon to speculate concerning the events surrounding the various "occasions of revelation," which purportedly shed light on ambiguities in the text of the Qur'ān itself. This structure and the details related to Muḥammad's interactions with Jews and Christians recorded in the biographical works became the primary source material used by western scholars to explain the Qur'ān's conversation with themes derived from biblical literature and Christian theology. For many of them, their focus was on discovering the various textual sources that went into the formation of the Qur'ān. Additionally, these methods allowed western scholars to fix the time and historical context out of which the Qur'ān emerged and to theorize about which heretical groups may have influenced Muḥammad's beliefs. One example of this is the supposed group of Mary-worshippers who many postulate is behind the Qur'ān's apparent conception of the Trinity as God, Jesus, and Mary (Q 5:116).[75]

Reynolds has noted that the problem with these methods is that the biographical works on Muḥammad's life were themselves developed by Muslim exegetes in order to explain the Qur'ān, not the other way around: "The *sīra* itself is a product of exegesis (*tafsīr*) of the Qur'ān, and therefore it can hardly be used to explain the Qur'ān."[76] The reason for

74. Cf. ch. 3, n31.

75. Reynolds argues that when the Qur'ān's use of hyperbole and rhetoric is understood, the need for postulating the existence of Christian heretics as the source for Muḥammad's misunderstanding of Christian doctrines "disappears entirely." See Reynolds, "Qur'anic Rhetoric."

76. Reynolds, *Biblical Subtext*, 9.

this is due, in large part, to the ambiguous and referential nature of the Qur'ān.

The Qur'ān's ambiguities and referential nature led Wansbrough to challenge the prevalent methods scholars used to analyze both the Qur'ān and other Islamic sources. In 1977 and 1978 Wansbrough published two groundbreaking works, *Quranic Studies and The Sectarian Milieu.* In *Quranic Studies*, Wansbrough challenges the long held assumption by western scholars that the stories used by the *mufassirūn* are historical records. He bases his theory in this regard on the Qur'ān's allusions to biblical personalities and events. As Wansbrough notes, "Quranic allusion presupposes familiarity with the narrative material of Judaeo-Christian scripture, which was not so much reformulated as merely referred to. Narrative structure, on the other hand, emerged in the literature of haggadic (i.e., *tafsīr*) exegesis, in which the many lacunae were more or less satisfactorily filled."[77] Eventually, Muslim scholars came to limit themselves to extra-qur'ānic (and strictly "Islamic") material for elucidating the Qur'ān. Among the reasons identified for this development, according to Wansbrough, was the sectarian milieu (i.e., Muslim disputation with Jews and Christians). The Muslim community defined itself within this milieu and part of that self-definition was the development of a distinctly Islamic understanding of salvation history.[78]

In order to ascertain the Qur'ān's meaning, Reynolds, following the precedents established by Wansbrough, advocates the use of literary approaches versus historical approaches to the Qur'ān. Literary approaches are more effective in arriving at the Qur'ān's original meaning since they take the text seriously and interpret it the way it intends to be interpreted—in relation to biblical literature. By adopting this methodology, Reynolds has definitively shown that the classical *tafsīr* literature is notoriously unhelpful in many cases for arriving at the original meaning of the Qur'ān. As he states, "*tafsīr* literature in general, *even when it is read with a critical method*, cannot provide the scholar with privileged information on what the Qur'ān originally meant."[79] Indeed, the Qur'ān presumes familiarity with biblical personalities and events. Hence, read-

77. Wansbrough, *Quranic Studies*, 20.

78. "Salvation" in this context should not be understood in Christian terms. Rather, it refers to a particular perspective on sacred history that centers on God's choice of Muḥammad and the Islamic *umma* to restore what they believe has been corrupted by Jews and Christians.

79. Reynolds, *Biblical Subtext*, 12; emphasis added.

ing the Qur'ān in the way it intends to be read means one will read it in relation to biblical literature. This does not mean that its religious message is the same as the Bible or other extra-canonical literature. But it does mean that reading it alongside that literature helps elucidate the Qur'ān's meaning.

However, Schlorff rejects these types of approaches on theological and hermeneutical grounds since he believes they are syncretistic. Obviously, adopting this type of approach does not mean that every passage has a "Christian meaning." It does assume however that the Qur'ān intends for those texts that treat Christian topics and doctrines to be read through the lens of biblical literature and in conversation with the various Christian communities existing at the time of the its emergence, whether contemporary Muslims recognize this or not. For Christians, realizing this fact can help them to demythologize the Qur'ān and situate it within its proper literary (and historical) context. Theologically, reading the Qur'ān in this way can help clarify the mechanisms it employs to subvert the Bible's story of redemption. Foremost among those mechanisms is the redefinition of two key doctrines: revelation and prophetology.

Revelation and Prophetology in the Islamic Construal of Salvation History

For those residing in the Arab world, it is only natural that they deal with the preunderstandings their audience brings to the Bible when discussing Christ and Christian doctrines. These preunderstandings are shaped by qur'ānic terminology and concepts as interpreted through the lens of Muslim theologians. Particularly important in this regard is the Qur'ān's redefinition of revelation and prophetology. Christians residing in the Muslim world must address these two doctrines if they are to succeed in allowing the Bible to exert "narrative control" in its depiction of the story of redemption told by the prophets and preserved in biblical revelation.[80]

As noted earlier, the Qur'ān repeatedly asserts that it is in continuity with the "previous revelation" (i.e., the Bible). But that assertion is predicated on a radical redefinition of the mode, form, and content of *all* divine revelation. Buttressing that redefinition is the Qur'ān's notion of prophetology. Prophets and messengers are envisioned as those who safeguard and deliver God's message to humanity. Indeed, central to the

80. Cf. Curry, "Mission to Muslims," 234–35.

Muslim community's self-understanding is their view of the uniqueness of Muḥammad in the qur'ānic dispensation. Reuven Firestone explains:

> The Qur'ān, like all scripture, must conform to recognizable patterns of human utterances, and the Qur'ān indeed contains imagery according to established literary types known from the Bible. In the case of the Qur'ān and the Bible, the phenomenon is mimetic. This differs from the relationship between the New Testament and the Hebrew Bible, where the figural interpretation establishes a claim of fulfillment by the former over the later. Qur'ānic allusions to biblical themes mostly reflect rather than develop biblical themes, but they are not merely calques of earlier, fixed forms. They represent a historiography that conveys a new dispensation in the revelation of the Qur'ān, and that very revelation reveals its polemical environment in, for example, its record of argument regarding the modes of revelation: Jewish and pagan demands for Muḥammad to produce a scripture according to biblical paradigms. That new dispensation is burdened, however, by its relationship to Jewish scripture and must therefore be differentiated by the text itself, by its own polemic, and by its early interpretation.[81]

Through a process of redefinition and back projection, the Qur'ān's self-understanding of revelatory preeminence shapes (and subverts) Muslim approaches to the Bible in at least three ways. First, the *mode* of qur'ānic revelation via divine dictation becomes the defining mode for all previous revelations. Christians believe that God has inspired the Bible through a process of verbal inspiration. However, verbal inspiration of documents that display all the characteristics of being "ordinary" or human in origin defies Muslim expectations regarding the mode of revelation and renders their judgments of those documents suspect.[82]

Second, the Qur'ān is distinguished in Muslim minds by being one text in one language that is marked by distinct literary and stylistic features, and those features tacitly shape the expectations Muslims have of the *form* of previous revelation. The Bible's varying genres, historical circumstances, languages, and its notion of progressive revelation through history do not fit this mold. Additionally, the Qur'ān's elliptical discourse about the prophets effectively flattens the redemptive significance found

81. Firestone, "The Qur'ān and the Bible," 20.

82. I am using the word "ordinary" in the sense that Vanhoozer does in his description of the various genres one finds in the Bible. See Vanhoozer, "The Semantics of Biblical Literature," 85–92.

in the details of their lives that are preserved in the biblical narratives. Lumping all the prophets together and assuming they all brought the same message enables the Qur'ān to deconstruct and decontextualize those prophets and their messages so as to deduce a generic form of both prophethood and revelation, which is used by Muslim scholars to validate Muḥammad as the seal of the prophets and the Qur'ān as God's final revelation to humanity.

Finally, the Qur'ān ostensibly assumes that the essential *content* of all previous revelation is the same. As McAuliffe notes, "God has revealed his guidance [*hudā*] to many messengers and prophets, but each instance is best understood as a representation of the same message in a medium and manner specifically suited to its intended recipients. Theoretically, at least, there can be no discrepancy in the content of these revelations because they all proceed from the same source."[83] Indeed, Muslim theologians depict Islam as the restorer of this original message. This is why they position Islam as the "final" revelation from God. But Islam's self-designation as the final revelation from God should not be construed linearly:

> Muslims understand the Qur'ān to be not only the continuation of a long series of divine disclosures but also their culmination. As expressed in passages such as Q 46:12, the Qur'ān confirms and completes all previous revelations. . . . It would be a mistake [however] to understand the Islamic sense of scriptural culmination as strictly a linear progression. While the Qur'ān recognizes the supersessionist claims that Christianity makes against Judaism, the Islamic tradition does not relate itself to previous "People of the Book" in precisely the same fashion. . . . Islam is more profoundly a religion of restoration than a new dispensation. . . . As God's final act of revelation, the Qur'ān effectively abrogates all previous revelations or renders them otiose but does so by reclaiming, recovering, and restoring the primordial divine message. An oscillation between the perfected and the primordial is a defining feature of qur'ānic self-understanding.[84]

This helps to explain why later generations of Muslim scholars invalidated the Bible as a faithful witness to God's redemptive actions in the world. It fails to meet their expectations in terms of the *mode*, *form*, and *content* of revelation. Revelation has been redefined as guidance from

83 McAuliffe, "Prediction," 108–9.

84. Ibid.

God centering on the primordial message of *tawḥīd*. Any assertion that God's intentions for humanity are other than submission to his will and strict adherence to the doctrine of his unity is deemed a corruption of this primordial message.

Despite the Qur'ān's repeated assertion that it affirms what God revealed beforehand to Jews and Christians (in the Bible), it is clear that in terms of the mode, form, and content of revelation, the Qur'ān's assumed continuity with the Bible and its message of redemption lacks substance. That being stated, I have sought to show that when those verses that address Christian themes are repositioned within a hermeneutical context with biblical horizons they not only become more comprehensible but reveal many of the discrepancies between the details in the Qur'ān and Bible. Apologetically, the aim of such an approach should be to draw the Qur'ān into the Bible's horizons. The goal in this endeavor must be to allow the Bible's comprehensive and self-contained narrative fill in and correct the narrative formation lacking in the Qur'ān. The goal, in effect, is to separate the Qur'ān from the ideologies of the *mufassirūn* and the *tafsīr* which fuel the subversion of the grand biblical narrative and the organic relationship between that narrative and core Christian doctrines like the Trinity and Incarnation. Schlorff's approach, on the other hand, leaves these presuppositions unchallenged.

FUTURE RESEARCH

Though this book raises many questions, there are two areas that need further attention by Christian scholars. First, critical scholarship on the Qur'ān demonstrates that it is a text in conversation with biblical literature and the Christian communities in its provenance. This calls into question a number of the standard features in the Muslim construal of early Islamic history such as the purported "pagan" environment within which Muḥammad first proclaimed his message. Indeed, it calls into question many of the details surrounding the Muslim prophet himself. Most of these appear to be the creations of later Muslim scholars seeking to legitimize their particular message and book in the mold of a "biblical prophet." Yet many Christians, in their polemical responses to Islam, continue to assume the historical veracity of the materials Muslims use to reconstruct their early history. One way of mitigating many of the harsh polemical approaches adopted by Christians is to make them more aware of critical research on early Muslim origins. That research calls into question many of the sources from which Christians and others have constructed their polemical critiques of Islam and Muḥammad. More research needs to be done on the integrity of Islamic sources *and* how it is that Christians can formulate thoughtful responses to Islam's clear subversion of the biblical story.

Second, this book has a number of implications for those laboring in Muslim contexts. Though I have focused solely on how indigenous Christians use the Qur'ān in Arabic-speaking contexts, more research needs to be done on how the Qur'ān impacts the religious discourse of those in non-Arabic-speaking Islamic milieus. Obviously, this has repercussions on their approaches to evangelism and discipleship. But longer term, more needs to be done to investigate how things like the Qur'ān's redefinition of the notion of revelation and prophetology impacts how Muslim background believers are appropriating and understanding biblical faith.

CONCLUSION

This book has sought to demonstrate that Christians in Arabic-speaking milieus are justified in making positive apologetic use of qur'ānic points of contact in their discourse about the Bible and Christian doctrines. It has sought to shed light on how one can enter into the Qur'ān's hermeneutical circle and use it in order to draw the Qur'ān and, more importantly, the Muslim into the Bible's hermeneutical horizons. Support for the thesis has been based on an exegetical argument from Acts 17, the analysis of various medieval and contemporary Arabic texts, and a discussion of theological method in Arabic-speaking milieus.

It has been shown that the resignification of qur'ānic locutions entails establishing points of linguistic and conceptual contact for conveyance of biblical ideas. Apologetically, this can be used to demonstrate the referential and mimetic nature of the Qur'ān. Separating the Qur'ān from the corpus of Muslim *tafsīr* literature is crucial for situating these locutions within a Christocenteric context and hermeneutical framework provided by the Bible. Since the Qur'ān presumes its message is in concert with the "previous scriptures," these previous scriptures can be referred to explain certain parts of the Qur'ān and, more importantly, to counteract normative Islam's subversion of the Bible's redemptive story. The aim is to help Muslims view the Qur'ān as a product of a certain environment shaped by biblical awareness and allusions. Those allusions can provide points of contact for Muslims to understand the Qur'ān by virtue of repositioning certain texts and their allusions to biblical ideas within the hermeneutical context that gave them birth.

It has been shown that positive use of the Qur'ān does not automatically entail the fusion of biblical and qur'ānic horizons so that both are demonstrated to be conveying the same message at each and every point. It has been argued that many of the Qur'ān's allusive references to biblical events, personalities, and Christian doctrines can be used to direct Muslims into the world of the Bible's discourse and its story of redemption. Obviously, if the apologist's goal does not include demonstrating how the Qur'ān's perceived continuity with biblical revelation is limited and ends in discontinuity at a number of key points, then one's use of the Qur'ān may end in the dangerous fusion of horizons that Schlorff warns against in his critique of the new hermeneutic. Positive use of the Qur'ān must, like Paul's approach on Mars Hill, ultimately be used to demonstrate discontinuity. And that discontinuity is only corrected when one allows the Bible to exert narrative control over how one constructs his perception of this world's story-structured reality. In this way, the Christian theologian will have achieved his purpose of entering into the Qur'ān's hermeneutical circle while simultaneously absorbing that circle into the realm of the Bible's discourse about what constitutes the true content of revelation and God's redemptive purposes in sending his prophets and ultimately his Son to redeem humanity from sin and reassert his kingdom-control over the entirety of his creation. Ultimately, all positive use of the Qur'ān's linguistic and conceptual congruence with biblical ideas must be used to drive people towards repentance and faith in the God of the Bible. This, in turn, will demonstrate the necessity of dispensing with the major signposts of the standard Muslim narrative that undermine the Bible's story of human redemption in Christ. The Bible's self-contained and comprehensive narrative must be released and enabled to subvert all other competing narratives, particularly those that separate key biblical doctrines from their context within the broader story of redemption and restoration.

A final thought about Middle Eastern followers of Christ and westerners is in order. In utilizing the insights gained from research on the Qur'ān's relationship to biblical literature, Christians residing in the Arab world must guard against the temptation to make an artificial separation between that research and the implications it has for their proclamation of the gospel. Their obligation, like all other Christians, is "to contend for the faith that was once for all delivered to the saints" (Jude 3). If the two principles at the heart of the gospel—the indigenous principle and the pilgrim principle—teach us anything about the Bible's story, they teach us that it is inherently subversive of all stories, philosophies, and worldviews that would squelch its transformative power. God desires the gospel to be unleashed to do its work within all spheres of a particular culture—on its language, ethics, and social structures, including how those who confess faith in it identify themselves as heirs of it. For western missionaries, theologians, and those interested in the advance of God's kingdom among Arabic-speaking Muslims, they must adopt a position of humility and partnership as they work with Middle Easterners who follow Christ in difficult circumstances. These brothers and sisters are striving to "work out their salvation with fear and trembling" (Phil 2:12). No two sets of circumstances are the same; yet, God's purposes in the gospel are consistent as are his expectations for his children regardless of culture, time, or place.

Bibliography

Abdul-Haqq, Abdiyah Akbar. *Sharing Your Faith with a Muslim*. Minneapolis, MN: Bethany Fellowship, 1980.

Abū Qurrah, Thawdhurus, and Sidney H. Griffith. *A Treatise on the Veneration of the Holy Icons*. Louvain: Peeters, 1997.

Abu-Zayd, Nasr. "The Dilemma of the Literary Approach to the Qur'an." *AJCP* 23 (2003) 8–47.

Accad, Fouad Elias. *Building Bridges: Christianity and Islam*. Colorado Springs: NavPress, 1997.

Accad, Martin. "Christian Attitudes toward Islam and Muslims: A Kerygmatic Approach." In *Toward Respectful Understanding & Witness among Muslims: Essays in Honor of J. Dudley Woodberry*, edited by Evelyne A. Reisacher, 28–48. Pasadena, CA: William Carey Library, 2012.

———. "Corruption and/or Misinterpretation of the Bible: The Story of Islamic Usage of *Taḥrīf*." *TR* 24:2 (2003) 67–97.

———. "Muḥammad's Advent as the Final Criterion for the Authenticity of the Judeo-Christian Tradition." In *The Three Rings: Textual Studies in the Historical Trialogue of Judaism, Christianity, and Islam*, edited by Barbara Roggema, 217–36. Leuven: Peeters, 2005.

———. "The Ultimate Proof-Text: The Interpretation of John 20:17 in Muslim-Christian Dialogue (Second/Eighth–Eighth/Fourteenth Centuries)." In *Christians at the Heart of Islamic Rule: Church Life and Scholarship in 'Abbasid Iraq*, edited by David Thomas, 199–214. Leiden: Brill, 2003.

Aquinas, Thomas. "De rationibus fidei," translated by Joseph Kenny. *SFM* 6:4 (2010) 733–67.

Arbache, Samir. "Bible et liturgie chez les arabes chrétiens (VIe–IXe siècle)." In *The Bible in Arab Christianity*, edited by David Thomas, 37–48. Leiden: Brill, 2007.

Arberry, A. J. *The Koran Interpreted*. New York: George Allen & Unwin, 1955.

———. *Sufism: An Account of the Mystics of Islam*. London: Allen & Unwin, 1950.

Ayoub, Mahmoud M. "Towards an Islamic Christology, II: The Death of Jesus, Reality or Delusion: A Study of the Death of Jesus in Tafsīr Literature." *MW* 70:2 (1980) 91–121.

Bacha, Constantine. *Les oeuvres arabes de Théodore Aboucara évêque d'Haran*. Beirut: 1904.

Badawi, Elsaid M., and Muhammad Abdel Haleem. *Arabic-English Dictionary of Qur'anic Usage*. Leiden: Brill, 2008.

Bahnsen, Greg L. "The Encounter of Jerusalem with Athens." *ASTJ* 13 (1980) 4–40.

Bar-Asher, Meir M., Simon Hopkins, Sarah Stroumsa, and Bruno Chiesa. *A Word Fitly Spoken: Studies in Medieval Exegesis of the Hebrew Bible and the Qur'ān*. Jerusalem: Ben-Zvi Institute, 2007.

Barr, James. *The Semantics of Biblical Language*. London: Oxford University, 1961.

Bartholomew, Craig G., and Michael W. Goheen. *Living At the Crossroads: An Introduction to Christian Worldview*. Grand Rapids: Baker, 2008.

Basetti-Sani, Giulio. *The Koran in the Light of Christ: A Christian Interpretation of the Sacred Book of Islam*. Chicago: Franciscan Herald, 1977.

Bauckham, Richard. *Bible and Mission: Christian Witness in a Postmodern World*. Grand Rapids: Baker Academic, 2003.

Bavinck, Johan Herman. *An Introduction to the Science of Missions*. Philadelphia: Presbyterian and Reformed, 1960.

Beale, Gregory K. "Other Religions in New Testament Theology." In *Biblical Faith and Other Religions: An Evangelical Assessment*, edited by David W. Baker, 79–105. Grand Rapids: Kregel, 2004.

Beaumont, I. Mark. *Christology in Dialogue with Muslims: A Critical Analysis of Christian Presentations of Christ for Muslims from the Ninth to the Twentieth Centuries*. Colorado Springs: Paternoster, 2005.

Becker, C. H. "Christian Polemic and the Formation of Islamic Dogma." In *Muslims and Others in Early Islamic Society*, edited by Robert G. Hoyland, 241–57. Burlington, VT: Ashgate, 2004.

Bell, Richard, and W. Montgomery Watt. *Introduction to the Qur'ān*. Edinburgh: Edinburgh University, 1970.

Bellamy, James A. "Some Proposed Emendations to the Text of the Koran." *JAOS* 113:4 (1993) 562–73.

Berding, Kenneth, and Jonathan Lunde. *Three Views on the New Testament Use of the Old Testament*. Grand Rapids: Zondervan, 2008.

Berg, Herbert. *The Development of Exegesis in Early Islam: The Authenticity of Muslim Literature From the Formative Period*. Richmond, Surrey: Curzon, 2000.

Bertaina, David. "An Arabic Account of Theodore Abū Qurra in Debate at the Court of Caliph al-Ma'mūn: A Study in Early Christian and Muslim Literary Dialogues." PhD diss., Catholic University of America, 2007.

———. *Christian and Muslim Dialogues: The Religious Uses of a Literary Form in the Early Islamic Middle East*. Piscataway, NJ: Gorgias, 2011.

———. "The Debate of Theodore Abū Qurra." In *CMR* 1:556–64.

Bevans, Stephen B. *Models of Contextual Theology*. Maryknoll, NY: Orbis, 2002.

Biechler, James E. "Christian Humanism Confronts Islam: Sifting the Qur'an with Nicolas of Cusa." *JES* 13:1 (1976) 1–14.

Bijlefeld, Willem Abraham. "A Prophet and More Than a Prophet?: Some Observations on the Qur'ānic Use of the Terms 'Prophet' and 'Apostle.'" *MW* 59:1 (1969) 1–28.

Blau, Joshua. "A Melkite Arabic Literary *Lingua Franca* from the Second Half of the First Millenium." *BSOAS* 57:1 (1994) 14–16.

Bock, Darrell L. *Acts*. Baker Exegetical Commentary on the New Testament. Grand Rapids: Baker Academic, 2007.

Britton-Ashkelony, Brouria, and Ariyeh Kofsky. "Monasticism in the Holy Land." In *Christians and Christianity in the Holy Land: From the Origins to the Latin*

Kingdoms, edited by Ora Limor and Guy G. Stroumsa, 257–91. Abingdon: Brepols Marston, 2006.

Brown, Jonathan A. C. *Hadith: Muhammad's Legacy in the Medieval and Modern World*. Oxford: Oneworld, 2009.

Brown, Rick. "Who Was 'Allah' before Islam? Evidence that the Term 'Allah' Originated with Jewish and Christian Arabs." In *Toward Respectful Understanding & Witness among Muslims: Essays in Honor of J. Dudley Woodberry*, edited by Evelyne A. Reisacher, 147–78. Pasadena, CA: William Carey Library, 2012.

Bulliet, Richard W. *Conversion to Islam in the Medieval Period: An Essay in Quantitative History*. Cambridge: Harvard University, 1979.

Burman, Thomas E. "Polemic, Philology, and Ambivalence: Reading the Qur'ān in Latin Christendom." *JIS* 15:2 (2004) 181–209.

Calder, Norman. "*Tafsīr* from Ṭabarī to Ibn Kathīr." In *Approaches to the Qur'ān*, edited by G. R. Hawting and Abdul-Kader A. Shareef, 101–40. New York: Routledge, 1993.

Caner, Ergun Mehmet and Emir Fethi Caner. *Unveiling Islam: An Insider's Look at Muslim Life and Beliefs*. Grand Rapids: Kregel, 2002.

Carson, D. A. *Christ and Culture Revisited*. Grand Rapids: Eerdmans, 2008.

———. *Jesus the Son of God: A Christological Title often Overlooked, Sometimes Misunderstood, and Currently Disputed*. Wheaton, IL: Crossway, 2012.

Carson, D. A., and Douglas J. Moo. *An Introduction to the New Testament*. 2nd ed. Grand Rapids: Zondervan, 2005.

Chandler, Paul-Gordon. *Pilgrims of Christ on the Muslim Road: Exploring a New Path Between Two Faiths*. Lanham, MD: Cowley, 2007.

Charles, J. Daryl. "Engaging the (Neo) Pagan Mind: Paul's Encounter with Athenian Culture as a Model for Cultural Apologetics." *TJ* 16 (1995) 47–62.

———. "Jude's Use of Pseudepigrahical Source Material as a Literary Strategy." *NTS* 37:1 (1991) 130–45.

Clark, David K. *To Know and Love God: Method for Theology*. Wheaton, IL: Crossway, 2003.

Conzelmann, Hans. "The Address of Paul on the Areopagus." In *Studies in Luke-Acts*, edited by Leander E. Keck and J. Louis Martyn, 217–30. Philadelphia: Fortress, 1980.

Cook, Michael. *Early Muslim Dogma: A Source-Critical Study*. New York: Cambridge University, 1981.

Corduan, Winfried. *A Tapestry of Faiths: The Common Threads between Christianity & World Religions*. Downers Grove, IL: InterVarsity, 2002.

Cragg, Kenneth. *The Arab Christian: A History in the Middle East*. Louisville: Westminster, 1991.

Cumming, Joseph L. "Ṣifāt al-Dhāt in al-Ash'arī's Doctrine of God and Possible Christian Parallels." In *Toward Respectful Understanding & Witness among Muslims: Essays in Honor of J. Dudley Woodberry*, edited by Evelyne A. Reisacher, 111–46. Pasadena, CA: William Carey Library, 2012.

Curry, Theodore A. "Mission to Muslims." In *Theology and Practice of Mission: God, the Church, and the Nations*, edited by Bruce Riley Ashford, 227–37. Nashville: B&H Academic, 2011.

Daiber, Hans. "Masā'il wa Adjwiba." In *EI*² 6:636.

Dibelius, Martin. *The Book of Acts: Form, Style, and Theology*. Minneapolis, MN: Fortress, 2004.

Dick, Ignace. *Mujādalat Abī Qurra ma' al-Mutakallimīn al-Muslimīn fī Majlis al-Khalīfa al-Ma'mūn*. Aleppo: 2007.

Donner, Fred M. *Muhammad and the Believers at the Origins of Islam*. Cambridge, MA: The Belknap Press of Harvard University, 2010.

Dunning, Craig A. "Palestinian Muslims Converting to Christianity: Effective Evangelistic Methods in the West Bank." PhD diss., University of Pretoria, 2013.

Endress, Gerhard. *The Works of Yaḥyā Ibn 'Adī: An Analytical Inventory*. Wiesbaden: Reichert, 1977.

Engdahl, June. Review of *Pilgrims on the Muslim Road: Exploring a New Path between Two Faiths* by Paul-Gordon Chandler. http://www.answering-islam.org/reviews/mallouhi_engdahl.html.

Firestone, Reuven. "The Qur'ān and the Bible: Some Modern Studies of Their Relationship." In *Bible and Qur'ān: Essays in Scriptural Intertextuality*, edited by John C. Reeves, 1–22. Atlanta: Society of Biblical Literature, 2003.

Flemming, Dean E. *Contextualization in the New Testament: Patterns for Theology and Mission*. Downers Grove, IL: InterVarsity, 2005.

Frank, Richard M. *Beings and Their Attributes: The Teaching of the Basrian School of the Mu'tazila in the Classical Period*. Albany, NY: State University of New York, 1978.

Gaudeul, Jean-Marie. *Called from Islam to Christ: Why Muslims Become Christians*. London: Monarch, 1999.

Gardet, Louis. "'Ilm al-Kalām." In EI^2 3:1141.

Gärtner, Bertil E. *The Areopagus Speech and Natural Revelation*, translated by Carolyn Hannay King. Uppsala: C. W. K. Gleerup, 1955.

Ghattas, Raouf, and Carol B. Ghattas. *A Christian Guide to the Qur'an: Building Bridges in Muslim Evangelism*. Grand Rapids: Kregel, 2009.

Gibson, Margaret Dunlop, ed. *An Arabic Version of the Acts of the Apostles and the Seven Catholic Epistles, from an Eighth or Ninth Century MS in the Convent of St. Catherine on Mount Sinai, with a Treatise 'On the Triune Nature of God.'* Studia Sinaitica 7. London: C. J. Clay and Sons, 1899.

Gilliot, Claude. "Creation of a Fixed Text." In *The Cambridge Companion to the Qur'ān*, edited by Jane Dammen McAuliffe, 41–57. New York: Cambridge University, 2006.

Goddard, Hugh. *Christians and Muslims: From Double Standards to Mutual Understanding*. Richmond Surrey, United Kingdom: Curzon, 1995.

Graf, Georg. "Christlich-Arabische Texte. Zwei Disputationen zwischen Muslîmen und Christen." In *Griechische,Koptische und Arabische Texte zur Religion und Religiösen Literatur in Ägyptens Spätzeit*, edited by Friedrich Bilabel and Adolf Grohmann, 1–31. Heidelberg: 1934.

Greenham, Ant. "Muslim Conversions to Christ: An Investigation of Palestinian Converts Living in the Holy Land." PhD diss., Southeastern Baptist Theological Seminary, 2004.

Greear, James D. "*Theosis* and Muslim Evangelism: How the Recovery of a Patristic Understanding of Salvation Can Aid Evangelical Missionaries in the Evangelization of Islamic Peoples." PhD diss., Southeastern Baptist Theological Seminary, 2003.

Greeson, Kevin. *Camel Training Manual: How Muslims Are Coming to Faith in Christ*. Arkadelphia, AR: WIGTake, 2007.

Griffith, Sidney H. "'Ammār al-Baṣrī's Kitāb al-Burhān: Christian Kalām in the First Abbasid Century." In *The Beginnings of Christian Theology in Arabic*, 141–85. Burlington, VT: Ashgate, 1983.

———. "*Answers for the Shaykh:* A 'Melkite' Arabic Text From Sinai and the Doctrines of the Trinity and the Incarnation in 'Arab Orthodox' Apologetics." In *The Encounter of Eastern Christianity with Early Islam*, edited by Emmanouela Grypeou et al., 277–309. Boston: Brill, 2006.

———. *Arabic Christianity in the Monasteries of Ninth-Century Palestine*. Brookfield, Vt: Variorum, 1992.

———. "Arguing From Scripture: The Bible in the Christian/Muslim Encounter in the Middle Ages." In *Scripture and Pluralism: Reading the Bible in the Religiously Plural Worlds of the Middle Ages and Renaissance*, edited by Thomas J. Heffernan et al., 29–59. Boston: Brill, 2005.

———. *The Church in the Shadow of the Mosque: Christians and Muslims in the World of Islam*. Princeton, NJ: Princeton, 2008.

———. "From Aramaic to Arabic: The Languages of the Monasteries of Palestine in the Byzantine and Early Islamic Periods." *DOP* 51 (1997) 11–31.

———. "Kenneth Cragg on Christians and the Call to Islam." *RSR* 20:1 (1994) 29–35.

———. "Muhammad and the Monk Baḥīrā: Reflections on a Syriac and Arabic Text from the Early Abbasid Times." *OC* 79 (1995) 146–74.

———. "A Ninth Century Summa Theologiae Arabica." In *Actes du premier congress international d'études arabes chrétiennes (Goslar, Septembre 1980)*, edited by Khalil Samir Samir, 123–41. Rome: Pontificium Institutum Studiorum Orientalium, 1982.

———. "The Qur'ān in Arab Christian Texts: The Development of an Apologetical Argument: Abū Qurrah in the *Mağlis* of Al-Ma'mūn." *PO* 24 (1999) 203–33.

———. "Syriacisms in the 'Arabic Qur'ān': Who Were 'Those Who Said "Allāh is Third of Three"' according to *al-Mā'ida* 73?" In *A Word Fitly Spoken: Studies in Medieval Exegesis of the Hebrew Bible and the Qur'ān*, edited by Meir M. Bar-Asher et al., 83–110. Jerusalem: Ben-Zvi Institute, 2007.

———. *Theodore Abū Qurrah: The Intellectual Profile of an Arab Christian Writer of the First Abbasid Century*. Tel Aviv: Tel Aviv University, 1992.

Griffith, Sidney H., ed. *The Beginnings of Christian Theology in Arabic: Muslim-Christian Encounters in the Early Islamic Period*. Burlington, VT: Ashgate, 2002.

Grunebaum, G. E. von. "I'djāz." In *EI*[2] 3:1180–20.

Harlan, Mark Alan. "A Model for Theologizing in Arab Muslim Contexts." PhD diss., Fuller Theological Seminary, 2005.

Hayek, Michel, ed. *'Ammār al-Basrī: apologie et controverses*. Beirut: Dar El-Mashreq, 1977.

Hays, Richard B. *Echoes of Scripture in the Letters of Paul*. New Haven: Yale University, 1989.

Hemer, Colin J. "The Speeches of Acts II: The Areopagus Speech." *TB* 40 (1989) 239–59.

Hengel, Martin. *The "Hellenization" of Judaea in the First Century after Christ*. Philadelphia: Trinity Press International, 1989.

Hesselgrave, David J., and Edward Rommen. *Contextualization: Meanings, Methods, and Models*. Pasadena, CA: William Carey Library, 2000.

Hiebert, Paul G. "Form and Meaning in the Contextualization of the Gospel." In *The Word among Us: Contextualizing Theology for Mission Today*, edited by Dean S. Gilliland, 101–20. Dallas: Word, 1989.

———. *Transforming Worldviews: An Anthropological Understanding of How People Change*. Grand Rapids: Baker Academic, 2008.

Hoyland, Robert G. *Seeing Islam as Others Saw It: A Survey and Evaluation of Christian, Jewish, and Zoroastrian Writings on Early Islam*. Princeton, NJ: Darwin, 1997.

Ibn ʿAdī, Yaḥyā. *Jawāb ʿan Radd Abī ʿIsā al-Warrāq ʿalā al-Naṣārā fī al-Ittiḥād*, edited and translated by Emilio Platti. Corpus Scriptorum Christianorium Orientalium 490 and 491. Leuven: E. Peeters, 1987.

Ibn Hishām, *Sīrat al-Nabī*, edited by Muḥammad ʿAbd al-Ḥamīd. Cairo: Maktabat al-Tijārīya al-Kubrā, 1937.

Ibn Isḥāq, *The Life of Muhammad*, translated by Alfred Guillaume. Oxford: Oxford University, 1995.

al-Jaṭlāwī, al-Hādī. *Madkhal ilā al-Uslūbīya: Tanẓīran wa Taṭbīqan*. Ayoun, Lebanon: Dar al-Bayda, 1992.

———. *Qaḍāyā al-Lugha fī Kutub al-Tafsīr: Dirāsa fī al-Manhaj wa al-Tāʾwīl wa al-Iʿjāz*. Sfax, Tunisia: Dar Muhammad Ali al-Hami, 1998.

al-Jaṭlāwī, al-Hādī et al., eds. *Al-Maʿnā al-Ṣaḥīḥ li-Injīl al-Masīḥ*. Beirut: Dar al-Farabi, 2008.

Jeffery, Arthur. *The Foreign Vocabulary of the Qurʾan*. Leiden: Brill, 2007.

———. *Materials for the History of the Text of the Qurʾān*. Baroda: Oriental Institute, 1938.

———. *The Qurʾan as Scripture*. New York: R.F. Moore, 1952.

Jenkins, Philip. *The Next Christendom: The Coming of Global Christianity*. New York: Oxford University, 2002.

Al-Kalima Editorial Committee. "A Response to Jay Smith's Criticisms of Common Ground and of 'the True Meaning of the Gospel.'" *SFM* 5:5 (2009) 15–20.

———. "Translation Project." http://www.al-kalima.com/translation_project.html.

Keating, Sandra Toenies. *Defending the "People of Truth" in the Early Islamic Period: The Christian Apologies of Abū Rāʾiṭah*. Leiden: Brill, 2006.

Khiok-Khng, Yeo. *What Has Jerusalem to Do with Beijing: Biblical Interpretation from a Chinese Perspective*. Harrisburg, PA: Trinity, 1998.

Khoury, Paul. *Exégèse chrétienne du Coran*. Matériaux pour servir á l'étude de la controverse théologique islamo-chrétienne de langue arabe du VIIIe au XIIe siècle 5. Würzburg and Altenberge: Echter and Oros Verlag, 1999.

Kraft, Kathryn Ann. "Community and Identity among Arabs of a Muslim Background Who Choose to Follow a Christian Faith." PhD diss., University of Bristol, 2007.

Lamoreaux, John C., ed. *Theodore Abū Qurrah*. Provo, Utah: Brigham Young University, 2005.

Latourette, Kenneth Scott. *A History of the Expansion of Christianity*. 7 vols. Grand Rapids: Zondervan, 1938.

Lazarus-Yafeh, Hava. *Intertwined Worlds: Medieval Islam and Bible Criticism*. Princeton, NJ: Princeton University, 1992.

———. "Is there a Concept of Redemption in Islam?" In *Types of Redemption*, edited by R. Zwi Werblowsky, 168–80 in Leiden: Brill, 1970.

Livingstone, Greg. *Planting Churches in Muslim Cities: A Team Approach*. Grand Rapids: Baker, 1993.

Losie, Lynn Allan. "Paul's Speech on the Areopagus: A Model of Cross-Cultural Evangelism." In *Mission in Acts: Ancient Narratives in Contemporary Context*, edited by Robert L. Gallagher and Paul Hertig, 221–38. Maryknoll, NY: Orbis, 2004.

Lüling, Günter. *A Challenge to Islam for Reformation: The Rediscovery and Reliable Reconstruction of a Comprehensive Pre-Islamic Christian Hymnal Hidden in the Koran under Earliest Islamic Reinterpretations*. Delhi: Motilal Banarsidass, 2003.

Luxenberg, Christoph. *The Syro-Aramaic Reading of the Koran: A Contribution to the Decoding of the Language of the Koran*. Berlin: H. Schiler, 2007.

Madigan, Daniel A. *The Qur'ān's Self Image: Writing and Authority in Islam's Scripture*. Princeton, NJ: Princeton University, 2001.

Mallouhi, Mazhar. "Comments on the Insider Movement." *SFM* 5:5 (2009) 3–14.

al-Mallūḥī, Maẓhar. *Ḍā'i'a fī al-Madīna*. Beirut: Dar al-Jil, 1991.

———. *Laḥẓat Mawt*. Beirut: Maktabat al-Thaqafa, 1988.

———. *Al-Layl al-Ṭawīl*. Beirut: Maktabat al-Thaqafa, 1988.

———. *Al-Rāḥil*. Beirut: Dar al-Jil, 1991.

al-Mallūḥī, Maẓhar, et al., eds. *Qirā'a Sharqīya li-Injīl Luqā*. Beirut: Dar al-Jil, 1998.

al-Mallūḥī, Maẓhar, et al., eds. *Nash'at al-'Ālam wa al-Basharīya: Qirā'a Mu'āṣira li-Sifr al-Takwīn*. Beirut: Dar al-Jil, 2001.

al-Mallūḥī, Maẓhar, et al., eds. *Qirā'a Ṣūfīya li-Injīl Yūḥannā*. Beirut: Dar al-Jil, 2004.

McAuliffe, Jane Dammen. "The Prediction and Prefiguration of Muḥammad." In *Bible and Qur'ān: Essays in Scriptural Intertextuality*, edited by John C. Reeves, 107–31. Atlanta: Society of Biblical Literature, 2003.

Mikhail, Wageeh Y. F. "The Missiological Significance of Early Christian Arab Theology with Special Reference to the Abbasid Period (750–1258)." ThM thesis, Calvin Theological Seminary, 2004.

Miller, Duane Alexander. "Living among the Breakage: Contextual Theology-Making and Ex-Muslim Christians." PhD., diss. University of Edinburgh, 2014.

Mini-Consultation on Reaching Muslims. "Lausanne Occasional Paper 13: Christian Witness to Muslims." *Lausanne Committee for World Evangelization*. June 16–27, 1980.

Moreau, A. Scott. *Contextualization in World Missions: Mapping and Assessing Evangelical Models*. Grand Rapids: Kregel, 2012.

Moreau, A. Scott, Gary Corwin, and Gary B. McGee. *Introducing World Missions: A Biblical, Historical, and Practical Survey*. Grand Rapids: Baker Academic, 2004.

Motzki, Harald. *Ḥadīth: Origins and Developments*. Burlington, VT: Ashgate, 2004.

Mouw, Richard J. *When the Kings Come Marching in: Isaiah and the New Jerusalem*. Rev. ed. Grand Rapids: Eerdmans, 2002.

Nasry, Wafik. *Abū Qurrah wa al-Ma'mūn, al-Muǧādalah*. Beirut: CEDRAC, 2010.

———. *The Caliph and the Bishop: A 9th Century Muslim-Christian Debate: Al-Ma'mūn and Abū Qurrah*. Beirut: CEDRAC, 2008.

Nicholson, R. A. *The Mystics of Islam*. New York: Schocken, 1975.

Newman, N. A., ed. *The Early Christian-Muslim Dialogue: A Collection of Documents from the First Three Islamic Centuries, 632–900 A.D.: Translations with Commentary*. Hatfield, Pa.: Interdisciplinary Biblical Research Institute, 1993.

Nickel, Gordon D. *Narratives of Tampering in the Earliest Commentaries on the Qur'ān*. Boston: Brill, 2011.

O'Shaughnessy, Thomas J. *The Koranic Concept of the Word of God*. Istituto Biblico, Rome, 1948.

Osborn, Eric F. "Justin Martyr and the Logos Spermatikos." *SM* 42 (1993) 143–59.

Ott, Craig, and Harold A. Netland. *Globalizing Theology: Belief and Practice in an Era of World Christianity*. Grand Rapids: Baker, 2006.

Parshall, Phil. *Muslim Evangelization: Contemporary Approaches to Contextualization*. Waynesboro, GA: Gabriel, 2003.

———. *New Paths in Muslim Evangelism: Evangelical Approaches to Contextualization*. Grand Rapids: Baker, 1980.

Parsons, Martin. *Unveiling God: Contextualising Christology for Islamic Culture*. Pasadena, CA: William Carey Library, 2005.

Pikkert, Peter. *Protestant Missionaries to the Middle East: Ambassadors of Christ or Culture?* Hamilton, Ontario: WEC Canada, 2008.

Qureshi, Nabeel. *Seeking Allah, Finding Jesus: A Devout Muslim Encounters Christianity*. Grand Rapids: Zondervan, 2014.

Qushayrī, 'Abd al-Karīm ibn al-Hawāzin. *Principles of Sufism*, translated by Barbara R. Von Schlegell. Berkeley: Mizan, 1990.

Qutb, Sayyid. *Basic Principles of the Islamic Worldview*. North Haledon, NJ: Islamic Publications International, 2006.

Register, Ray G. *Dialogue and Interfaith Witness with Muslims: A Guide and Sample Ministry in the U.S.A*. Kingsport, TN: Moody, 1979.

Reinink, Gerrit J. "Early Christian Reactions to the Building of the Dome of the Rock in Jerusalem." *XV* 2:8 (2001) 227–41.

Reynolds, Gabriel Said. *The Emergence of Islam: Classical Traditions in Contemporary Perspective*. Minneapolis: Fortress, 2012.

———. "The Muslim Jesus: Dead or Alive?" *BSOAS* 72:2 (2009) 237–58.

———. "On the Presentation of Christianity in the Qur'ān and the Many Aspects of Qur'anic Rhetoric." *Al-Bayān* 12 (2014) 42–54.

———. Qur'ānic Studies and Its Controversies." In *The Qur'ān in Its Historical Context*, edited by Gabriel Said Reynolds, 1–24. New York: Routledge, 2007.

———. *The Qur'ān and Its Biblical Subtext*. New York: Routledge, 2010.

———. "Remembering Muḥammad." *Numen* 58 (2011) 188–206.

Rippin, Andrew. "Literary Analysis of *Qur'ān*, *Tafsīr*, and *Sīra*: The Methodologies of John Wansbrough." In *Approaches to Islam in Religious Studies*, edited by Richard C. Martin, 151–63. Tucson: University of Arizona, 1985.

Robinson, George G. "The Gospel and Evangelism." In *Theology and Practice of Mission: God, the Church, and the Nations*, edited by Bruce Riley Ashford, 76–91. Nashville: B&H Academic, 2011.

Roggema, Barbara. *The Legend of Sergius Baḥīrā: Eastern Christian Apologetics and Apocalyptic in Response to Islam*. Boston: Brill, 2009.

Rowe, C. Kavin. *World Upside Down: Reading Acts in the Graeco-Roman Age*. New York: Oxford University, 2009.

Saadi, Abdul-Massih. "Nascent Islam in Syriac Sources." In *The Qur'ān in Its Historical Context*, edited by Gabriel Said Reynolds, 217–22. New York: Routledge, 2007.

Saeed, Abdullah. "The Charge of Distortion of Jewish and Christian Scriptures." *MW* 92 (2002) 419–36.

Sahas, Daniel J. *John of Damascus on Islam: The "Heresy of the Ishmaelites."* Leiden: Brill, 1972.

Saleh, Walid A. "A Fifteenth-Century Muslim Hebraist: Al-Biqāʿī and His Defense of Using the Bible to Interpret the Qur'ān." *Speculum* 83 (2008) 629–54.

Samir, Samir Khalil. "The Earliest Arab Apology for Christianity (c. 750)." In *Christian Arabic Apologetics During the Abbasid Period,* 750–1258, edited by Samir Khalil Samir and Jørgen S. Nielsen, 57–114. New York: Brill, 1994.

Sanneh, Lamin O. *Translating the Message: The Missionary Impact on Culture.* Maryknoll, NY: Orbis, 1989.

al-Sayyid, Riḍwān. *Al-Islām al-Muʿāṣar: Naẓarīyāt fī al-Ḥāḍir wa al-Mustaqbal.* Beirut: Dar al-ʿAlum al-ʿArabiya, 1986.

———. *Mafāhīm al-Jamāʿāt fī al-Islām.* Beirut: Dar al-Tatwir lil-Tabaʿa wa al-Nashr, 1984.

Schacht, Joseph. *The Origins of Muhammadan Jurisprudence.* Oxford: Clarendon, 1953.

Schimmel, Annemarie. *Mystical Dimensions of Islam.* Chapel Hill: University of North Carolina, 1975.

Schlorff, Samuel P. "The Hermeneutical Crisis in Muslim Evangelism." *EMQ* 16:3 (1980) 143–51.

———. *Missiological Models in Ministry to Muslims.* Upper Darby, PA: Middle East Resources, 2006.

Schnabel, Eckhard J. "Contextualising Paul in Athens: The Proclamation of the Gospel before Pagan Audiences in the Graeco-Roman World." *RT* 12:2 (2005) 172–90.

———. *Paul the Missionary: Realities, Strategies and Methods.* Downers Grove, IL: InterVarsity, 2008.

Schreiter, Robert J. *Constructing Local Theologies.* Maryknoll, NY: Orbis, 1985.

Shahid, Irfan. "Arab Christianity before the Rise of Islam." In *Christianity: A History in the Middle East,* edited by Habib Badr, 435–51. Beirut: Middle East Council of Churches, 2005.

———. *Byzantium and the Arabs in the Fifth Century.* Washington, DC: Dumbarton Oaks, 1989.

———. *Byzantium and the Arabs in the Fourth Century.* Washington, DC: Dumbarton Oaks, 1984.

———. *Byzantium and the Arabs in the Sixth Century.* Washington, DC: Dumbarton Oaks, 1995.

Simnowitz, Adam. Review of *Pilgrims on the Muslim Road: Exploring a New Path between Two Faiths,* by Paul-Gordon Chandler. http://www.answering-islam.org/Reviews/chandler_mallouhi.html.

Small, Keith E. *Textual Criticism and Qur'an Manuscripts.* Lanham, MD: Lexington, 2011.

Stephens, Paul. "Factors Contributing to and Inhibiting Growth of Muslim Background Believer Groups in Arabland." DMin Project. Columbia International University, 2009.

Stern, Ryan K. "The Challenge of Contextualization in Muslim Ministry." MA thesis, Reformed Theological Seminary, 2008.

Stonehouse, N. B. *Paul before the Areopagus and Other New Testament Studies.* Grand Rapids: Eerdmans, 1957.

Swanson, Mark N. "An Apology for the Christian Faith." In *The Orthodox Church in the Arab World, 700-1700: An Anthology of Sources,* edited by Samuel Nobel et al., 40–59. DeKalb: Northern Illinois University, 2014.

———. "Are Hypostases Attributes? An Investigation into Modern Egyptian Christian Appropriation of the Medieval Arabic Apologetic Heritage." *PO* 16 (1990) 239–50.

———. "Arabic as a Christian Language." http://www.luthersem.edu/mswanson/papers/Indonesia%20Arabic.pdf.

———. "Beyond Prooftexting: Approaches to the Qur'ān in Some Early Arabic Christian Apologies." *MW* 88:3–4 (1998) 297–319.

———. "The Christian al-Ma'mūn Tradition." In *Christians at the Heart of Islamic Rule: Church Life and Scholarship in 'Abbasid Iraq*, edited by David Thomas, 63–92. Leiden: Brill, 2003.

———. "Early Christian-Muslim Theological Conversation among Arabic-Speaking Intellectuals." http://www.luthersem.edu/mswanson/papers/Indonesia%20Intellectuals.pdf.

———. "Fī Taṯlīt Allāh al-Wāḥid." In *Christian Muslim Relations: A Biographical History*, edited by David Thomas et al. *MR* 1:330–33.

———. "Some Considerations for the Dating of Fī Taṯlīṯ Allāh al-Wāḥid (Sinai Ar. 154) and al-Ǧāmiʿ Wuǧūh al-Īmān (London, British Library Or. 4950)." *PO* 18 (1993) 115–41.

———. "Thinking Through Islam." *WW* 22:3 (2002) 264–74.

Tennent, Timothy C. *Christianity at the Religious Roundtable: Evangelicalism in Conversation with Hinduism, Buddhism, and Islam*. Grand Rapids: Baker, 2002.

———. "Followers of Jesus (Isa) in Islamic Mosques: A Closer Examination of C-5 "High Spectrum" Contextualization." *IJFM* 23:3 (2006) 101–15.

———. *Invitation to World Missions: A Trinitarian Missiology for the Twenty-First Century*. Grand Rapids: Kregel Publications, 2010.

———. *Theology in the Context of World Christianity: How the Global Church is Influencing the Way We Think about and Discuss Theology*. Grand Rapids: Zondervan, 2007.

Thomas, David. *Christian Doctrines in Islamic Theology*. Leiden: Brill, 2008.

Tottoli, Robert. *Biblical Prophets in the Qur'ān and Muslim Literature*. Richmond, Surrey: Curzon, 2002.

Trimingham, J. Spencer. *Christianity among the Arabs in Pre-Islamic Times*. New York: Longman, 1979.

Tritton, Arthur Stanley. *The Caliphs and Their Non-Muslim Subjects: A Critical Study of the Covenant of 'Umar*. London: F. Cass, 1970.

Ṭūfī, Sulayman ibn 'Abd al-Qawi. *Muslim Exegesis of the Bible in Medieval Cairo: Najm al-Dīn al-Ṭūfī's (d. 716/1316) Commentary on the Christian Scriptures*. Translated, annotated, and introduced by Lejla Demiri. History of Christian-Muslim Relations 19. Boston: Brill, 2013.

van Ess, Josef. "Disputationspraxis in der islamischen Theologie. Ein vorläufige Skizze." *REI* 44 (1976) 23–60.

Vanhoozer, Kevin J. *The Drama of Doctrine: A Canonical-Linguistic Approach to Christian Theology*. Louisville: Westminster John Knox, 2005.

———. "'One Rule to Rule Them All?' Theological Method in an Era of World Christianity." In *Globalizing Theology: Belief and Practice in an Era of World Christianity*, edited by Craig Ott and Harold A. Netland, 85–126. Grand Rapids: Baker, 2006.

———."The Semantics of Biblical Literature: Truth and Scripture's Diverse Literary Forms." In *Hermeneutics, Authority, and Canon*, edited by D. A. Carson and John D. Woodbridge, 53–104. Grand Rapids: Academie, 1986.

Volf, Miroslav. *Allah: A Christian Response*. New York: HarperOne, 2011.

Walls, Andrew F. *The Cross-Cultural Process in Christian History: Studies in the Transmission and Appropriation of Faith*. Maryknoll, NY: Orbis, 2002.

———. *The Missionary Movement in Christian History: Studies in Transmission of Faith*. Maryknoll, NY: Orbis, 1996.

Wansbrough, John E. *Quranic Studies: Sources and Methods of Scriptural Interpretation*. Amherst, NY: Prometheus, 2004.

———. *The Sectarian Milieu: Content and Composition of Islamic Salvation History*. Oxford: Oxford University, 1978.

Warrāq, Muḥammad ibn Hārūn and David Thomas. *Anti-Christian Polemic in Early Islam: Abū ʿĪsā Al-Warrāq's "Against the Trinity."* New York: Cambridge University, 1992.

———. *Early Muslim Polemic Against Christianity: Abū ʿĪsā al-Warrāq's "Against the Incarnation."* New York: Cambridge University, 2002.

Watt, W. Montgomery. *The Formative Period of Islamic Thought*. Oneworld, 1998.

Wilde, Clare. "Early Christian Arabic Texts: Evidence for Non-ʿUthmānic Qur'ān Codices, or Early Approaches to the Qur'ān?" In *New Perspectives on the Qur'ān: The Qur'ān in Its Historical Context 2*, edited by Gabriel Said Reynolds, 358–71. New York: Routledge, 2011.

———. "Produce Your Proof if You Are Truthful (Q 2:111): The Qur'ān in Christian Arabic Texts (750–1258 C.E.)." PhD diss., The Catholic University of America, 2011.

Wilson, Harry K. "The Stigma of Baptism in the Evangelization of Muslims." PhD diss., Southwestern Baptist Theological Seminary, 1995.

Wolfson, Harry A. "The Muslim Attributes and the Christian Trinity." *HTR* 49: (1956) 1–18.

———. "Philosophical Implications of the Problem of Divine Attributes in the Kalam." *JAOS* 79:2 (1959) 73–80.

———. *The Philosophy of the Kalam*. Cambridge, MA: Harvard, 1976.

Wright, Christopher J. H. *The Mission of God: Unlocking the Bible's Grand Narrative*. Downers Grove, IL: InterVarsity, 2006.

Ye'or, Bat. *The Decline of Eastern Christianity under Islam: From Jihad to Dhimmitude: Seventh-Twentieth Century*. Madison, NJ: Fairleigh Dickinson, 1996.

Index of Subjects

New Testament and, 42–44
theological fidelity and, 136–39
Chalcedonian orthodoxy, 4–5, 13
Abū Qurra's exegesis and, 94–99
Christianity
in Arab-Muslim milieus, 129–60
biblical literature in, 150–54
cultural plasticity of, 133–35
Greek philosophy and, 24, 56–57
limitations of qur'ānic interpretations in, 33–35
revelation and prophetology and, 154–57
theological translatability in, 132–36
translation and diffusion in, 136–39
use of Qur'ān in, 1
Christian-Muslim disputation literature, 10n40, 69–72
Christology
Abū Qurra's disputation with *mutakallimūn* and, 86, 91–99
al-Kalima *logos*-apology and, 110–21
al-Kalima theology and, 109–10
canonic principle and, 136–39
dyophysite interpretations, 35–37
qur'ānic interpretations and, 14–15, 32–33, 99–104
qur'āninc point of contact and, 63–64
redemption narrative and, 131–32
themes in*Tathlith* from, 72–80, 82–85
Christology in Dialogue with Muslims, 39
Church of the East (Nestorians), 5
church planting, 38
Clement of Alexandria, 140–41
contextual theology
Betrothal Model of, 27–31, 129–30, 139–46
Christian qur'ānic interpretations and, 24, 31–32, 35, 61–64, 100–104
grand Biblical narrative and, 130–39
language and meaning in Qur'ān and, 148–50
locus of responsibility in, 142–46
conversion
in evangelical apologetics, 37–40
to Islam, by early Jews and Christians, 8–9
to Islam, Christian theology and, 13–14
Coptic language, Arab Christianity and, 5
Council of Ephesus, 4
Cragg, Kenneth, 30
creation
noncanonical texts and, 44n9
in *Tathlīth,* 80–85
cross-cultural missionary, classification of Paul as, 45
crucifixion and resurrection
Abū Qurra's exegesis and, 97–99
in al-Kalima theology, 121–26
noncanonical texts and, 44n9
qur'ānic interpretations and, 33, 66
in Tathlīth, 84–85
cultural diversity
contextual theology and, 140–46
hermeneutics of contextual theology and, 146–48
linear theology and, 142–46
non-negotiable theology and, 136–39
theological translatability and, 132–36

dhimmīs classification, of early Jews and Christians, 8–9
divine origin in Christianity
Abū Qurra's exegesis and, 94–99
al-Kalima *logos*-apology and, 110–21
noncanonical references in New Testament and, 58–61
Qur'ān as point of contact and, 65–66
dyophysite Christology, 35–37
Abū Qurra's exegesis and, 94–99
dyothelite treatises, 13

ecclesiology
Christian qur'ānic interpretations and, 34–35
in evangelical apologetics, 38–40

Index of Authors

Index of Biblical Passages

GALATIANS

COLOSSIANS

1 TIMOTHY

TITUS

REVELATION

Index of Qur'ānic Passages